D1376589

EVERYMAN, I will go with thee,

and be thy guide,

In thy most need to go by thy side

RAPHAEL HOLINSHED, or HOLLINGSHEAD

Probably belonged to a Cheshire family
and may have attended Christ's College,
Cambridge, in 1544. About 1560 he came
to London and was employed as a trans-
lator. Holinshed died in about 1580.

Holinshed's Chronicle

As used in Shakespeare's Plays

EDITED BY
ALLARDYCE & JOSEPHINE NICOLL

DENT: LONDON, MELBOURNE AND TORONTO
EVERYMAN'S LIBRARY
DUTTON: NEW YORK

No. 800 Hardback ISBN 0 460 00800 5

INTRODUCTION

EVERYTHING that bears upon the work of William Shakespeare has its own peculiar value, and chief among all the materials we possess for a study of his craft are the books which he used for the foundation of his plays. He sought widely for themes, situations, ideas and language, reworking old dramas, turning into tragedy and comedy ancient tales of Italy, discussing thoughts of Montaigne and Pythagoras. Above all the books of Shakespeare's library stand out two, the *Lives* of Plutarch and the *Chronicle* of Holinshed, the former used as the basis of the Roman plays, the latter for that of the Histories, of *Lear*, of *Macbeth*, of *Cymbeline*. Each of these two works Shakespeare must have known almost by heart ; each of these must have lain open on his desk as he penned scenes and dialogue. Through a study of each we may delve deeply into his dramatic methods and his dramatic purpose.

In presenting this selection of such passages in Holinshed as Shakespeare drew upon in his plays, it must be emphasised that the orientation of the present editors is towards drama rather than history. It is valuable to see wherein Shakespeare deviated from his sources, but it tells us nothing to note how history, as rewritten from more recently discovered documents and after generations of research, has been misinterpreted in his plays. The prime consideration is the dramatic work of Shakespeare, which, as a thing of art, stands apart from, and independent of, all actuality as expressed by historians. As a consequence no effort has been made in this volume to point out the shortcomings of Holinshed or to indicate those scenes in the plays where Shakespeare, basing his work on contemporary chroniclers, was misled.

That Holinshed has his grievous shortcomings need

hardly be emphasised. In the first place, it must be understood that the modern ways of scholarship, although they were being dimly recognised at this period, were still confused by gossip, rumour and anecdote, which, in the Middle Ages, had stood for history. The medieval mind was credulous ; the characteristic of the modern mind is scientific acumen, and this the chroniclers of the Elizabethan period hardly possessed. A tale told by some far-off author, unsubstantiated and perhaps anonymous, finds as prominent a place as the accurate description in a contemporary official document of some formal event. A dragon, a prophetic comet, is as seriously narrated as a battle and a murder. In the second place, Holinshed's book is frankly a compilation. Its originator and part author, Raphael Holinshed, perhaps, according to Anthony à Wood, a minister of the Gospel, seems about 1570 to have planned out this work which was to be a compendious survey of history, starting with Noah and devoting special attention to the three kingdoms. Realising that such a work could not be undertaken unaided, Holinshed, while reserving for himself the history of England, commissioned William Harrison to pen his well-known *Description* of that country, Richard Stanyhurst and Edmund Campion to write the *Description* of Ireland and Richard Hooker to cover its history. Their joint efforts appeared in 1577 as *The Chronicles of England, Scotlande, and Irelande . . . faithfully gathered & set forth by Raphaell Holinshed*. Ten years later the whole collection, " newlie augmented & continued (with manifold matters of singular note & worthie memorie) to the year 1586," was reprinted. It would appear that Shakespeare read the work in the second and not in the first edition, for certain phrases in the former were repeated by him almost *verbatim* in several of his plays. As Holinshed's will was proved on April 24, 1582, he can hardly himself have had much to do with the 1587 reprint.

Regarding the *Chronicles* as a Shakespearean source-book and not as a history, we may present it to modern readers in one of two ways. The whole compilation might be reissued (as it was in the year 1807), the Shakespearean amateur being left to wade through its thousands of pages searching for that which had appealed to the dramatist. This, the ideal way, obviously would be impossible within the limits of an Everyman's Library volume, and, even if it had been possible, would have demanded the ideal reader, amply leisured and scholarly of eye. The other method, adopted here and in Mr. W. G. Boswell-Stone's *Shakespeare's Holinshed* of 1896, necessitates a departure from the original ordering of material. Here Shakespeare's plays are taken as the standard, and such passages from the chronicler are presented as seem to have a bearing on those plays, with a few indications of the acts and scenes most coloured by the Holinshed matter. With other books, straightforward selections would have been possible, but Holinshed's vast work, when cut down to the limits here given, must have seemed largely unintelligible and would in any case have been of little value either to the lover of Shakespeare or to the student. In the arrangement here the usual First Folio order of the plays has been retained.

It must not be assumed, of course, that all the matter common to Shakespeare and to Holinshed was necessarily derived from the latter by the former. Sometimes Shakespeare may have gone to Holinshed's sources, sometimes he found that preceding dramatists had taken themes from the *Chronicles* and had worked them up into plays. The story of *Lear* had been put on the stage before Shakespeare's time, and the history of *King John* was evidently derived more from an already existing drama than from Holinshed's prose account. Each play, therefore, must be studied separately and considered by itself, and in the consideration of each the reader must, if he wishes to use Holinshed aright, ask himself what Shakespeare was attracted by in the story presented to him, what he found unsuitable for dramatic treatment and what he took over almost unaltered from his original. There is, it is true, less to be learned of Shakespeare's purposes here than there is in a study, let us say, of *Othello* and of Cinthio's tale of the Moor of Venice. A certain external necessity led Shakespeare towards the histories as it did not lead him towards the Othello story. The Elizabethan audiences were clamouring for knowledge of their own land. A new era had dawned, and with that new era nationalism had taken a fresh form. For ever were gone the vague, medieval ideals concerning a Holy Roman Empire, an all-embracing Catholic Church and a universal Latin tongue. England now stood by itself; its monarch was supreme; its Church was its own; its language vied with Latin, Spanish, and Italian. What more natural than that in the youthful theatres which were but one manifestation of this new spirit, audiences should cry for, and dramatists should provide records of, the more glorious and the more thrilling events in the national history? Nothing impeded them. The English stage was romantically free. No heavy Unities fettered the playwrights within circumscribed limits. A whole reign could be shown to those naïf and imaginative spectators for whom the bare platform became a city-street and a couple of hirelings were an army. As always, Shakespeare showed himself willing to fall in with the popular demand. His predecessors, the University Wits, had applied themselves to the history-play; even the academic authors, straining after neo-classic decorum, had started their tragic efforts with what was then thought to be English history, the story of Ferrex and Porrex. In approaching the stage, then, about 1590, Shakespeare found already an enthusiasm for this type of drama and found, moreover, certain examples of this type being played in London. Such examples were of two kinds. Some, such as Marlowe's *Edward II*, were dramas of genius, and these Shakespeare left alone. Certain reigns, because he would not enter into rivalry with works of undoubted artistry, were barred for him. Other plays, however, had not this distinctive mark, and several of these, such as those on the reigns of John and Henry VI, Shakespeare proceeded to rewrite, besides applying himself to reigns which, so far as we know, had not been dealt with before his time. External necessity, therefore, to a certain extent dictated to him both choice of theme and choice of kind.

These remarks are made because one of the most interesting and perhaps one of the most neglected aspects of Shakespeare's artistic life is the consideration of his choice of themes. The old-fashioned view that he was a careless genius, taking any old tale which met his eye, must, it seems, be put aside in favour of the other, which would, more sensibly, present Shakespeare as an artist, widely read and intelligently seeking for themes which might either prove eminently suitable for dramatic treatment or which might give him opportunities for developing certain ideas or types of character. In the Holinshed volume the most interesting stories from this point of view are those of *Macbeth*, *Cymbeline* and *Lear*. The first shows Shakespeare, courtier-like, choosing a theme designed to please the newly-crowned James I of England, a monarch who brought the Stuarts to England and thus united the long-severed kingdoms. One who superstitiously had renewed the practice of touching for the King's Evil and who himself had written a work on Demonology, must have looked with special interest upon this flattering tragedy written by one of his own company of players. In selecting the Macbeth theme Shakespeare left himself fairly free to develop a story in his own way. He was not here dealing with " historical " history but with a dim and distant past which even his rumour-loving and unscientific contemporaries felt need not be adhered to over scrupulously. We find accordingly that several elements in the original account are left untouched and that the killing of Duncan is made more thrilling by the adoption of the Holinshed record concerning the death of King Duff. For dramatic purposes, too, the youthful King Duncan of the chroniclers was turned into an aged monarch whose white hair reminded Lady Macbeth of her father. The stories of *Cymbeline* and of *King Lear* left the dramatist equally free. Both dealt with a prehistoric Britain, and could accordingly be rewritten, as the career of Henry IV could not. Out of the one Shakespeare created a rather amorphous tragi-comedy, full of vague romance' and misty fantasy ; out of the other he made one of his most powerful and poetic tragedies. The aged Lear is not with him brought back to a peaceful throne ; for Shakespeare's purpose the King, after passing through a soul-tormenting madness—itself virtually the creation of the dramatist—had to die, and with him had to perish the strong-minded Cordelia. A comparison of *Cymbeline* and *Lear* tells us much. In style both are close together, and *Lear*, had it not been for that sterner treatment, might have been as *Cymbeline* is. In each we see the dramatist at work; once as the stern creator from legendary fairy-tale of highest tragedy, once as the weaver of pleasant myth and dainty love-tale.

It is impossible here to indicate in detail the precise points of Shakespeare's indebtedness to Holinshed; indeed it were not of much use thus to indicate the portions chosen and neglected. That study, the value of which lies in the revelation of Shakespeare's method of dramatic composition, must be undertaken by each individual student of Shakespeare. Unless the passages in Holinshed are compared carefully with Shakespeare's reworking, little understanding can be gained into the ways of his art. In this book indication is given, in the left-hand margin, of the volume and the page in the *Chronicle* from which each selected part is taken. Where such a passage bears directly upon a scene in Shakespeare and does not merely provide general material for the plot as a whole, there is inserted at the end of the appropriate line a reference to act and scene of the play. These may serve at least as a general guide for the reader. As remarked above, the general plan of Mr. Boswell-Stone's edition has been followed, and to that edition the present editors wish to express their indebtedness. Perhaps sufficient is given here for the ordinary lover and student of Shakespeare's dramas, but it must be emphasised that this volume contains only a very small part of Holinshed's original, and that more detailed research into particular plays demands a direct investigation of the *Chronicle*, as well as a comparison of the *Chronicle* with earlier histories, and with later history-plays of non-Shakespearean authorship.

JOSEPHINE NICOLL.
ALLARDYCE NICOLL.

BIBLIOGRAPHICAL NOTE

THE Chronicles of Raphael Holinshed appeared in 1577 under the title: *The firste volume of the chronicles of England, Scotlande, and Irelande, conteyning the description and chronicles of England, from the first inhabiting unto the Conquest. The description and chronicles of Scotland, from the first originall of the Scottes nation, till the yeare 1571. The description and chronicles of Yrelande, from the firste originall, untill the yeare 1547. (The laste volume . . . conteyning the chronicles of Englande from William Conquerour untill this present tyme.)* The Chronicles were contained in three volumes.

Ten years later, in 1587, after Holinshed's death, there appeared an enlarged edition entitled: *The first and second volumes of Chronicles . . . newlie augmented and continued to the year 1586 by J. Hooker alias Vowell . . . and others* [Francis Thynne, Abraham Fleming and John Stow, etc.].

In 1806 a portion of the work was published in Arbroath as: *The Scottish Chronicle; or, a complete history and description of Scotland . . . continued from 1571 until 1586 by F. Botevile.*

A complete six-volume edition appeared between the years 1807 and 1808, entitled *Holinshed's Chronicles of England, Scotland and Ireland.*

In 1917 R. S. Wallace and Alma Hansen edited Holinshed's Chronicles: Richard II, 1398-1400, and Henry V; another edition, with Henry IV added to the title, appeared in 1923.

Shakespeare's debt to Holinshed's Chronicles is illustrated in the following works: *The history of Makbeth, from which Shakespeare took his tragedy of Macbeth. Reprinted from Holinshed's Chronicle*, 1843; *Shakespeare's Macbeth: with the chapters of Hollinshed's 'Historie of Scotland' on which the play is based*, 1862; another ed., 1864; *Macbeth, by William Shakespeare. With the Historie of Macbeth, from R. Holinshed's Chronicle of Scotland, 1577*, 1886; *Shakspere's Holinshed: The Chronicle and the Historical Plays compared*, by W. G. Boswell-Stone, 1896. See also the German work by L. Riechelmann: *Zu Richard II. Shakespeare und Holinshed*, 1860.

An interesting study of this period is given in W. H. D. Rouse's *England in the Sixteenth Century*, 1906 and 1913.

As noted in the Introduction, the work of Boswell-Stone has been taken as the basis for this edition. The text, however, has been compared with the original and various alterations have been made in regard to the passages selected. Words in italics are those which Shakespeare directly borrowed for his dramatic dialogue.

CONTENTS

JOHN

[There is no doubt that Shakespeare based his play of *King John* on the older anonymous chronicle-history drama, entitled *The Troublesome Raigne of Iohn King of England*, which, first published in 1591, was reprinted in 1611 as by W. Sh. and in 1622 as by W. Shakespeare. His use of Holinshed was therefore at second-hand, although for the King's outburst when he learns of the supposed murder of Arthur it would seem that he had in mind the corresponding passage in the chronicler. This, however, appears to be the only (and it is doubtful) evidence to show Shakespeare's acquaintanceship with the original narrative. From the point of view of history, the most noticeable fact is the strange omission from both the old *Troublesome Raigne* and *King John* of the events connected with the sealing of Magna Charta.]

[H. iii. 157] Iohn the yoongest son of Henrie the [I. i] second was proclaimed king of England, beginning his reigne the sixt daie of April, in the yeare of our Lord 1199. . . . This man, so soone as his brother Richard was deceassed, sent Hubert archbishop of Canturburie, and William Marshall earle of Striguill (otherwise called Chepstow) into England, both to proclaime him king, and also to see his peace kept ; togither with Geffrey Fitz Peter lord cheefe iustice, and diuerse other barons of the realme ; whilest he himselfe went to Chinon where his brothers treasure laie, which was foorthwith deliuered vnto him by Robert de Turneham : and therewithall the castell of Chinon and Sawmer and diuerse other places, which were in the custodie of the foresaid Robert. But Thomas de Furnes nephue to the said Robert de Turneham deliuered the citie and castell of Angiers vnto Arthur duke of Britaine. For, by generall consent of the nobles and peeres of the countries of *Aniou, Maine, and Touraine*, Arthur was receiued as the liege and souereigne lord of the same countries.

For euen at this present, and so soone as it was knowne
that king Richard was deceased, diuerse cities and townes,
on that side of the sea belonging to the said Richard
whilest he liued, fell at ods among themselues, some of
them indeuouring to preferre king Iohn, other labouring
rather to be vnder the gouernance of Arthur duke of
Britaine : considering that he seemed by most right to
be their cheefe lord, forsomuch as he was sonne to Geffrey
elder brother to Iohn.

Now whilest king Iohn was thus occupied in recouering
his brothers treasure, and traueling with his subiects to
reduce them to his obedience, queene Elianor his mother,
by the helpe of Hubert archbishop of Canturburie and
other of the noble men and barons of the land, trauelled as
diligentlie to procure the English people to receiue their
oth of allegiance to be true to king Iohn. . . .

[H. iii. 158] Surelie queene Elianor the kings mother
was sore against hir nephue Arthur, rather mooued thereto
by enuie conceiued against his mother, than vpon any
iust occasion giuen in the behalfe of the child, for that she
saw, if he were king, how his mother Constance would
looke to beare most rule within the realme of England,
till hir sonne should come to lawfull age, to gouerne of
himselfe. . . .

When this dooing of the queene was signified vnto the
said Constance, she, doubting the suertie of hir sonne,
committed him to the trust of the French king, who,
receiuing him into his tuition, promised to defend him
from all his enimies, and foorthwith furnished the holds
in Britaine with French souldiers. . . . . .

In the meane time [John's] mother [Acts II.–III.]
queene Elianor, togither with capteine Marchades,
entred into Aniou, and wasted the same, bicause they
of that countrie had receiued Arthur for their souereigne
lord and gouernour. And, amongst other townes and
fortresses, they tooke the citie of Angiers, slue manie
of the citizens, and committed the rest to prison.

Finallie [John] entred into Aniou, and, comming to the
citie of Angiers, appointed certeine bands of his footmen, &
all his light horssemen to compasse the towne about, whilest
he, with the residue of the footmen, & all the men of armes,

did go to assault the gates. Which enterprise with fire
and sword he so manfullie executed, that the gates being
in a moment broken open, the citie was entered and
deliuered to the souldiers for a preie. So that of the
citizens some were taken, some killed, and the wals of the
citie beaten flat to the ground.

RICHARD'S WILL

[*H*. iii. 155–156] [Richard] feeling himselfe to wax
weaker and weaker, preparing his mind to death, which
he perceiued now to be at hand, he ordeined his testament,
or rather reformed and added sundrie things vnto the
same which he before had made, at the time of his going
foorth towards the holie land.

Unto his brother Iohn he assigned the crowne of
England, and all other his lands and dominions, causing
the Nobles there present to sweare fealtie vnto him.

[*H*. iii. 160] King Philip made Arthur duke of Britaine,
knight, and receiued of him his homage for Aniou, Poictiers,
Maine, Touraine, and Britaine. Also somewhat before
the time that the truce should expire ; to wit, on the
morrow after the feast of the Assumption of our ladie, and
also the day next following, the two kings talked by
commissioners, in a place betwixt the townes of Buteuant
and Guleton. Within three daies after, they came
togither personallie, and communed at full of the variance
depending betweene them. But the French king shewed
himselfe stiffe and hard in this treatie, demanding the
whole countrie of Veulquessine to be restored vnto him,
as that which had beene granted by Geffrey earle of Aniou,
the father of king Henrie the second, vnto Lewis le Grosse,
to haue his aid then against king Stephan. Moreouer, he
demanded, that Poictiers, Aniou, Maine, and Touraine,
should be deliuered and wholie resigned vnto Arthur duke
of Britaine.

But these, & diuerse other requests which he made,
king Iohn would not in any wise grant vnto, and so they
departed without conclusion of anie agreement.

[*H*. iii. 161] Finallie, vpon the Ascension day in this
second yeare of his reigne, they came eftsoones to a
communication betwixt the townes of Vernon and Lisle

Dandelie; where finallie they concluded an agreement, with a marriage to be had betwixt Lewes the sonne of king Philip, and *the ladie Blanch*, daughter of Alfonso king of Castile the 8 of that name, & neece to K. Iohn by his sister Elianor.

In consideration whereof, king Iohn, besides the summe of *thirtie thousand markes* in siluer, as in respect of *dowrie* assigned to his said neece, resigned his title to the citie of Eureux, and also vnto all those townes which the French king had by warre taken from him, the citie of Angiers onelie excepted, which citie he receiued againe by couenants of the same agreement. The French king restored also to king Iohn (as *Rafe Niger* writeth) the citie of Tours, and all the castels and fortresses which he had taken within Touraine. . . . The king of England likewise did homage vnto the French king for Britaine, and againe (as after you shall heare) receiued homage for the same countrie, and for the countie of Richmont, of his nephue Arthur. . . .

By this conclusion of marriage betwixt the said Lewes and Blanch, the right of king Iohn went awaie ; which he lawfullie before pretended vnto the citie of Eureux, and vnto those townes in the confines of Berrie, Chateau Roux or Raoul, Cressie and Isoldune, and likewise vnto the countrie of Veuxin or Veulquessine, which is a part of the territorie of Gisors : the right of all which lands, townes and countries was released to the king of France by K. Iohn, who supposed that by his affinitie, and resignation of his right to those places, the peace now made would haue continued for euer. And, in consideration thereof, he procured furthermore, that the foresaid Blanch should be conueied into France to hir husband with all speed. That doone he returned into England.

[*H.* iii. 162] King Iohn and Philip king of France met togither neere the towne of Vernon, where Arthur duke of Britaine (as vassall to his vncle king Iohn) did his homage vnto him for the duchie of Britaine, & those other places which he held of him on this side and beyond the riuer of Loir, and afterward, still mistrusting his vncles curtesie, he returned backe againe with the French king, and would not commit himselfe to his said vncle, who (as he supposed) did beare him little good will.

THE ELECTION OF THE ARCHBISHOP

[*H*. iii. 170-171] But after the pope was fullie informed of the manner of their elections, he disanulled them both, and procured by his papall authoritie the moonks of Canturburie (of whome manie were then come to Rome about that matter) to choose one *Stephan Langton* the cardinall of S. Chrysogon, and Englishman borne, and of good estimation and learning in the court of Rome, to be their archbishop. . . .

The king, sore offended in his mind that the bishop of Norwich was thus put beside that dignitie, to the which he had aduanced him, . . . wrote his letters vnto the pope, giuing him to vnderstand for answer, that he would neuer consent that Stephan, which had beene brought vp & alwaies conuersant with his enimies the Frenchmen, should now inioy the rule of the bishoprike and dioces of Canturburie. . . . He added hereto, that for the liberties of his crowne he would stand to the death, if the matter so required.

[*H*. iii. 171-172] The pope perceiuing that king Iohn continued still in his former mind (which he called obstinacie), sent ouer his bulles into England, directed to William bishop of London, to Eustace bishop of Elie, and to Mauger bishop of Worcester, commanding them that, vnlesse king Iohn would suffer peaceablie the archbishop of Canturburie to occupie his see, and his moonks their abbie, they should put both him and his land vnder the sentence of interdiction, denouncing him and his land plainelie accurssed.

[*H*. iii. 175] The pope sent two *legats* into England, the one named *Pandulph* a lawier, and the other Durant a templer, who, comming vnto king John, exhorted him with manie terrible words to leaue his stubborne disobedience to the church, and to reforme his misdooings. The king for his part quietlie heard them, and, bringing them to Northampton, being not farre distant from the place where he met them vpon his returne foorth of Wales, had much conference with them ; but at length, when they perceiued that they could not haue their purpose, neither for restitution of the goods belonging to preests which he had seized vpon, neither of those that apperteined to certeine other persons, which the king had gotten also into his hands, by meanes of the controuersie betwixt him and the pope, the legats departed, leauing him accursed, and the land interdicted, as they found it at their comming.

In the meane time pope Innocent, after the returne of his legats out of England, perceiuing that king Iohn would not be ordered by him, determined, with the consent of his cardinals and other councellours, and also at the instant suit of the English bishops and other prelats being there with him, to depriue king Iohn of his kinglie state ; and so first absolued all his subiects and vassals of their oths of allegiance made vnto the same king, and after depriued him by solemne protestation of his kinglie administration and dignitie, and lastlie signified that his depriuation vnto the French king and other christian princes ; admonishing them to pursue king Iohn, being thus depriued, forsaken, and condemned, as a common enimie to God and his church. He ordeined furthermore, that whosoeuer imploied goods or other aid to vanquish and ouercome that disobedient prince, should remaine in assured peace of the church. . . .

But yet, that it might appeare to all men, that nothing could be more ioifull vnto his holinesse, than to haue king Iohn to repent his trespasses committed, and to aske forgiuenesse for the same, he appointed Pandulph, which latelie before was returned to Rome, with a great number of English exiles, to go into France, togither with Stephan the archbishop of Canturburie, and the other English bishops ; giuing him in commandement that, repairing vnto the French king, he should communicate with him all that which he had appointed to be doone against king Iohn, and to exhort the French king to make warre vpon him, as a person for his wickednesse excommunicated.

[*H*. iii. 164] Queene Elianor, that was regent in those parties, being put in great feare with the newes of this sudden sturre, got hir into Mirabeau, a strong towne situat in the countrie of Aniou, and foorthwith dispatched a messenger with letters vnto king Iohn, requiring him of speedie succour in this hir present danger. In the meane time, Arthur following the victorie, shortlie after followed hir, and woone Mirabeau, where he tooke his grandmother within the same ; whom he yet intreated verie honorablie, and with great reuerence (as some haue reported). ¶ But other write far more trulie, that she was not taken, but escaped into a tower, within the which she was straitlie besieged. Thither came also to aid Arthur all the Nobles and men of armes in Poictou, and namelie the . . . earle of March, according to appointment betwixt them : so that by this meanes Arthur had a great armie togither in the field.

King Iohn, in the meane time, hauing receiued his mothers letters, and vnderstanding thereby in what danger she stood, was maruellouslie troubled with the strangenesse of the newes, and with manie bitter words accused the French king as an vntrue prince, and a fraudulent league-breaker ; and in all possible hast speedeth him foorth, continuing his iournie for the most part both day and night to come to the succour of his people. To be briefe, he vsed such diligence, that he was vpon his enimies necks yer they could vnderstand any thing of his comming, or gesse what the matter meant when they saw such a companie of souldiers as he brought with him to approch so neere the citie. . . .

And hauing thus put them all to flight, they pursued the chase towards the towne of Mirabeau, into which the enimies made verie great hast to enter; but such speed was vsed by the English souldiers at that present, that they entred and wan the said towne before their enimies could come neere to get into it. Great slaughter was made within Mirabeau it selfe, and Arthur, with the residue of the armie that escaped with life from the first bickering, was taken ; who, being herevpon committed to prison, first at Falais, and after within the citie of Rouen, liued not long after, as you shall heare.

THE DEATH OF ARTHUR

[*H*. iii. 165] It is said that king Iohn caused his [IV.] nephue Arthur to be brought before him at Falais, and there went about to persuade him all that he could to forsake his freendship and aliance with the French king, and to leane and sticke to him, being his naturall vncle. But Arthur, like one that wanted good counsell, and abounding too much in his owne wilfull opinion, made a presumptuous answer; not onelie denieng so to doo, but also commanding king Iohn to restore vnto him the realme of England, with all those other lands and possessions which king Richard had in his hand at the houre of his death. . . . King Iohn, being sore mooued with such words thus vttered by his nephue, appointed (as before is said) that he should be straitlie kept in prison, as first in Falais, and after at Roan within the new castell there. . . .

Shortlie after, king Iohn, comming ouer into England, caused himselfe to be crowned againe at Canturburie by the hands of Hubert the archbishop there, on the fourteenth day of Aprill, and then went backe againe into Normandie, where, immediatlie vpon his arriuall, a rumour was spred through all France, of the death of his nephue Arthur. True it is that great suit was made to haue Arthur set at libertie, as well by the French king, as by William de Riches a valiant baron of Poictou, and diuerse other Noble men of the Britains, who when they could not preuaile in their suit, they banded themselues togither, and, ioining in confederacie with Robert earle of Alanson, the vicount Beaumont, William de Fulgiers, and other, they began to leuie sharpe wars against king Iohn in diuerse places, insomuch (as it was thought) that, so long as Arthur liued, there would be no quiet in those parts: wherevpon it was reported that king Iohn, through persuasion of his councellors, appointed certeine persons to go vnto Falais, where Arthur was kept in prison, vnder the charge of Hubert de Burgh, and there to put out the yoong gentlemans eies.

But through such resistance as he made against one of the tormentors that came to execute the kings commandment (for the other rather forsooke their prince and countrie, than they would consent to obeie the kings authoritie heerein) and such lamentable words as he vttered, Hubert de Burgh did preserue him from that iniurie; not doubting but rather to haue thanks than displeasure at the kings hands, for deliuering him of such

infamie as would haue redounded vnto his highnesse, if
the yoong gentleman had beene so cruellie dealt withall.
For he considered, that king Iohn had resolued vpon this
point onelie in his heat and furie . . . and that afterwards,
vpon better aduisement, he would both repent himselfe
so to haue commanded, and giue them small thanke that
should see it put in execution. Howbeit, to satisfie his
mind for the time, and to staie the rage of the Britains, he
caused it to be bruted abroad through the countrie, that the
kings commandment was fulfilled ; and that Arthur also
through sorrow and greefe was departed out of this life.
For the space of fifteene daies this rumour incessantlie ran
through both the realmes of England and France, and there
was ringing for him through townes and villages, as it had
beene for his funerals.

But when the Britains were nothing pacified, but
rather kindled more vehementlie to worke all the mischeefe they could deuise, in reuenge of their souereignes
death, there was no remedie but to signifie abroad
againe, that Arthur was as yet liuing and in health.
Now when the king heard the truth of all this matter, he
was nothing displeased for that his commandement was
not executed, sith there were diuerse of his capteins which
vttered in plaine words, that he should not find knights to
keepe his castels, if he dealt so cruellie with his nephue.
For if it chanced any of them to be taken by the king of
France or other their aduersaries, they should be sure to
tast of the like cup. But now touching the maner in
verie deed of the end of this Arthur, writers make sundrie
reports. Neuerthelesse certeine it is, that, in the yeare
next insuing, he was remooued from Falais vnto the castell
or tower of Rouen, out of the which there was not any that
would confesse that euer he saw him go aliue. Some
haue written, that, as he assaied to haue escaped out of
prison, and proouing to clime ouer the wals of the castell,
he fell into the riuer of Saine, and so was drowned. Other
write, that through verie greefe and languor he pined awaie,
and died of naturall sicknesse. But some affirme, that
king Iohn secretlie caused him to be murthered and made
awaie, so as it is not throughlie agreed vpon, in what sort
he finished his daies ; but verelie king Iohn was had in
great suspicion, whether worthilie or not, the lord knoweth.

[*H*. iii. 167-168]   Queene Elianor the mother of king Iohn departed this life, consumed rather through sorrow and anguish of mind, than of any other natural infirmitie.

[*H*. iii. 180]   There was in this season an heremit, whose name was Peter, dwelling about Yorke; a man in great reputation with the common people, bicause that, either inspired with some spirit of prophesie, as the people beleeued, or else hauing some notable skill in art magike, he was accustomed to tell what should follow after. And for so much as oftentimes his saiengs prooued true, great credit was giuen to him as to a verie prophet. . . . This Peter, about the first of Ianuarie last past, had told the king that, at the feast of the Ascension, it should come to passe, that he should be cast out of his kingdome. And (whether, to the intent that his words should be the better beleeued, or whether vpon too much trust of his owne cunning) he offered himselfe to suffer death for it, if his prophesie prooued not true. Herevpon being committed to prison within the castell of Corf, when the day by him prefixed came, without any other notable damage vnto king Iohn, he was, by the kings commandement, drawne from the said castell vnto the towne of Warham, & there hanged, togither with his sonne.

[*H*. iii. 163]   About the moneth of December, there were seene in the prouince of Yorke fiue moones, one in the east, the second in the west, the third in the north, the fourth in the south, and the fift as it were set in the middest of the other; hauing manie stars about it, and went fiue or six times incompassing the other, as it were the space of one houre, and shortlie after vanished awaie.

PHILIP ORDERED TO DETHRONE JOHN

[*H*. iii. 176]   [Philip] was easilie persuaded thereto [V] of an inward hatred that he bare vnto our king, and therevpon with all diligence made his prouision of men, ships, munition and vittell, in purpose to passe ouer into England.

[*H*. iii. 176-177]   As [John] lay thus readie, neere to the coast, to withstand and beat backe his enimies, there arriued at Douer two Templers, who, comming before the

king, declared vnto him that they were sent from Pandulph
the popes legat, who for his profit coueted to talke with
him; for he had (as they affirmed) meanes to propone,
whereby he might be reconciled both to God and his
church, although he were adiudged, in the court of Rome,
to haue forfeited all the right which he had to his kingdome.

The king, vnderstanding the meaning of the messengers,
sent them backe againe to bring ouer the legat, who
incontinentlie came ouer to Douer; of whose arriuall
when the king was aduertised, he went thither, and
receiued him with all due honour and reverence. Now
after they had talked togither a little, and courteouslie
saluted each other (as the course of humanitie required) the
legat (as it is reported) vttered these words following. . . .

These words being thus spoken by the legat, king
Iohn, as then vtterlie despairing in his matters, when
he saw himselfe constreined to obeie, was in a great
perplexitie of mind, and as one full of thought, looked
about him with a frowning countenance; waieng with
himselfe what counsell were best for him to follow. At
length, oppressed with the burthen of the imminent
danger and ruine, against his will, and verie loth so to
haue doone, he promised vpon his oth to stand to the
popes order and decree. Wherefore shortlie after (in like
manner as pope Innocent had commanded) he tooke the
crowne from his owne head, and deliuered the same to
Pandulph the legat; neither he, nor his heires at anie
time thereafter to receiue the same, but at the popes
hands. . . .

Then Pandulph, keeping the crowne with him for the
space of fiue daies in token of possession thereof, at
length (as the popes vicar) gaue it him againe.

[H. iii. 180] The people much blamed king Iohn for
this extreame dealing, bicause that the heremit was
supposed to be a man of great vertue, and his sonne
nothing guiltie of the offense committed by his father (if
any were) against the king. Moreouer, some thought
that he had much wrong to die, bicause the matter fell
out euen as he had prophesied; for, the day before the
Ascension day, king Iohn had resigned the superioritie of
his kingdome (as they tooke the matter) vnto the pope,

and had doone to him homage, so that he was no absolute king indeed, as authors affirme. One cause, and that not the least which mooued king Iohn the sooner to agree with the pope, rose through the words of the said heremit, that did put such a feare of some great mishap in his hart, which should grow through the disloialtie of his people, that it made him yeeld the sooner.

The Nobles, supposing that longer delaie therein was not to be suffered, assembled themselues togither at the abbeie of Burie (vnder colour of going thither to doo their deuotions to the bodie of S. Edmund which laie there inshrined) where they vttered their complaint of the kings tyrannicall manners. . . .

And therfore, being thus assembled in the queere of the church of S. Edmund, they receiued a solemne oth vpon the altar there, that, if the king would not grant to the same liberties, with others which he of his owne accord had promised to confirme to them, they would from thencefoorth make warre vpon him, till they had obteined their purpose, and inforced him to grant, not onelie to all these their petitions, but also yeeld to the confirmation of them vnder his seale, for euer to remaine most stedfast and inuiolable.

[*H*. iii. 190] [They] resolued with themselues to seeke for aid at the enimies hands ; and therevpon Saer earle of Winchester, and Robert Fitz Walter, with letters vnder their seales, were sent vnto Lewes the sonne of Philip the French king, offering him the crowne of England, and sufficient pledges for performance of the same, and other couenants to be agreed betwixt them ; requiring him with all speed to come vnto their succour.

[*H*. iii. 191] The pope, desirous to helpe king Iohn all that he might (bicause he was now his vassall), sent his legat Gualo into France, to disswade king Philip from taking anie enterprise in hand against the king of England. But king Philip, though he was content to heare what the legat could saie, yet by no meanes would be turned from the execution of his purpose ; alledging that king Iohn was not the lawfull king of England, hauing first vsurped and taken it awaie from his nephue Arthur the lawfull inheritour, and that now sithens, as an enimie to

his owne roiall dignitie, he had giuen the right of his
kingdome awaie to the pope (which he could not doo
without consent of his nobles) and therefore through his
owne fault he was worthilie depriued of all his kinglie
honor. . . .

Lewes, on the morrow following, being the 26 of Aprill
by his fathers procurement, came into the councell
chamber, and with frowning looke beheld the legat;
where by his procurator he defended the cause that moued
him to take vpon him this iournie into England, dis-
prouing not onelie the right which king Iohn had to the
crowne, but also alledging his owne interest, not onelie by
his new election of the barons, but also in the title of his
wife, whose mother the queene of Castile remained onelie
aliue of all the brethren and sisters of Henrie the second,
late King of England.

Lewes . . . imbarking himselfe with his people, and
all necessarie prouisions for such a iournie, tooke the
sea, and arriued at a place called Stanchorre in the Ile of
Tenet, vpon the 21 day of Maie; and shortlie after
came to Sandwich, & there landed with all his people,
where he also incamped vpon the shore by the space of
three daies. In which meane time there came vnto him a
great number of those lords and gentlemen which had
sent for him; and there euerie one apart and by himselfe
sware fealtie and homage vnto him, as if he had beene
their true and naturall prince.

King Iohn, about the same time that Lewes thus arriued,
came to Douer, meaning to fight with his aduersaries by
the way as they should come forward towards London.
But yet, vpon other aduisement taken, he changed his
purpose, bicause he put some doubt in the Flemings and
other strangers, of whome the most part of his armie
consisted, bicause he knew that they hated the French men
no more than they did the English. Therefore, furnishing
the castell of Douer, with men, munition, and vittels, he
left it in the keeping of Hubert de Burgh, a man of
notable prowesse & valiancie, and returned himselfe vnto
Canturburie, and from thence tooke the high waie towards
Winchester. Lewis, being aduertised that king Iohn was
retired out of Kent, passed through the countrie without

anie incounter, and wan all the castels and holds as he
went, but Douer he could not win. . . .

[*H.* iii. 191–192]   On the other part [he] tooke an oth to
mainteine and performe the old lawes and customes of
the realme, and to restore to euerie man his rightfull
heritage and lands ; requiring the barons furthermore to
continue faithfull towards him, assuring them to bring
things so to passe, that the realme of England should
recouer the former dignitie, and they their ancient
liberties.   Moreouer he vsed them so courteouslie, gaue
them so faire words, and made such large promises, that
they beleeued him with all their harts. . . .

The rumour of this pretended outward courtesie, being
once spred through the realme, caused great numbers of
people to come flocking to him ; among whome were
diuerse of those which before had taken part with king
Iohn, as William earle Warren, William earle of Arundell,
William earle of Salisburie, William Marshall the yoonger,
and diuerse other ; supposing verelie that the French
kings sonne should now obteine the kingdome. . . .

The cheefest points (as we find) that were laid by
Lewes his procurators against king Iohn were these:
that, by the murther committed in the person of his
nephue Arthur, he had beene condemned in the parlement
chamber, before the French king, by the peeres of France ;
and that, being summoned to appeare, he had obstinatelie
refused so to doo, and therefore had by good right forfeited
not onelie his lands within the precinct of France, but
also the realme of England, which was now due vnto the
said Lewes, as they alledged, in right of the ladie Blanch
his wife, daughter to Elianor queene of Spaine.   But the
pope refelled all such allegations as they produced for
proofe hereof, & seemed to defend king Iohns cause verie
pithilie ; but namelie, in that he was vnder the protection
of him as supreme lord of England.

[*H.* iii. 201]   The earle of Penbroke, and other the lords
that tooke part with king Henrie, hauing aduertisement,
that a new supplie of men was readie to come and aid
Lewes, they appointed Philip de Albenie and Iohn Marshall
to associat with them the power of the cinque ports, and
to watch for the comming of the aduersaries, that they

might keepe them from landing; who on saint Bartholo-
mews day set forth from Caleis, in purpose to arriue in
the Thames, and so to come vp the riuer to London.
Howbeit Hubert de Burgh, capiteine of the castell of
Douer, togither with the said Philip de Albenie and Iohn
Marshall, with other such power as they could get togither
of the cinque ports, hauing not yet aboue the number of
40 ships great & small, vpon the discouering of the French
fleet, (which consisted of 80 great ships, besides other
lesser vessels well appointed and trimmed,) made foorth
to the sea. And, first coasting aloofe from them, till
they had got the wind on their backs, came finallie with
their maine force to assaile the Frenchmen, and, with helpe
of their crossebowes and archers at the first ioining, made
great slaughter of their enimies; and so, grapling togither,
in the end the Englishmen bare themselues so manfullie,
that they vanquished the whole French fleet, and obteined
a famous victorie.

[H. iii. 193]   About the same time, or rather in   [V. iv.]
the yeare last past as some hold, it fortuned that the
vicount of Melune, a French man, fell sicke at London,
and, perceiuing that death was at hand, he called vnto him
certeine of the English barons, which remained in the
citie, vpon safeguard thereof, and to them made this
protestation: "I lament" (saith he) "your destruction
and desolation at hand, bicause ye are ignorant of the
perils hanging ouer your heads. For this vnderstand,
that Lewes, and with him 16 earles and barons of France,
haue secretlie sworne (if it shall fortune him to conquere
this realme of England, & to be crowned king) that he
will kill, banish, and confine all those of the English
nobilitie (which now doo serue vnder him, and persecute
their owne king) as traitours and rebels; and furthermore
will dispossesse all their linage of such inheritances as
they now hold in England. And bicause" (saith he)
"you shall not haue doubt hereof, I, which lie here at the
point of death, doo now affirme vnto you, and take it on
the perill of my soule, that I am one of those sixteen that
haue sworne to performe this thing: wherefore I aduise
you to prouide for your owne safeties, and your realmes
which you now destroie; and keepe this thing secret

which I haue vttered vnto you." After this speech was
vttered he streightwaies died.

When these words of the lord of Melune were opened
vnto the barons, they were, and not without cause, in
great doubt of themselues, for they saw how Lewes had
alredie placed and set Frenchmen in most of such castels
and townes as he had gotten, the right whereof indeed
belonged to them. And againe, it greeued them much
to vnderstand, how, besides the hatred of their prince,
they were euerie sundaie and holiedaie openlie accursed
in euerie church, so that manie of them inwardlie relented,
and could haue bin contented to haue returned to king
Iohn, if they had thought that they should thankfullie
haue beene receiued.

[H. iii. 197] It is reported by writers, that amongst
other things, as there were diuerse, which withdrew the
hearts of the Englishmen from Lewes, the consideration of
the confession which the vicount of Melune made at the
houre of his death, was the principall.

[H. iii. 194] Thus, the countrie being [V. v.–vii.]
wasted on each hand, the king hasted forward till he came
to Wellestreme sands, where passing the washes he lost
a great part of his armie, with horsses and carriages ; so
that it was iudged to be a punishment appointed by God,
that the spoile, which had beene gotten and taken out
of churches, abbeies, and other religious houses, should
perish, and be lost by such means togither with the
spoilers. Yet the king himselfe, and a few other, escaped
the violence of the waters, by following a good guide.
But, as some haue written, he tooke such greefe for the
losse susteined at this passage, that immediatlie therevpon
he fell into an ague ; the force and heat whereof, togither
with his immoderate feeding on rawe peaches, and
drinking of new sider, so increased his sicknesse, that he
was not able to ride, but was faine to be carried in a litter
presentlie made of twigs, with a couch of strawe vnder him,
without any bed or pillow, thinking to haue gone to Lincolne ; but the disease still so raged and grew vpon him,
that he was inforced to staie one night at the castell of
Laford, and, on the next day with great paine, caused
himselfe to be caried vnto Newarke, where, in the castell,

through anguish of mind, rather than through force of sicknesse, he departed this life the night before the nineteenth day of October, in the yeare of his age fiftie and one, and after he had reigned seauenteene yeares, six moneths, and seauen and twentie daies.

There be which haue written, that, after he had lost his armie, he came to the abbeie of Swineshead in Lincolneshire, and, there vnderstanding the cheapenesse and plentie of corne, shewed himselfe greatlie displeased therewith, as he that for the hatred which he bare to the English people, that had so traitorouslie reuolted from him vnto his aduersarie Lewes, wished all miserie to light vpon them; therevpon said in his anger, that he would cause all kind of graine to be at a farre higher price, yer manie daies should passe. Wherevpon a moonke, that heard him speake such words, being mooued with zeale for the oppression of his countrie, gaue the king poison in a cup of ale, wherof he first tooke the assaie, to cause the king not to suspect the matter, and so they both died in manner at one time. . . .

The men of warre that serued vnder his ensignes, being for the more part hired souldiers and strangers, came togither, and marching foorth with his bodie, each man with his armour on his backe, in warlike order, conueied it vnto Worcester, where he was pompouslie buried in the cathedrall church before the high altar; not for that he had so appointed (as some write) but bicause it was thought to be a place of most suertie for the lords and other of his freends there to assemble, and to take order in their businesse now after his deceasse.

[*H.* iii. 197] Immediatlie after the death of his father king Iohn, William Marshall earle of Penbroke, generall of his fathers armie, brought this yoong prince with his brother and sisters vnto Glocester, and there called a councell of all such lords as had taken part with king Iohn. Anon, after it was once openlie knowne, that the sonnes and daughters of the late deceassed prince were brought into a place of safetie, a great number of the lords and cheefe barons of the realme hasted thither (I meane not onelie such as had holden with king Iohn, but also diuerse other, which, vpon certeine knowledge had of his death,

were newlie reuolted from Lewes) in purpose to aid
yoong king Henrie, to whome of right the crowne did
apperteine. . . .

When the barons had heard this earles words, after
some silence and conference had, they allowed of his
saiengs, and immediatlie, with one consent, proclaimed the
yoong gentleman king of England ; whome the bishops of
Winchester and Bath did crowne and annoint with all
due solemnities at Glocester, vpon the day of the feast
of the apostles Simon & Iude, in presence of the legat.

Appearance and Character of John

[*H.* iii. 196] He was comelie of stature, but of looke
and countenance displeasant and angrie ; somewhat cruell
of nature, as by the writers of his time he is noted ; and
not so hardie as doubtfull in time of perill and danger.
But this seemeth to be an enuious report vttered by those
that were giuen to speake no good of him whome they
inwardlie hated. Howbeit some giue this witnesse of
him (as the author of the booke of Bernewell abbeie and
other) : that he was a great and mightie prince, but yet
not verie fortunate, much like to Marius the noble
Romane, tasting of fortune both waies ; bountifull and
liberall vnto strangers, but of his owne people (for their
dailie treasons practised towards him) a great oppressour ;
so that he trusted more to forreners than to them, and
therfore in the end he was of them vtterlie forsaken.

Verelie, whosoeuer shall consider the course of the
historie written of this prince, he shall find, that he hath
beene little beholden to the writers of that time in which
he liued ; for scarselie can they afoord him a good word,
except when the trueth inforceth them to come out with
it as it were against their willes. The occasion whereof
(as some thinke) was, for that he was no great freend to
the clergie. . . .

Certeinelie it should seeme the man had a princelie
heart in him, and wanted nothing but faithful subiects
to have assisted him in reuenging such wrongs as were
doone and offered by the French king and others.

Moreouer, the pride and pretended authoritie of the

cleargie he could not well abide, when they went about to wrest out of his hands the prerogatiue of his princelie rule and gouernment. True it is, that to mainteine his warres which he was forced to take in hand, as well in France as elsewhere, he was constreined to make all the shift he could deuise to recouer monie, and, bicause he pinched their pursses, they conceiued no small hatred against him ; which when he perceiued, and wanted peraduenture discretion to passe it ouer, he discouered now and then in his rage his immoderate displeasure, as one not able to bridle his affections, (a thing verie hard in a stout stomach), and thereby missed now and then to compasse that which otherwise he might verie well haue brought to passe.

RICHARD II

[The theme of *Richard II* is drawn almost exclusively from Holinshed. Clearly, the subject was one which had a decided fascination for contemporaries. The anonymous play called *The Life and Death of Iacke Straw, A notable Rebell in England* (printed 1593) has the King as a central figure. A drama which introduced Henry IV and the killing of Richard II was performed at the Globe on February 2, 1601, just before the ill-fated insurrection of Essex ; this may have been Shakespeare's, although it was described contemporaneously as an " *exoleta tragoedia* " and as " old and long out of use." Later, on April 30, 1611, Dr. Simon Forman saw a Richard play, clearly not Shakespeare's, at the Globe ; while a drama to which has been given the title of *Thomas of Woodstock* is preserved in the famous Egerton manuscript 1994. The last mentioned is of special importance because, as Dr. Boas has suggested, its existence may have caused Shakespeare to restrict his action to Richard's last years and to permit little of a comic note in his tragedy.]

THE QUARREL OF HEREFORD AND NORFOLK

[*H*. iii. 493–494] In this parlement holden at Shrewsburie, Henrie, duke of Hereford, accused Thomas Mowbraie duke of Norfolke of certeine words which he should vtter in talke had betwixt them, as they rode togither latelie before betwixt London and Brainford ; sounding highlie to the kings dishonor. And for further proofe thereof, he presented a supplication to the king, wherein he appealed the duke of Norfolke in field of battell, for a traitor, false and disloiall to the king, and enimie vnto the realme. This supplication was red before both the dukes, in presence of the king ; which doone, the duke of Norfolke tooke vpon him to answer it, declaring that whatsoeuer the duke of Hereford had said against him other than well, he lied falslie like a vntrue knight as he was. And, when the king asked of the duke of Hereford what he said to it, he, taking his hood off his head, said : " My souereign lord, euen as the supplication which I tooke you importeth, right so I saie for truth, that Thomas Mowbraie, duke of Norfolke, is a traitour, false and disloiall to your roiall maiestie, your crowne, and to all the states of your realme."

Then the duke of Norfolke being asked what he said to this, he answered: " Right deere lord, with your fauour that I make answer vnto your coosine here, I saie (your reuerence saued) that Henrie of Lancaster, duke of Hereford, like a false and disloiall traitor as he is, dooth lie, in that he hath or shall say of me otherwise than well." " No more," said the king, " we haue heard inough "; and herewith commanded the duke of Surrie, for that turne marshall of England, to arrest in his name the two dukes; the duke of Lancaster, father to the duke of Hereford, the duke of Yorke, the duke of Aumarle, constable of England, and the duke of Surrie, marshall of the realme, vndertooke as pledges bodie for bodie for the duke of Hereford; but the duke of Northfolke was not suffered to put in pledges, and so vnder arrest was led vnto Windsor castell, and there garded with keepers that were appointed to see him safelie kept.

Now after the dissoluing of the parlement at Shrewsburie, there was a daie appointed about six weeks after, for the king to come vnto Windsor, to heare and to take some order betwixt the two dukes, which had thus appealed ech other. There was a great scaffold erected within the castell of Windsor for the king to sit with the lords and prelats of his realme; and so, at the daie appointed, he with the said lords & prelats being come thither and set in their places, the duke of Hereford appellant, and the duke of Norfolke defendent, were sent for to come & appeare before the king, sitting there in his seat of iustice. And then began sir Iohn Bushie to speake for the king; declaring to the lords how they should vnderstand, that where the duke of Hereford had presented a supplication to the king, who was there set to minister iustice to all men that would demand the same, as apperteined to his roiall maiestie, he therefore would now heare what the parties could say one against an other: and withall the king commanded the dukes of Aumarle and Surrie, (the one being constable, and the other marshall,) to go vnto the two dukes, appellant and defendant, requiring them, on his behalfe, to grow to some agreement; and,

for his part, he would be readie to pardon all that had
been said or doone amisse betwixt them, touching anie
harm or dishonor to him or his realme ; but they answered
both assuredlie, that it was not possible to haue anie
peace or agreement made betwixt them.

When he heard what they had answered, he commanded
that they should be brought foorthwith before his presence,
to heare what they would say. Herewith an herald in
the kings name with lowd voice commanded the dukes to
come before the king, either of them to shew his reason,
or else to make peace togither without more delaie. When
they were come before the king and lords, the king spake
himselfe to them, willing them to agree, and make peace
togither : "for it is" (said he) "the best waie ye can
take." The duke of Norfolke with due reuerence herevnto
answered, it could not be so brought to passe, his honor
saued. Then the king asked of the duke of Hereford,
what it was that he demanded of the duke of Norfolke,
"and what is the matter that ye can not make peace
togither, and become friends ? "

Then stood foorth a knight, who, asking and obteining
licence to speake for the duke of Hereford, said : " Right
deare and souereigne lord, here is Henrie of Lancaster,
duke of Hereford and earle of Derbie, who saith, and I for
him likewise say, that Thomas Mowbraie, duke of Norfolke,
is a false and disloiall traitor to you and your roiall
maiestie, and to your whole realme : and likewise the
duke of Hereford saith, and I for him, *that* Thomas
Mowbraie, duke of Norfolke, *hath receiued eight thousand*
nobles to pay the *souldiers* that keep your towne of Calis ;
which he hath not doone as he ought: and furthermore
the said duke of Norfolke hath beene the occasion of *all*
the treason that hath beene contriued in your realme *for*
the space of *these eighteene yeares*, &, by his false sug-
gestions and malicious counsell he hath caused to die
and to be murdered your right deere vncle, the duke of
Glocester, sonne to king Edward. Moreouer, the duke
of Hereford saith, and I for him, that he will proue this
with his bodie against the bodie of the said duke of
Norfolke within lists." The king herewith waxed angrie,
and asked the duke of Hereford, if these were his woords;

who answered : " Right deere lord, they are my woords ; and hereof I require right, and the battell against him."

There was a knight also that asked licence to speake for the duke of Norfolke, and, obteining it, began to answer thus : " Right deere souereigne lord, here is Thomas Mowbraie, duke of Norfolke, who answereth and saith, and I for him, that all which Henrie of Lancaster hath said and declared (sauing the reuerence due to the king and his councell) is a lie ; and the said Henrie of Lancaster hath falselie and wickedlie lied as a false and disloiall knight, and both hath beene, and is, a traitor against you, your crowne, roiall maiestie, & realme. This will I proue and defend as becommeth a loiall knight to doo with my bodie against his : right deere lord, I beseech you therefore, and your councell, that it maie please you, in your roiall discretion to consider and marke, what Henrie of Lancaster, duke of Hereford, such a one as he is, hath said."

The king then demanded of the duke of Norfolke, if these were his woords, and whether he had anie more to saie. The duke of Norfolke then answered for himselfe : " Right deere sir, true it is, that I haue receiued so much gold to paie your people of the towne of Calis ; which I haue doone, and I doo auouch that your towne of Calis is as well kept at your commandement as euer it was at anie time before, and that there neuer hath beene by anie of Calis anie complaint made vnto you of me. Right deere and my souereigne lord, for the voiage that I made into France, about your marriage, I neuer receiued either gold or siluer of you, nor yet for the voiage that the duke of Aumarle & I made into Almane, where we spent great treasure. Marie, true it is, that *once* I laid *an ambush* to haue slaine the *duke of Lancaster*, that there sitteth; but neuerthelesse he hath pardoned me thereof, and there was good peace made betwixt vs, for the which I yeeld him hartie thankes. This is that which I haue to answer, and I am readie to defend my selfe against mine aduersarie; I beseech you therefore of right, and to haue the battell against him in vpright iudgement."

After this, when the king had communed with his

councell a little, he commanded the two dukes to stand
foorth, that their answers might be heard. The K. then
caused them once againe to be asked, if they would agree
and make peace togither, but they both flatlie answered
that they would not : and withall the duke of Hereford
cast downe his gage, and the duke of Norfolke tooke it
vp. The king, perceiuing this demeanor betwixt them,
sware by saint Iohn Baptist, that he would neuer seeke
to make peace betwixt them againe. And therefore sir
Iohn Bushie in name of the king & his councell declared,
that the king and his councell had commanded and
ordeined, that they should haue a daie of battell appointed
them at Couentrie.

THE MURDER OF GLOUCESTER

[*H*. iii. 489] [Richard] sent vnto Thomas Mowbraie,
earle marshall and of Notingham, to make the duke
secretlie awaie.

The earle prolonged time for the executing of the kings
commandement, though the king would haue had it
doone with all expedition, wherby the king conceiued no
small displeasure, and sware that it should cost the earle
his life if he quickly obeied not his commandement. The
earle thus, as it seemed, in maner inforced, called out the
duke at midnight, as if he should haue taken ship to passe
ouer into England, and there in the lodging called the
princes In, he caused his seruants to cast featherbeds
vpon him, and so smoother him to death ; or otherwise
to strangle him with towels (as some write.) This was
the end of that noble man, fierce of nature, hastie, wilfull,
and giuen more to war than to peace : and in this greatlie
to be discommended, that he was euer repining against
the king in all things, whatsoeuer he wished to haue
forward. . . . His bodie was afterwards with all funerall
pompe conueied into England, and buried at his owne
manor of Plashie within the church there ; in a sepulchre
which he in his life time had caused to be made, and
there erected.

[*H*. iii. 511–512] It was further conteined in that
bill, that as the same Bagot rode on a daie behind the

duke of Norfolke in the Sauoy street toward Westminster, the duke asked him what he knew of the manner of the duke of Glocester his death, and he answered that he knew nothing at all: "but the people" (quoth he) "doo saie that you haue murthered him." Wherevnto the duke sware great othes that it was vntrue, and that he had saued his life contrarie to the will of the king, and certeine other lords, by the space of three weeks, and more; affirming withall, that he was neuer in all his life time more affraid of death, than he was at his comming home againe from Calis at that time, to the kings presence, by reason he had not put the duke to death. "And then" (said he) "the king appointed one of his owne seruants, and certeine other that were seruants to other lords to go with him to see the said duke of Glocester put to death;" swearing that, as he should answer afore God, it was neuer his mind that he should haue died in that sort, but onelie for feare of the king and sauing of his owne life.

[H. iii. 488] Upon this multiplieng of woords [I. ii.] in such presumptuous maner by the duke against the king, there kindeled such displeasure betwixt them, that it neuer ceassed to increase into flames, till the duke was brought to his end. . . .

The king . . . determined to suppresse both the duke and other of his complices, and tooke more diligent regard to the saiengs & dooings of the duke than before he had doone. And as it commeth to passe that those, which suspect anie euill, doo euer deeme the worst; so he tooke euerie thing in euill part, insomuch that he complained of the duke vnto his brethren the dukes of Lancaster and Yorke, in that he should stand against him in all things and seeke his destruction, the death of his counsellors, and ouerthrow of his realme.

The two dukes of Lancaster and Yorke, to deliuer the kings mind of suspicion, made answer, that they were not ignorant, how their brother of Glocester, as a man sometime rash in woords, would speake oftentimes more than he could or would bring to effect, and the same proceeded of a faithfull hart, which he bare towards the king; for that it grieued him to vnderstand, that the

confines of the English dominions should in anie wise be
diminished : therefore his grace ought not to regard his
woords, sith he should take no hurt thereby. These
persuasions quieted the king for a time, till he was informed of the practise which the duke of Glocester had
contriued (as the fame went among diuerse persons) to
imprison the king. For then the duke of Lancaster and
Yorke, first reprouing the duke of Glocester for his too
liberall talking, vttering vnaduisedlie woords that became
not his person . . . and, perceuing that he set nothing
by their woords, were in doubt least, if they should remaine in the court still, he would, vpon a presumptuous
mind, in trust to be borne out by them, attempt some
outragious enterprise. Wherefore they thought best to
depart for a time into their countries, that by their
absence he might the sooner learne to staie himselfe for
doubt of further displeasure. But it came to passe,
that their departing from the court was the casting awaie
of the duke of Glocester. For after that they were gone,
there ceassed not such as bare him euill will, to procure
the K. to dispatch him out of the way.

The Meeting of Hereford and Norfolk

[*H*. iii. 494-495] At the time appointed the   [I. iii.]
king came to Couentrie, where the two dukes were readie,
according to the order prescribed therein ; comming
thither in great arraie, accompanied with the lords and
gentlemen of their linages. The king caused a sumptuous
scaffold or theater, and roiall listes there to be erected
and prepared. The sundaie before they should fight,
after dinner, the duke of Hereford came to the king (being
lodged about a quarter of a mile without the towne in a
tower that belonged to sir William Bagot) to take his
leaue of him. The morow after, being the day appointed
for the combat, about the spring of the daie, came the
duke of Norfolke to the court to take leaue likewise of
the king. The duke of Hereford armed him in his tent,
that was set vp neere to the lists ; and the duke of Norfolke
put on his armor, betwixt the gate & the barrier of the
towne, in a beautiful house, hauing a faire perclois of

wood towards the gate, that none might see what was
doone within the house.

The duke of Aumarle that daie, being high constable
of England, and the duke of Surrie, marshall, placed
themselues betwixt them, well armed and appointed;
and, when they saw their time, they first entered into the
lists with a great companie of men apparelled in silke
sendall, imbrodered with siluer, both richlie and curiouslie,
euerie man hauing a tipped staffe to keepe the field in
order.   About the houre of prime, came to the barriers
of the lists the duke of Hereford, mounted on a white
courser, barded with greene & blew veluet imbrodered
sumptuouslie with swans and antelops of goldsmiths
woorke; armed at all points.   The constable and marshall
came to the barriers, demanding of him what he was.
He answered: "*I am Henrie of Lancaster*, duke of Hereford, which am come hither to doo mine indeuor against
Thomas Mowbraie, duke of Norfolke, as *a traitor* vntrue
to God, the *king*, his realme, *and me*." Then incontinentlie he sware vpon the holie euangelists, that his
quarrell was true and iust, and vpon that point he
required to enter the lists.   Then he put vp his sword,
which before he held naked in his hand, and, putting
downe his visor, made a crosse on his horsse; and, with
speare in hand, entered into the lists, and descended from
his horsse, and set him downe in a chaire of greene veluet,
at the one end of the lists, and there reposed himselfe,
abiding the comming of his aduersarie.

Soone after him, entred into the field with great triumph
king Richard, accompanied with all the peeres of the
realme. . . . The king had there aboue ten thousand
men in armour, least some fraie or tumult might rise
amongst his nobles, by quarelling or partaking.   When
the king was set in his seat, (which was richlie hanged and
adorned,) a king at armes made open proclamation, prohibiting all men in the name of the king, and of the high
constable and marshall, to enterprise or attempt to
approch or touch any part of the lists vpon paine of death,
except such as were appointed to order or marshall the
field.   The proclamation ended, an other herald cried:
"Behold here Henrie of Lancaster, duke of Hereford,

appellant, which is entred into the lists roiall to doo his
deuoir against Thomas Mowbraie, duke of Norfolke,
defendant ; vpon paine to be found false and recreant ! "

The duke of Norfolke houered on horssebacke at the
entrie of the lists, his horsse being barded with crimosen
veluet, imbrodered richlie with lions of siluer and mulberie
trees ; and, when he had made his oth before the constable and marshall that his quarrell was iust and true,
he entred the field manfullie, saieng alowd : " God aid
him that hath the right ! " and then he departed from
his horsse, & sate him downe in his chaire, which was of
crimosen veluet, courtined about with white and red
damaske.   The lord marshall viewed their speares, to
see that they were of equall length, and deliuered the
one speare himselfe to the duke of Hereford, and sent
the other vnto the duke of Norfolke by a knight.   Then
the herald proclamed that the trauerses & chaires of the
champions should be remooued ; commanding them on
the kings behalfe to mount on horssebacke, & addresse
themselues to the battell and combat.

The duke of Hereford was quicklie horssed, and closed
his bauier, and cast his speare into the rest, and when the
trumpet sounded set forward couragiouslie towards his
enimie six or seuen pases.   The duke of Norfolke was not
fullie set forward, when *the king* cast *downe his warder*
and the heralds cried, "Ho, ho!"   Then the king caused
their speares to be taken from them, and commanded
them to repaire againe *to their chaires*, where they remained
two long houres, while the king and his councell de-
liberatlie consulted what order was best to be had in
so weightie a cause.   Finallie, after they had deuised,
and fullie determined what should be doone therein, the
heralds cried silence; and sir Iohn Bushie, the kings
secretarie, read the sentence and determination of the
king and his councell, in a long roll, the effect wherof
was, that Henrie duke of Hereford should within fifteene
daies depart out of the realme, and not to returne before
the terme of ten yeares were expired, except by the king
he should be repealed againe, and this *vpon paine of*
death; and that Thomas Mowbraie, duke of Norfolke,
bicause he had sowen sedition in the relme by his words,

should likewise auoid the realme, and *neuer to returne* againe into England, nor approch the borders or confines thereof *vpon paine of* death; and that the king would staie the profits of his lands, till he had leuied thereof such summes of monie as the duke had taken vp of the kings treasuror for the wages of the garrison of Calis, which were still vnpaid.

When these iudgements were once read, the king called before him both the parties, and made them to sweare that the one should neuer come in place where the other was, willinglie ; nor keepe any company to gither in any forren region ; which oth they both receiued humblie, and so went their waies. The duke of Norfolke departed sorowfullie out of the relme into Almanie, and at the last came to Venice, where he for thought and melancholie deceassed : for he was in hope (as writers record) that he should haue beene borne out in the matter by the king, which when it fell out otherwise, it greeued him not a little. The duke of Hereford tooke his leaue of the king at Eltham, who there released foure yeares of his banishment : so he tooke his iornie ouer into Calis, and from thence went into France, where he remained. . . .

A woonder it was to see what number of people ran after him in euerie towne and street where he came, before he tooke the sea ; lamenting and bewailing his departure, as who would saie, that when he departed, the onelie shield, defense, and comfort of the commonwealth was vaded and gone.

The Trouble in Ireland and at Home

[*H*. iii. 496–497] In this meane time the king [I. iv.] being aduertised that the wild Irish dailie wasted and destroied the townes and villages within the English pale, and had slaine manie of the souldiers which laie there in garison for defense of that countrie, determined to make eftsoones a voiage thither, & prepared all things necessarie for his passage now against the spring.

[*H*. iii. 496] The common brute ran, that the king had set *to farme* the *realme* of England vnto sir William Scroope, earle of Wiltshire, and then treasuror of England,

to sir Iohn Bushie, sir William Bagot, and sir Henrie
Greene, knights.

[*H.* iii. 496]   But yet to content the kings mind, manie
blanke charters were deuised, and brought into the citie,
which manie of the substantiall and wealthie citizens were
faine to seale, to their great charge, as in the end appeared.
And the like charters were sent abroad into all shires
within the realme, whereby great grudge and murmuring
arose among the people : for, when they were so sealed,
the kings officers wrote in the same what liked them, as
well for charging the parties with paiment of monie, as
otherwise.

[*H.* iii. 502]   The spiritualitie alledged against him, that
he, at his going into Ireland, exacted manie notable
summes of monie, beside plate and iewels, without law
or custome, contrarie to his oth taken at his coronation.

[*H.* iii. 496–497]   In this meane time the duke   [II. i.]
of Lancaster departed out of this life at the bishop of
Elies place in Holborne. . . .

The death of this duke gaue occasion of increasing more
hatred in the people of this realme toward the king, for
he seized into his hands all the goods that belonged to him,
and also receiued all the rents and reuenues of his lands
which ought to haue descended vnto the duke of Hereford
by lawfull inheritance ; in reuoking his letters patents,
which he had granted to him before, by vertue wherof he
might make his attorneis generall to sue liuerie for him, of
any maner of inheritances or possessions that might from
thencefoorth fall vnto him ; and that his homage might
be respited, with making reasonable fine : whereby it was
euident, that the king meant his vtter vndoing. . . .

This hard dealing was much misliked of all the nobilitie,
and cried out against of the meaner sort ; but namelie the
duke of Yorke was therewith sore mooued ; who, before
this time, had borne things with so patient a mind as he
could, though the same touched him verie neere, as the
death of his brother the duke of Glocester, the banishment
of his nephue the said duke of Hereford, and other mo
iniuries in great number ; which, for the slipperie youth
of the king, he passed ouer for the time, and did forget
aswell as he might. . . .

Herevpon he with the duke of Aumarle his sonne went
to his house at Langlie. . . .

When these iusts were finished, the king departed
toward Bristow, from thence to passe into Ireland ;
leauing the queene with hir traine still at Windesor : he
appointed for his lieutenant generall *in* his *absence* his
vncle the duke of *Yorke* : and so in the moneth of Aprill,
as diuerse authors write, he set forward from Windesor,
and finallie tooke shipping at Milford, and from thence,
with two hundred ships, and a puissant power of men of
armes and archers, he sailed into Ireland.

[*H*. iii. 428]   There was a new and strange subsidie or
taske granted to be leuied for the kings vse, and towards
the charges of this armie that went ouer into France with
the earle of Buckingham ; to wit, of euerie preest secular
or regular, six shillings eight pence, and as much of euerie
nunne, and of euerie man & woman married or not married,
being 16 yeares of age, (beggers certenlie knowne onlie
excepted,) foure pence for euerie one.   Great grudging &
manie a bitter cursse followed about the leuieng of this
monie,& much mischeefe rose thereof,as after it appeared.

Moreouer, this yeare he caused seuenteene shires of
the realme, by waie of putting them to their fines, to
paie no small summes of monie, for redeeming their
offenses, that they had aided the duke of Glocester, the
earles of Arundell, and Warwike, when they rose in armor
against him.   The nobles, gentlemen, and commons of
those shires were inforced also to receiue a new oth to
assure the king of their fidelitie in time to come ;   and
withall certeine prelats and other honorable personages
were sent into the same shires to persuade men to this
paiment, and to see things ordered at the pleasure of the
prince :   and suerlie the fines which the nobles, and other
the meaner estates of those shires were constreined to paie,
were not small, but exceeding great, to the offense of manie.

[*H*. iii. 497–498]   Now whilest he was thus occupied in
deuising how to reduce them into subiection, and taking
orders for the good staie and quiet gouernment of the countrie, diuerse of the nobilite, aswell prelats as other, and
likewise manie of the magistrats and rulers of the cities,
townes, and communaltie, here in England, perceiuing

dailie how the realme drew to vtter ruine, not like to be recouered to the former state of wealth whilest king Richard liued and reigned, (as they tooke it,) deuised with great deliberation, and considerate aduise, to send and signifie by letters vnto duke Henrie, whome they now called (as he was in deed) duke of Lancaster and Hereford, requiring him with all conuenient speed to conueie himselfe into England; promising him all their aid, power, and assistance, if he, expelling K. Richard, as a man not meet for the office he bare, would take vpon him the scepter, rule, and diademe of his natiue land and region.

He, therefore, being thus called vpon by messengers and letters from his freends, and cheeflie through the earnest persuasion of Thomas Arundell, late archbishop of Canturburie, who . . . had beene remooued from his see, and banished the realme by king Richards means, got him downe to Britaine, togither with the said archbishop; where he was ioifullie receiued of the duke and duchesse, and found such freendship at the dukes hands, that there were certeine ships rigged, and made readie for him, at a place in base *Britaine* called *Le port blanc*, as we find in the chronicles of Britaine; and, when all his prouision was made readie, he tooke the sea, togither with the said *archbishop of Canturburie*, and his nephue Thomas Arundell, sonne and heire to the late earle of Arundell. . . . There were also with him, *Reginald lord Cobham, sir Thomas Erpingham*, and *sir Thomas Ramston*, knights, *Iohn Norburie, Robert Waterton*, & *Francis Coint*, esquires: few else were there, for (as some write) he had not past fifteene lances, as they tearmed them in those daies, that is to saie, men of armes, furnished and appointed as the vse then was. ¶ Yet other write, that the duke of Britaine deliuered vnto him three thousand men of warre, to attend him, and that he had eight ships well furnished for the warre, where *Froissard* yet speaketh but of three. Moreouer, where *Froissard* and also the chronicles of Britaine auouch, that he should land at Plimmouth, by our English writers it seemeth otherwise: for it appeareth by their assured report, that he, approching to the shore, did not streight take land, but lay houering aloofe, and shewed himselfe now in this place, and now in that, to see what countenance was made by the people, whether they meant enuiouslie to resist him, or freendlie to receiue him.

[*H*. iii. 496] About the same time, the earle of Arundels sonne, named Thomas, which was kept in the duke of Exeters house, escaped out of the realme, by meanes of one William Scot, mercer ; and went to his vncle Thomas Arundell, late archbishop of Canturburie, as then soiourning at Cullen.

[*H*. iii. 498] When the lord gouernor, Edmund duke of Yorke, was aduertised, that the duke of Lancaster kept still the sea, and was readie to arriue, (but where he ment first to set foot on land, there was not any that vnderstood the certeintie,) he sent for the lord chancellor, Edmund Stafford, bishop of Excester, and for the lord treasuror, William Scroope, earle of Wiltshire, and other of the kings priuie councell, as Iohn Bushie, William Bagot, Henrie Greene, and Iohn Russel, knights : of these he required to know what they thought good to be doone in this matter, concerning the duke of Lancaster, being on the seas. Their aduise was, to depart from London vnto S. Albons, and there to gather an armie to resist the duke in his landing ; but, to how small purpose their counsell serued, the conclusion thereof plainlie declared, for the most part that were called, when they came thither, boldlie protested, that they would not fight against the duke of Lancaster, whome they knew to be euill dealt withall. . . .

The duke of Lancaster, after that he had coasted alongst the shore a certeine time, & had got some intelligence how the peoples minds were affected towards him, landed about the beginning of Iulie in Yorkshire, at a place sometime called Rauenspur, betwixt Hull and Bridlington ; and with him not past threescore persons, as some write : but he was so ioifullie recieued of the lords, knights, and gentlemen of those parts, that he found means (by their helpe) forthwith to assemble a great number of people, that were willing to take his part. The first that came to him were the lords of Lincolneshire, and other countries adioining ; as the lords Willoughbie, Ros, Darcie, and Beaumont.

[*H*. iii. 499–500] Sir Thomas Persie, earle of Worcester,

lord steward of the kings house, either being so commanded
by the king, or else vpon displeasure (as some write) for
that the king had proclaimed his brother the earle of
Northumberland, traitor, brake his white staffe, (which is
the representing signe and token of his office,) and without
delaie went to duke Henrie. When the kings seruants of
houshold saw this (for it was doone before them all) they
dispersed themselues, some into one countrie, and some
into an other.

[*H*. iii. 499]   But here you shall note, that it   [II. ii.]
fortuned at the same time in which the duke of Hereford or
Lancaster (whether ye list to call him) arriued thus in
England, the seas were so troubled by tempests, and the
winds blew so contrarie for anie passage to come ouer
foorth of England to the king, remaining still in Ireland,
that, for the space of six weeks, he recieued no aduertisements from thence : yet at length, when the seas became
calme, and the wind once turned anie thing fauourable,
there came ouer a ship ; whereby the king vnderstood the
manner of the dukes arriuall, and all his proceedings till
that daie in which the ship departed from the coast of
England : wherevpon he meant foorthwith to haue
returned ouer into England, to make resistance against
the duke ; but through persuasion of the duke of Aumarle
(as was thought) he staied, till he might haue all his ships,
and other prouision, fullie readie for his passage.

[*H*. iii. 498]   The lord treasuror, Bushie, Bagot, and
Greene, perceiuing that the commons would cleaue vnto,
and take part with, the duke, slipped awaie ; leauing the
lord gouernour of the realme, and the lord chancellor, to
make what shift they could for themselues. Bagot got
him to Chester, and so escaped in*to Ireland*; the other
fled *to* the *castell* of *Bristow*, in hope there to be in
safetie.

[*H*. iii. 498]   At [Bolingbroke's] comming   [II. iii.]
vnto Doncaster, the earle of Northumberland, and his
sonne, sir Henrie Persie, wardens of the marches against
Scotland, with the earle of Westmerland, came vnto him ;
where he sware vnto those lords, that he would demand
no more, but the lands that were to him descended by
inheritance from his father, and in right of his wife.

Moreouer, he vndertooke to cause the paiment of taxes and tallages to be laid downe, & to bring the king to good gouernment, & to remooue from him the Cheshire men, which were enuied of manie ; for that the king esteemed of them more than of anie other ; happilie, bicause they were more faithfull to him than other, readie in all respects to obeie his commandements and pleasure. From Doncaster, hauing now got a mightie armie about him, he marched foorth with all speed through the countries, comming by Euesham vnto Berkelie : within the space of three daies, all the kings castels in those parts were surrendred vnto him.

The duke of Yorke, whome king Richard had left as gouernour of the realme in his absence, hearing that his nephue the duke of Lancaster was thus arriued, and had gathered an armie, he also assembled a puissant power of men of armes and archers ; (as before yee haue heard ;) but all was in vaine, for there was not a man that willinglie would thrust out one arrow against the duke of Lancaster, or his partakers, or in anie wise offend him or his freends. The duke of Yorke, therefore, passing foorth towards Wales to meet the king, at his comming foorth of Ireland, was receiued into the castell of Berkelie, and there remained, till the comming thither of the duke of Lancaster, whom (when he perceiued that he was not able to resist, on the sundaie, after the feast of saint Iames, which, as that yeare came about, fell vpon the fridaie) he came foorth into the church that stood without the castell, and there communed with the duke of Lancaster. With the duke of Yorke were the bishop of Norwich, the lord Berkelie, the lord Seimour, and other ; with the duke of Lancaster were these : Thomas Arundell, archbishop of Canturburie, (that had beene banished,) the abbat of Leicester, the earles of Northumberland and Westmerland, Thomas Arundell, sonne to Richard, late earle of Arundell, the baron of Greistoke, the lords Willoughbie and Ros, with diuerse other lords, knights, and other people, which dailie came to him from euerie part of the realme : those that came not were spoiled of all they had, so as they were neuer able to recouer themselues againe, for their goods, being then taken awaie, were neuer restored. And thus,

what for loue, and what for feare of losse, they came
flocking vnto him from euerie part.

[*H*. iii. 499]   In the meane time, he sent the   [II. iv.]
earle of Salisburie ouer into England, to gather a power
togither, by helpe of the kings freends in Wales, and
Cheshire, with all speed possible ; that they might be
readie to assist him against the duke, vpon his arriuall,
for he meant himselfe to follow the earle, within six daies
after.   The earle, passing ouer into Wales, landed at
Conwaie, and sent foorth letters to the kings freends, both
in Wales and Cheshire, to leauie their people, & to come
with all speed to assist the K., whose request, with great
desire, & very willing minds, they fulfilled, hoping to haue
found the king himself at Conwaie ; insomuch that, within
foure daies space, there were to the number of fortie
thousand men assembled, readie to march with the king
against his enimies, if he had beene there himselfe in
person.

But, when they missed the king, there was a brute spred
amongst them, that *the king* was suerlie *dead* ; which
wrought such an impression, and euill disposition, in the
minds of the Welshmen and others, that, for anie persuasion
which the earle of Salisburie might vse, they would not go
foorth with him, till they saw the king : onelie they were
contented to staie foureteene daies to see if he should come
or not ; but, when he came not within that tearme, they
would no longer abide, but scaled & departed awaie ;
wheras if the king had come before their breaking vp, no
doubt, but they would haue put the duke of Hereford in
aduenture of a field : so that the kings lingering of time,
before his comming ouer, gaue opportunitie to the duke to
bring things to passe as he could haue wished, and took
from the king all occasion to recouer afterwards anie forces
sufficient to resist him.

[*H*. iii. 496]   In this yeare in a manner throughout all
the realme of England, old *baie trees withered*, and, afterwards, contrarie to all mens thinking, grew greene againe ;
a strange sight, and supposed to import some vnknowne
euent.

[*H*. iii. 498]   The forsaid dukes, with their   [III. i.]
power, went towards Bristow, where (at their comming)

they shewed themselues before the towne & castell; being
an huge multitude of people. There were inclosed within
the castell, the lord William Scroope, earle of Wiltshire and
treasuror of England, sir Henrie Greene, and sir Iohn
Bushie, knights, who prepared to make resistance; but,
when it would not preuaile, they were taken and brought
foorth bound as prisoners into the campe, before the duke
of Lancaster. On the morow next insuing, they were
arraigned before the constable and marshall, and found
giltie of treason, for misgouerning the king and realme;
and foorthwith had their heads smit off.

[*H.* iii. 499] At length, about eighteene [III. ii.]
daies after that the king had sent from him the earle of
Salisburie, he tooke the sea, togither with the dukes of
Aumarle, Excester, Surrie, and diuerse others of the
nobilitie, with the bishops of London, Lincolne, and
Carleill. They landed neere the castell of Barclowlie in
Wales, about the feast of saint Iames the apostle, and
staied a while in the same castell, being aduertised of the
great forces which the duke of Lancaster had got togither
against him; wherewith he was maruellouslie amazed,
knowing certeinelie that those, which were thus in armes
with the duke of Lancaster against him, would rather
die than giue place, as well for the hatred as feare which
they had conceiued at him. Neuerthelesse he, departing
from Barclowlie, hasted with all speed towards Conwaie,
where he vnderstoode the earle of Salisburie to be still
remaining.

He therefore taking with him such Cheshire men as he
had with him at that present (in whom all his trust was
reposed) he doubted not to reuenge himselfe of his aduersaries, & so at the first he passed with a good courage; but
when he vnderstood as he went thus forward, that all the
castels, euen from the borders of Scotland vnto Bristow,
were deliuered vnto the duke of Lancaster; and that likewise the nobles and commons, as well of the south parts,
as the north, were fullie bent to take part with the same
duke against him; and further, hearing how his trustie
councillors had *lost their heads at Bristow*, he became so
greatlie discomforted, that sorowfullie lamenting his miserable state, he vtterlie despaired of his owne safetie, and

calling his armie togither, which was not small, licenced euerie man to depart to his home.

The souldiers, being well bent to fight in his defense, besought him to be of good cheere, promising with an oth to stand with him against the duke, and all his partakers vnto death; but this could not incourage him at all, so that, in the night next insuing, he stole from his armie, and, with the dukes of Excester and Surrie, the bishop of Carleill, and sir Stephan Scroope, and about halfe a score others, he got him to the castell of Conwaie, where he found the earle of Salisburie; determining there to hold himselfe, till he might see the world at some better staie; for what counsell to take to remedie the mischeefe thus pressing vpon him he wist not.

[*H.* iii. 500–501] King Richard being thus [III. iii.] come vnto the castell of Flint, on the mondaie, the eighteenth of August, and the duke of Hereford being still aduertised from houre to houre by posts, how the earle of Northumberland sped, the morow following being tues-daie, and the nineteenth of August, he came thither, & mustered his armie before the kings presence; which vndoubtedlie made a passing faire shew, being verie well ordered by the lord Henrie Persie, that was appointed generall, or rather (as we maie call him) master of the campe, vnder the duke, of the whole armie.

[*H.* iii. 500] [Northumberland] came before the towne, and then sending an herald to the king, requested a safe conduct from the king, that he might come and talke with him; which the king granted, and so the earle of Northumberland, passing the water, entred the castell, and comming to the king, declared to him, that, if it might please his grace to vndertake, that there should be a parlement assembled, in the which iustice might be had against such as were enimies to the common-wealth, and had procured the destruction of the duke of Glocester, and other noblemen, and herewith pardon the duke of Hereford of all things wherin he had offended him, the duke would be readie to come to him *on his knees*, to craue of him forgiuenesse, and, as an humble subiect, to obeie him in all dutifull seruices.

[*H.* iii. 501] Then the earle of Northumberland, passing

foorth of the castell to the duke, talked with him a while
in sight of the king, being againe got vp to the walles, to
take better view of the armie, being now aduanced within
two bowe shootes of the castell, to the small reioising (ye
may be sure) of the sorowfull king. The earle of
Northumberland, returning to the castell, appointed the
king to be set to dinner (for he was fasting till then) and,
after he had dined, the duke came downe to the castell
himselfe, and entred the same all armed, his bassenet
onelie excepted ; and being within the first gate, he staied
there, till the king came foorth of the inner part of the
castell vnto him.

The king, accompanied with the bishop of Carleill, the
earle of Salisburie, and sir Stephan Scroope, knight, (who
bare the sword before him,) and a few other, came foorth
into the vtter ward, and sate downe in a place prepared
for him. Foorthwith, as the duke got sight of the king,
he shewed a reuerend dutie as became him, in bowing his
knee, and, comming forward, did so likewise the second
and third time, till the king tooke him by the hand, and
lift him vp, saieng : "Deere cousine, ye are welcome."
The duke, humblie thanking him, said : "My souereigne
lord and king, the cause of my comming at this present,
is (your honor saued) to haue againe restitution of my
person, my lands and heritage, through your fauourable
licence." The king hervnto answered : "Deere cousine,
I am readie to accomplish your will, so that ye may inioy
all that is yours, without exception."

Meeting thus togither, they came foorth of the castell,
and the king there called for wine, and after they had
dronke, they mounted on horssebacke, and rode . . . to
London.

The Declaration of the Parliament of 1399

[*H.* iii. 512] There was no man in the realme [IV. i.]
to whom king Richard was so much beholden, as to the
duke of Aumarle : for he was the man that, to fulfill his
mind, had set him in hand with all that was doone against
the said duke, and the other lords. . . . There was also
conteined in the said bill, that Bagot had heard the duke

of Aumarle say, that he had rather than twentie thousand pounds that the duke of Hereford were dead ; not for anie feare he had of him, but for the trouble and mischeefe that he was like to procure within the realme.

After that the bill had beene read and heard, the duke of Aumarle rose vp and said, that as touching the points conteined in the bill concerning him, they were vtterlie false and vntrue ; which he would proue with his bodie, in what manner soeuer it should be thought requisit. . . .

On the saturdaie next insuing, sir William Bagot and the said John Hall were brought both to the barre, and Bagot was examined of certeine points, and sent againe to prison. The lord Fitzwater herewith rose vp, and said to the king, that where the duke of Aumarle excuseth himselfe of the duke of Glocester's death, " I say " (quoth he) " that he was *the* verie *cause of* his *death* " ; and so he appealed him of treason, offering by throwing downe his hood as a gage to proue it with his bodie. There were twentie other lords also that threw downe their hoods, as pledges to proue the like matter against the duke of Aumarle. The duke of Aumarle threw downe his hood to trie it against the lord Fitzwater, as against him that lied falselie, in that he had charged him with, by that his appeale. These gages were deliuered to the constable and marshall of England, and the parties put vnder arrest.

The duke of Surrie stood vp also against the lord Fitzwater, auouching that where he had said that the appellants were causers of the duke of Gloucesters death, it was false, for they were constrained to sue the same appeale, in like manner as the said lord Fitzwater was compelled to giue iudgement against the duke of Glocester, and the earle of Arundell ; so that the suing of the appeale was doone by constraint, and if he said contrarie he lied : and therewith he threw downe his hood. The lord Fitzwater answered herevnto, that he was not present in the parlement house, when iudgement was giuen against them, and all the lords bare witnesse thereof. Moreouer, where it was alledged that the duke of *Aumarle* should send *two of* his seruants *to Calis*, to murther the duke of Glocester, the said duke of Aumarle said, that if the duke of Norfolke affirme it, he lied falselie, and that he would

proue with his bodie ; throwing downe an other hood
which he had borowed. The same was likewise deliuered
to the constable and marshall of England, and the king
licenced the duke of Norfolk to returne, that he might
arraigne his appeale.

RICHARD IN THE TOWER

[*H*. iii. 503]   To bring the matter without slander the
better to passe, diuerse of the kings seruants, which by
licence had accesse to his person, comforted him (being
with sorrow almost consumed, and in manner halfe dead)
in the best wise they could, exhorting him to regard his
health, and saue his life.

And first, they aduised him willinglie to suffer himselfe
to be deposed, and to resigne his right of his owne accord,
so that the duke of Lancaster might without murther or
battell obteine the scepter and diademe, after which (they
well perceiued) he gaped : by meane whereof they thought
he might be in perfect assurance of his life long to continue.
Whether this their persuasion proceeded by the suborning
of the duke of Lancaster and his fauourers, or of a sincere
affection which they bare to the king, as supposing it
most sure in such an extremitie, it is vncerteine ; but
yet the effect followed not, howsoeuer their meaning was :
notwithstanding, the king, being now in the hands of his
enimies, and vtterlie despairing of all comfort, was easilie
persuaded to renounce his crowne and princelie preheminence, so that, in hope of life onelie, he agreed to all
things that were of him demanded.   And so (as it should
seeme by the copie of an instrument hereafter following)
he renounced and voluntarilie was deposed from his
roiall crowne and kinglie dignitie ; the mondaie being
the nine and twentith daie of September, and feast of
S. Michaell the archangell, in the yeare of our Lord 1399,
and in the three and twentith yeare of his reigne.

[*H*. iii. 504]   Now foorthwith, in our presences and
others, he subscribed the same, and after deliuered it vnto
the archbishop of Canturburie, saieng that if it were in his
power, or at his assignement, he would that the duke of
Lancaster there present should be his successour, and king

after him . . . desiring and requiring the archbishop of Yorke, & the bishop of Hereford, to shew and make report vnto the lords of the parlement of his voluntarie resignation, and also of his intent and good mind that he bare towards his cousin the duke of Lancaster, to haue him his successour and their king after him.

[*H*. iii. 505] Immediatlie as the sentence was in this wise passed, and that by reason thereof the realme stood void without head or gouernour for the time, the duke of Lancaster, rising from the place where before he sate, and standing where all those in the house might behold him, in reuerend manner made a signe of the crosse on his forhead, and likewise on his brest, and, after silence by an officer commanded, said vnto the people, there being present, these words following.

The duke of Lancaster laieth challenge
or claime to the crowne.

" In the name of the Father, and of the Sonne, & of the Holie-ghost. I Henrie of Lancaster claime the realme of England and the crowne, with all the appurtenances, as I that am descended by right line of the blood comming from that good lord king Henrie the third ; and through the right that God of his grace hath sent me, with the helpe of my kin, and of my freends, to recouer the same, which was in point to be vndoone for default of good gouernance and due iustice."

After these words thus by him vttered, he returned and sate him downe in the place where before he had sitten. Then the lords hauing heard and well perceiued this claime thus made by this noble man, ech of them asked of other what they thought therein. At length, after a little pausing or staie made, the archbishop of Canturburie, hauing notice of the minds of the lords, stood vp & asked the commons if they would assent to the lords, which in their minds thought the claime of the duke made, to be rightfull and necessarie for the wealth of the realme and them all : whereto the commons with one voice cried, " Yea, yea, yea ! " After which answer, the said archbishop, going to the duke, and kneeling downe before him on his knee, addressed to him all his purpose in few words.

The which when he had ended, he rose, &, taking the duke
by the right hand, led him vnto the kings seate, (the archbishop of Yorke assisting him,) and with great reuerence
set him therein, after that the duke had first vpon his knees
made his praier in deuout manner vnto almightie God.

[*H.* iii. 512] On wednesdaie following, request was
made by the commons, that sith king Richard had
resigned, and was lawfullie deposed from his roiall dignitie,
he might haue iudgement decreed against him, so as the
realme were not troubled by him, and that the causes of
his deposing might be published through the realme for
satisfieng of the people : which demand was granted.
Wherevpon the bishop of Carleill, a man both learned,
wise, and stout of stomach, boldlie shewed foorth his
opinion concerning that demand ; affirming that there was
none amongst them woorthie or meet to giue iudgement
vpon so noble a prince as king Richard was, whom they
had taken for their souereigne and liege lord, by the space
of two & twentie yeares and more : " And I assure you "
(said he) " there is not so ranke a traitor, nor so errant a
theef, nor yet so cruell a murtherer apprehended or
deteined in prison for his offense, but he shall be brought
before the iustice to heare his iudgement ; and will ye
proceed to the iudgement of an anointed king, hearing
neither his answer nor excuse ? I say, that the duke of
Lancaster, *whom* ye *call king*, hath more trespassed to
K. Richard & his realme, than king Richard hath doone
either to him, or vs : " . . . As soone as the bishop
had ended this tale, he was attached by the earle marshall,
and committed to ward in the abbeie of saint Albons.

[*H.* iii. 504–505] Upon the morrow after, being tuesdaie,
and the last daie of September, all the lords spirituall and
temporall, with the commons of the said parlement,
assembled at Westminster, where, in the presence of them,
the archbishop of Yorke, and the bishop of Hereford,
according to the kings request, shewed vnto them the
voluntarie renouncing of the king, with the fauour also
which he bare to his cousine of Lancaster to haue him
his successour. And moreouer shewed them the schedule
or bill of renouncement, signed with king Richards owne
hand ; which they caused to be read first in Latine, as it

was written, and after in English. This doone, the
question was first asked of the lords, if they would admit
and allow that renouncement : the which when it was of
them granted and confirmed, the like question was asked
of the commons, and of them in like manner confirmed.
After this, it was then declared, that, notwithstanding the
foresaid renouncing, so by the lords and commons admitted
and confirmed, it were necessarie, in auoiding of all
suspicions and surmises of euill disposed persons, to haue
in writing and registred the manifold crimes and defaults
before doone by king Richard, to the end that they might
first be openlie declared to the people, and after to remaine
of record amongst other of the kings records for euer.

All this was doone accordinglie, for the articles, which
before yee haue heard, were drawne and ingrossed vp,
and there shewed readie to be read ; but, for other causes
more needfull as then to be preferred, the reading of those
articles at that season was deferred.

[H. iii. 502] After this was a parlement called by
the duke of Lancaster, vsing the name of king Richard in
the writs directed foorth to the lords, and other states for
their summons. This parlement began the thirteenth
daie of September, in the which manie heinous points of
misgouernance and iniurious dealings in the administration
of his kinglie office, were laid to the charge of this noble
prince king Richard : the which (to the end the commons
might be persuaded, that he was an vnprofitable prince to
the common-wealth, and worthie to be deposed) were
ingrossed vp in 33 solemne articles.

[H. iii. 504] The King with glad countenance . . .
said openlie that he was readie to renounce and resigne
all his kinglie maiestie in maner and forme as he before had
promised. And although he had and might sufficientlie
haue declared his renouncement by the reading of an other
meane person ; yet, for the more suertie of the matter,
and for that the said resignation should haue his full
force and strength, himselfe therefore read the scroll of
resignation, in maner and forme as followeth.

[H. iii. 501] The next day after his comming to London,
the king from Westminster was had to the Tower, and
there committed to safe custodie.

[*H*. iii. 514] By force of this act king Henrie thought himselfe firmelie set on a sure foundation, not needing to feare any storme of aduerse fortune. But yet shortlie after he was put in danger to haue beene set besides the seat, by a conspiracie begun in the abbat of Westminsters house, which had it not beene hindred, it is doubtfull whether the new king should haue inioied his roialtie, or the old king (now a prisoner) restored to his principalitie.

[*H*. iii. 507] Shortlie after Richard's resignation, [V. i.] he was conueied to the castell of Leeds in Kent, & fro*m* thence to Pomfret, where he departed out of this miserable life (as after you shall heare).

[*H*. iii. 501] As for the duke, he was receiued   [V. ii–iii.] with all the ioy and pompe that might be of the Londoners, and was lodged in the bishops palace, by Paules church. It was a woonder to see what great concursse of people, & what number of horsses, came to him on the waie as he thus passed the countries, till his comming to London, where (vpon his approach to the citie) the maior rode foorth to receiue him, and a great number of other citizens. Also the cleargie met him with procession ; and such joy appeared in the countenances of the people, vttering the same also with words, as the like not lightlie beene seene. For in euerie towne and village where he passed, children reioised, women clapped their hands, and men cried out for ioy. But to speake of the great numbers of people that flocked togither in the fields and streets of London at his comming, I here omit ; neither will I speake of the presents, welcommings, lauds, and gratifications made to him by the citizens and communaltie.

[*H*. iii. 501] Manie euill disposed persons, assembling themselues togither in great numbers, intended to haue met with [Richard], and to haue taken him from such as had the conueieng of him, that they might haue slaine him. But the maior and aldermen gathered to them the worship-full commoners and graue citizens, by whose policie, and not without much adoo, the other were reuoked from their euill purpose.

[*H*. iii. 513] It was finallie enacted, that such as were appellants in the last parlement against the duke of

Glocester and other, should in this wise following be ordred. The dukes of Aumarle, Surrie, and Excester, there present, were iudged to loose their names of dukes, togither with the honors, titles, and dignities therevnto belonging.

THE ABBOT'S CONSPIRACY

[*H*. iii. 514–515] But now to speak of the conspiracie, which was contriued by the abbat of Westminster as cheefe instrument thereof. Ye shall vnderstand, that this abbat (as it is reported) vpon a time heard king Henrie saie, when he was but earle of Derbie, and yoong of yeares, that princes had too little, and religious men too much. He therfore doubting now, least if the king continued long in the estate, he would remooue the great beame that then greeued his eies, and pricked his conscience, became an instrument to search out the minds of the nobilitie, and to bring them to an assemblie and councell, where they might consult and commen togither, how to bring that to effect, which they earnestlie wished and desired ; that was, the destruction of king Henrie, and the restoring of king Richard. For there were diuerse lords that shewed themselues outwardlie to fauor king Henrie, where they secretlie wished & sought his confusion. The abbat, after he had felt the minds of sundrie of them, called to his house, on a day in the terme time, all such lords & other persons which he either knew or thought to be as affectioned to king Richard, so enuious to the prosperitie of king Henrie ; whose names were: Iohn Holland earle of Huntington, late duke of Excester ; Thomas Holland earle of Kent, late duke of Surrie ; Edward earle of Rutland, late duke of Aumarle, sonne to the duke of Yorke ; Iohn Montacute earle of Salisburie ; Thomas lord Spenser, late earle of Glocester ; Thomas the bishop of Carleill ; sir Thomas Blunt ; and Maudelen, a priest, one of king Richards chappell, a man as like him in stature and proportion in all lineaments of bodie, as vnlike in birth, dignitie, and conditions.

The abbat highlie feasted these lords, his speciall freends, and, when they had well dined, they withdrew into a secret chamber, where they sat downe in councell, and, after much talke & conference had about the bringing of their purpose to passe concerning the destruction of king Henrie, at length by the aduise of the earle of Huntington it was deuised, that they should take vpon them a solemne iusts to be enterprised betweene him and 20 on his part, & the earle of Salisburie and 20 with him, at Oxford; to the which triumph K. Henrie should be desired, &, when he should be most busilie marking the martiall pastime, he suddenlie should be slaine and destroied, and so by that means king Richard, who as yet liued, might be restored to libertie, and haue his former estate & dignitie. It was further appointed, who should assemble the people; the number and persons which should accomplish and put in execution their deuised enterprise. Hervpon was an indenture sextipartite made, sealed with their seales, and signed with their hands, in the which each stood bound to other, to do their whole indeuour for the accomplishing of their purposed exploit. Moreouer, they sware on the holie euangelists to be true and secret each to other, euen to the houre and point of death.

When all things were thus appointed, the earle of Huntington came to the king vnto Windsore, earnestlie requiring him, that he would vouchsafe to be at Oxenford on the daie appointed of their iustes; both to behold the same, and to be the discouerer and indifferent iudge (if anie ambiguitie should rise) of their couragious acts and dooings. The king, being thus instantlie required of his brother in law, and nothing lesse imagining than that which was pretended, gentlie granted to fulfill his request. Which thing obteined, all the lords of the conspiracie departed home to their houses, as they noised it, to set armorers on worke about the trimming of their armour against the iusts, and to prepare all other furniture and things readie, as to such an high & solemne triumph apperteined. The earle of Huntington came to his house and raised men on euerie side, and prepared horsse and harnesse for his compassed purpose; and, when he had all things readie, he departed towards Oxenford, and, at his comming thither, he found all his mates and con-

federates there, well appointed for their purpose, except
the earle of Rutland, by whose follie their practised
conspiracie was brought to light and disclosed to king
Henrie. For this earle of Rutland, departing before
from Westminster to see his father the duke of Yorke,
as he sat at dinner, had his counterpane of the indenture
of the confederacie in his bosome.

The father, espieng it, would needs see what it was;
and, though the sonne humblie denied to shew it, the
father, being more earnest to see it, by force tooke it
out of his bosome; and perceiuing the contents therof,
in a great rage caused his horsses to be sadled out of
hand, and spitefullie reproouing his sonne of treason, for
whome he was become suertie and mainpernour for his
good abearing in open parlement, he incontinentlie
mounted on horssebacke to ride towards Windsore to
the king, to declare vnto him the malicious intent of his
complices. The earle of Rutland, seeing in what danger
he stood, tooke his horsse, and rode another waie to
Windsore in post, so that he got thither before his father,
and, when he was alighted at the castell gate, he caused
the gates to be shut, saieng that he must needs deliuer
the keies to the king. When he came before the kings
presence, he kneeled downe on his knees, beseeching him
of mercie and forgiuenesse, and, declaring the whole
matter vnto him in order as euerie thing had passed,
obteined pardon. Therewith came his father, and, being
let in, deliuered the indenture, which he had taken from
his sonne, vnto the king, who thereby perceiuing his
sonnes words to be true, changed his purpose for his
going to Oxenford.

RICHARD'S DEATH

[*H.* iii. 517] One writer, which seemeth to [V. iv.–v.]
haue great knowledge of king Richards dooings, saith,
that king Henrie, sitting on a daie at his table, sore
sighing, said: "*Haue I no* faithfull *freend* which will
deliuer me of him, whose life will be my death, and whose
death will be the preseruation of my life?" This saieng
was much noted of them which were present, and

especiallie of one called sir Piers of Exton. This knight incontinentlie departed from the court, with eight strong persons in his companie, and came to Pomfret, commanding the esquier, that was accustomed to sew and take the assaie before king Richard, to doo so no more, saieng : " Let him eat now, for he shall not long eat." King Richard sat downe to dinner, and was serued without courtesie or assaie ; wherevpon, much maruelling at the sudden change, he demanded of the esquier whie he did not his dutie : " Sir " (said he) " I am otherwise commanded by sir Piers of Exton, which is newlie come from K. Henrie." When king Richard heard that word, he tooke the keruing knife in his hand, and strake the esquier on the head, saieng: *The diuell take Henrie of Lancaster and thee togither!*" And with that word, sir Piers entred the chamber, well armed, with eight tall men likewise armed, euerie of them hauing a bill in his hand.

King Richard, perceiuing this, put the table from him, &, steping to the formost man, wrung the bill out of his hands, & so valiantlie defended himselfe, that he slue foure of those that thus came to assaile him. Sir Piers, being half dismaied herewith, lept into the chaire where king Richard was woont to sit, while the other foure persons fought with him, and chased him about the chamber. And in conclusion, as king Richard trauersed his ground, from one side of the chamber to an other, & comming by the chaire, where sir Piers stood, he was felled with a stroke of a pollax which sir Piers gaue him vpon the head, and therewith rid him out of life ; without giuing him respit once to call to God for mercie of his passed offenses. It is said, that sir Piers of Exton, after he had thus slaine him, wept right bitterlie, as one striken with the pricke of a giltie conscience, for murthering him, whome he had so long time obeied as king.

THE FORTUNES OF THE REBELS

[*H.* iii. 516] The lord Hugh Spenser, other- [V. vi.] wise called earle of Glocester, as he would haue fled into Wales, was taken and carried to Bristow, where (according to the earnest desires of the commons) he was beheaded. . . . Manie other that were priuie to this conspiracie, were taken, and put to death, some at Oxford, as sir Thomas Blunt, sir Benet Cilie, knight, . . . but sir Leonard Brokas, and [others] . . . , were drawne, hanged, and beheaded at London. There were nineteene in all executed in one place and other, and the heads of the cheefe conspirators were set on polles ouer London bridge, to the terror of others. Shortlie after, the abbat of Westminster, in whose house the conspiracie was begun, (as is said,) gooing betweene his monasterie & mansion, for thought fell into a sudden palsie, and shortlie after, without speech, ended his life. The bishop of Carleill was impeached, and condemned of the same conspiracie ; but the king, of his mercifull clemencie, pardoned him of that offense ; although he died shortlie after, more through feare than force of sicknesse, as some haue written.

Richard's Funeral

[*H*. iii. 517] After he was thus dead, his bodie was imbalmed, and seered, and couered with lead, all saue the face, to the intent that all men might see him, and perceiue that he was departed this life : for as the corps was conueied from Pomfret to London in all the townes and places where those that had the conueiance of it did staie with it all night, they caused dirige to be soong in the euening, and masse of *Requiem* in the morning ; and as well after the one seruice as the other, his face discouered, was shewed to all that coueted to behold it.

Thus was the corps first brought to the Tower, and after through the citie, to the cathedrall church of saint Paule, bare faced ; where it laie three daies togither, that all men might behold it. There was a solemne obsequie doone for him, both at Paules, and after at Westminster, at which time, both at dirige ouernight, and in the morning at the masse of *Requiem*, the king and the citizens of London were present. When the same was ended, the corps was commanded to be had vnto Langlie, there to be buried in the church of the friers preachers.

Richard's Character

[*H*. iii. 507–508] He was seemelie of shape and fauor,
& of nature good inough, if the wickednesse & naughtie
demeanor of such as were about him had not altered it.

His chance verelie was greatlie infortunate, which fell
into such calamitie, that he tooke it for the best waie
he could deuise to renounce his kingdome, for the which
mortall men are accustomed to hazard all they haue to
atteine therevnto. But such misfortune (or the like)
oftentimes falleth vnto those princes, which, when they
are aloft, cast no doubt for perils that maie follow. He
was prodigall, ambitious, and much giuen to the pleasure
of the bodie. . . .

Furthermore, there reigned abundantlie the filthie sinne
of leacherie and fornication, with abhominable adulterie,
speciallie in the king.

Character of York

[*H*. iii. 464] Verelie a man of a gentle nature, wished
that the state of the common-wealth might haue beene
redressed without losse of any mans life, or other cruell
dealing.

[*H*. iii. 485] A man rather coueting to liue in pleasure,
than to deale with much businesse, and the weightie
affaires of the realme.

Character of Bushie

[*H*. iii. 490] sir Iohn Bushie, a knight of Lincolneshire,
accompted to be an exceeding cruell man, ambitious, and
couetous beyond measure.

[*H*. iii. 490] Sir Iohn Bushie, in all his talke, when he
proponed any matter vnto the king, did not attribute to
him titles of honour, due and accustomed ; but inuented
vnused termes, and such strange names as were rather
agreeable to the diuine maiestie of God, than to any
earthlie potentate. The prince, being desirous inough of
all honour, and more ambitious than was requisite,
seemed to like well of his speech and gaue good eare to
his talke.

FIRST PART OF KING HENRY THE FOURTH

[*Henry IV*, Shakespeare's most popular history play, derives its serious matter from Holinshed, although Falstaff and his boon companions who give to the work its peculiar character are of Shakespeare's invention, inspired by some rambling scenes of riot in *The Famous Victories of Henry the fifth: Containing the Honourable Battell of Agin-court* (printed 1598, but probably acted before 1588). It is not certain whether Shakespeare drew directly from *The Famous Victories* or whether, as Professor Morgan thinks, a lost play on this subject was the origin of the two extant dramas. The connection between *The Famous Victories* and Shakespeare's plays was fully appreciated by contemporaries, for the former in 1617 was reissued "as it was Acted by the Kinges Maiesties Servants"—evidently an endeavour on the part of a bookseller to confuse the two dramas. It is unnecessary here to do more than mention the fact that Sir John Falstaff grew out of another character, Sir John Oldcastle, whose name, though changed, peers out from certain lines of Shakespeare's play.]

[*H.* iii. 520] Owen Glendouer, according to his accustomed manner, robbing and spoiling within the English borders, caused all the forces of the shire of Hereford to assemble togither against them, vnder the conduct of Edmund Mortimer, earle of March. But, comming to trie the matter by battell, whether by treason or otherwise, so it fortuned, that the English power was discomfited, the earle taken prisoner, and aboue *a thousand of his people* slaine in the place. The *shame*full villanie vsed by the *Welshwomen* towards the *dead* carcasses, was such as honest eares would be ashamed to heare, and continent toongs to speake thereof. The dead bodies might not be buried, without great summes of monie giuen for libertie to conueie them awaie. . . .

Archembald, *earle Dowglas*, sore displeased in his mind for this ouerthrow, procured a commission to inuade England, and that to his cost, as ye may likewise read in the Scotish histories. For, *at* a place called *Homildon*, they were so fiercelie assailed by the Englishmen vnder the leading of the lord Persie, surnamed Henrie Hotspur, and George earle of March, that with violence of the English shot they were quite vanquished and put to flight, on the Rood daie in haruest, with a great slaughter made by the Englishmen. . . . There were slaine . . . three and *twentie knights*, besides *ten thousand* of the commons; and of prisoners among other were these: *Mordacke earle of Fife*, son to the gouernour, Archembald earle Dowglas, (which in the fight lost one of his eies,) Thomas erle of *Murrey*, George earle of *Angus*, and (as some writers haue) the *earles* of *Atholl & Menteith*; with fiue hundred other of meaner degrees.

[*H*. iii. 521–522] Henrie, earle of Northum- [I. iii.] berland, with his brother Thomas, earle of Worcester, and his sonne the lord Henrie Persie, surnamed Hotspur, which were to king Henrie, in the beginning of his reigne, both faithfull freends, and earnest aiders, began now to enuie his wealth and felicitie; and especiallie they were greeued, bicause the king demanded of the earle and his sonne such Scotish *prisoners* as were taken *at Homeldon* and Nesbit: for, of all the captiues which were taken in the conflicts foughten in those two places, there was deliuered to the kings possession onelie *Mordake earle of Fife*, the duke of Albanies sonne; though the king did diuers and sundrie times require deliuerance of the residue, and that with great threatnings : wherewith the Persies being sore offended, (for that they claimed them as their owne proper prisoners, and their peculiar preies,) by the counsell of the lord Thomas Persie, earle of Worcester, whose studie was euer (as some write) to procure malice, and set things in a broile, came to the king vnto Windsore, (vpon a purpose to prooue him,) and there required of him, that either by ransome or otherwise, he would cause to be deliuered out of prison Edmund Mortimer earle of March, their cousine germane, whom (as they reported) Owen Glendouer kept in filthie prison, shakled with irons; onelie for that he tooke his part, and was to him faithfull and true.

The king began not a little to muse at this request, and not without cause : for in deed it touched him somewhat neere, sith this Edmund was sonne to Roger earle of March, sonne to the ladie Philip, daughter of Lionell duke

of Clarence, the third sonne of king Edward the third;
which Edmund, at *king Richards* going into Ireland, was
proclaimed heire apparant to the crowne and realme;
whose aunt, called Elianor, the lord Henrie Persie had
married ; and therefore king Henrie could not well beare,
that anie man should be earnest about the aduancement
of that linage. The king, when he had studied on the
matter, made answer, that the earle of March was not taken
prisoner for his cause, nor in his seruice, but willinglie
suffered himselfe to be taken, bicause he would not withstand the attempts of Owen Glendouer, and his complices;
& therefore he would neither ransome him, nor releeue him.

The Persies with this answer and fraudulent excuse were
not a little fumed, insomuch that Henrie Hotspur said
openlie : " Behold, the heire of the relme is robbed of his
right, and yet the robber with his owne will not redeeme
him ! " So in this furie the Persies departed, minding
nothing more than to depose king Henrie from the high type
of his roialtie, and to place in his seat their cousine Edmund
earle of March, whom they did not onelie deliuer out of
captiuitie, but also (to the high displeasure of king Henrie)
entered in league with the foresaid Owen Glendouer. . . .

King Henrie, not knowing of this new confederacie, and
nothing lesse minding than that which after happened,
gathered a great armie to go againe into Wales ; whereof
the earle of Northumberland and his sonne were aduertised
by the earle of Worcester, and with all diligence raised all
the power they could make, and sent to the Scots, which
before were taken prisoners at Homeldon, for aid of men :
promising to the earle of Dowglas the towne of Berwike,
and a part of Northumberland, and, to other Scotish lords,
great lordships and seigniories, if they obteined the vpper
hand. The Scots, in hope of gaine, and desirous to be
reuenged of their old greefes, came to the earle with a great
companie well appointed.

The Persies, to make their part seeme good, deuised
certeine articles, by the aduise of Richard Scroope, archbishop of Yorke, cousin to the lord Scroope, whome king
Henrie had caused to be beheaded at Bristow.

[*H*. iii. 521] Edmund Mortimer, earle of March,
prisoner with Owen Glendouer, whether for irkesomnesse

of cruell captiuitie, or feare of death, or for what other cause, it is vncerteine agreed to take part with Owen against the king of England; and tooke to wife the daughter of the said Owen.

[*H.* iii. 520] The king was not hastie to purchase the deliuerance of the earle March, bicause his title to the crowne was well inough knowen and therefore suffered him to remaine in miserable prison; wishing both the said earle, and all other of his linage, out of this life, with God and his saincts in heauen, so they had beene out of the waie, for then all had beene well inough as he thought.

[*H.* iii. 522] These articles being shewed to [II. iii.] diuerse noblemen, and other states of the realme, mooued them to fauour their purpose, in so much that manie of them did not onelie promise to the Persies aid and succour by words, but also by their writings and seales confirmed the same. Howbeit, when the matter came to triall, the most part of the confederates abandoned them, and at the daie of the conflict left them alone. Thus, after that the conspirators had discouered themselues, the lord Henrie Persie, desirous to proceed in the enterprise, vpon trust to be assisted by Owen Glendouer, the earle of March, & other, assembled an armie of men of armes and archers foorth of Cheshire and Wales.

[*H.* iii. 522] [Hotspur's] vncle Thomas Persie, earle of Worcester, that had the gouernement of the prince of Wales, who as then laie at London, in secret manner conueied himselfe out of the princes house; and comming to Stafford (where he met his nephue) they increased their power by all waies and meanes they could deuise.

[*H.* iii. 519] In the moneth of March appeared [III. i.] a blasing starre, first betweene the east part of the firmament and the north, flashing foorth fire and flames round about it, and, lastlie, shooting foorth fierie beams towards the north; foreshewing (as was thought) the great effusion of bloud that followed, about the parts of Wales and Northumberland. For much about the same time, Owen Glendouer (with his Welshmen) fought with the lord Greie of Ruthen, comming foorth to defend his possessions, which the same Owen wasted and destroied; and, as the fortune of that daies worke fell out, the lord Greie was taken prisoner and manie of his men were slaine. This hap lifted the Welshmen into high pride, and increased meruelouslie their wicked and presumptuous attempts.

[*H*. iii. 520]   About mid of August, the king, to chastise the presumptuous attempts of the Welshmen, went with a great power of men into Wales, to pursue the capteine of the Welsh rebels, Owen Glendouer; but in effect he lost his labor, for Owen coueied himselfe out of the waie into his knowen lurking places, and (as was thought) through art magike, he cased such foule weather of winds, tempest, raine, snow, and haile to be raised, for the annoiance of the kings armie, that the like had not beene heard of: in such sort, that the king was constreined to returne home, hauing caused his people to spoile and burne first a great part of the countrie.

[*H*. iii. 530]   [Henry] tooke his iournie directlie into Wales, where he found fortune nothing fauourable vnto him, for all his attempts had euill successe; in somuch that, losing fiftie of his cariages through abundance of raine and waters, he returned.

[*H*. iii. 521]   [The rebels] by their deputies, in the house of the archdeacon of Bangor, diuided the realme amongst them; causing a *tripartite indenture* to be made and *sealed* with their seales, by the couenants whereof, all *England from Seuerne and Trent, south and east*ward, was *assigned* to the earle of March: *all Wales, & the lands* beyond Seuerne *westward*, were appointed to Owen Glendouer: and all *the remnant from Trent northward*, to the lord Persie. . . .

This was doone (as some haue said) through a foolish credit giuen to a vaine prophesie, as though king Henrie was *the moldwarpe*, curssed of Gods owne mouth, and they three were the *dragon*, the *lion*, and the woolfe, which should diuide this realm betweene them.

THE PRINCE AND THE KING

[*H*. iii. 539]   Lord Henrie, prince of Wales,   [III. ii.] eldest sonne to king Henrie, got knowledge that certeine of his fathers seruants were busie to giue informations against him, whereby discord might arise betwixt him and his father: for they put into the kings head, not onelie

what euill rule (according to the course of youth) the
prince kept to the offense of manie, but also what great
resort of people came to his house ; so that the court was
nothing furnished with such a traine as dailie followed the
prince. These tales brought no small suspicion into the
kings head, least his sonne would presume to vsurpe the
crowne, he being yet aliue ; through which suspicious
gelousie, it was perceiued that he fauoured not his sonne,
as in times past he had doone.

The Prince (sore offended with such persons as, by
slanderous reports, sought not onelie to spot his good name
abrode in the realme, but to sowe discord also betwixt
him and his father) wrote his letters into euerie part of
the realme, to reprooue all such slanderous deuises of those
that sought his discredit. And to cleare himselfe the
better, (that the world might vnderstand what wrong he
had to be slandered in such wise,) about the feast of Peter
and Paule, to wit, the nine and twentith daie of June, he
came to the court with such a nunber of noble men and
other his freends that wished him well, as the like traine
had beene sildome seene repairing to the court at any one
time in those daies. . . .

Thus were the father and the sonne reconciled, betwixt
whom the said *pickthanks* had sowne diuision, insomuch
that the sonne, vpon a vehement conceit of vnkindnesse
sproong in the father, was in the waie to be worne out of
fauour. Which was the more likelie to come to passe, by
their informations that priuilie charged him with riot and
other vnciuill demeanor vnseemlie for a prince. Indeed
he was youthfullie giuen, growne to audacitie, and had
chosen him companions agreeable to his age ; with whome
he spent the time in such recreations, exercises, and
delights as he fansied. But yet (it should seeme by the
report of some writers) that his behauiour was not offensiue
or at least tending to the damage of anie bodie ; sith he
had a care to auoid dooing of wrong, and to tedder his
affections within the tract of vertue ; whereby he opened
vnto himselfe a redie passage of good liking among the
prudent sort, and was beloued of such as could discerne
his disposition, which was in no degree so excessiue, as that
he deserued in such vehement maner to be suspected.

[*H*. iii. 543] The king after expelled him out of his

priuie councell, banisht him the court, and made the duke of Clarence (his yoonger brother) president of councell in his steed.

THE PERCYS' REBELLION

[*H*. iii. 522]   King Henrie, aduertised of the proceedings of the Persies, foorthwith gathered about him such power as he might make, and, being earnestlie called vpon by the Scot, the earle of March, to make hast and giue battell to his enimies, before their power by delaieng of time should still too much increase, he passed forward with such speed, that he was in sight of his enimies, lieng in campe neere to Shrewesburie, before they were in doubt of anie such thing ; for the Persies thought that he would haue staied at Burton vpon Trent, till his councell had come thither to him to giue their aduise what he were best to doo.   But herein the enimie was deceiued of his expectation, sith the king had great regard of expedition and making speed for the safetie of his owne person ; where-vnto the earle of March incited him, considering that in *delaie* is danger, & losse in lingering.

[*H*. iii. 522]   The earle of Northumberland himselfe was not with them, but, being sicke, had promised vpon his amendement to repaire vnto them (as some write) with all conuenient speed.

[*H*. iii. 523]   The next daie in the morning earlie, being the euen of Marie Magdalene, they set their battels in order on both sides, and now, whilest the warriors looked when the token of battell should be giuen, the abbat of Shrewes-burie, and one of the clearks of the priuie seale, were sent from the king vnto the Persies, to offer them pardon, if they would come to any reasonable agreement.   By their persuasions, the lord Henrie Persie began to giue eare vnto the kings offers, & so sent with them his vncle the earle of Worcester, to declare vnto the king the causes of those troubles, and to require some effectuall reformation in the same.

[*H*. iii. 523]   Now when the two armies were incamped, the one against the other, the earle of Worcester and the lord Persie with their complices sent the articles (whereof I spake before), by Thomas Caiton and Roger Saluain, esquiers, to king Henrie, vnder their hands and seales ;

which articles in effect charged him with manifest periurie,
in that (contrarie to his oth receiued vpon the euangelists
at Doncaster, when he first entred the realm after his
exile) he had taken vpon him the crowne and roiall dignitie,
imprisoned king Richard, caused him to resigne his title,
and finallie to be murthered. Diuerse other matters they
laid to his charge, as leuieng of taxes and tallages, contrarie
to his promise, infringing of lawes & customes of the realme,
and suffering the earle of March to remaine in prison,
without trauelling to haue him deliuered. All which
things they, as procurors & protectors of the common-
wealth, tooke vpon them to prooue against him, as they
protested vnto the whole world.

King Henrie, after he had read their articles, with the
defiance which they annexed to the same, answered the
esquiers, that he was readie with dint of sword and fierce
battell to prooue their quarrell false, and nothing else than
a forged matter ; not doubting, but that God would aid
and assist him in his righteous cause, against the disloiall
and false forsworne traitors.

[*H*. iii. 523] It was reported for a truth, that now
when the king had condescended vnto all that was
resonable at his hands to be required, and seemed to
humble himselfe more than was meet for his estate, the
earle of Worcester (vpon his returne to his nephue) made
relation cleane contrarie to that the king had said, in such
sort that he set his nephues hart more in displeasure
towards the king, than euer it was before ; driuing him
by that meanes to fight whether he would or not.

[*H*. iii. 522] By reason of the kings sudden coming in
this sort, they staied from assaulting the towne of Shrewesburie, which enterprise they were readie at that instant to
haue taken in hand ; and foorthwith the lord Persie (as
a capteine of high courage) began to exhort the capteines
and souldiers to prepare themselues to battell, sith the
matter was growen to that point, that by no meanes it
could be auoided, "so that" (said he) "this daie shall
either bring vs all to aduancement & honor, or else, if
it shall chance vs to be ouercome, shall deliuer vs from the
kings spitefull malice and cruell disdaine : for plaieng the
men (as we ought to doo), better it is to die in battell for
the commonwealths cause, than through cowardlike feare

to prolong life, which after shall be taken from vs by sentence of the enimie."

[*H.* iii. 523–524] Then suddenlie blew the trumpets, the kings part crieng, " S. George ! vpon them ! " the aduersaries cried, " *Esperance ! Persie !* " and so the two armies furiouslie ioined. The archers on both sides shot for the best game, laieng on such load with arrowes, that manie died, and were driuen downe that never rose againe.

The Scots (as some write), which had the fore ward on the Persies side, intending to be reuenged of their old displeasures doone to them by the English nation, set so fiercelie on the kings fore ward, led by the earle of Stafford, that they made the same draw backe, and had almost broken their aduersaries arraie. The Welshmen also, which before had laine lurking in the woods, mounteines, and marishes, hearing of this battell toward, came to the aid of the Persies, and refreshed the wearied people with new succours. The king perceiuing that his men were thus put to distresse, what with the violent impression of the Scots, and the tempestuous stormes of arrowes, that his aduersaries discharged freely against him and his people,—it was no need to will him to stirre : for suddenlie, with his fresh battell, he approched and relieued his men ; so that the battell began more fierce than before. Here the lord Henrie Persie, and the earle Dowglas, a right stout and hardie capteine, not regarding the shot of the kings battell, nor the close order of the ranks, pressing forward togither, bent their whole forces towards the kings person ; comming vpon him with speares and swords so fiercelie, that the earle of March, the Scot, perceiuing their purpose, withdrew the king from that side of the field (as some write) for his great benefit and safegard (as it appeared) ; for they gaue such a violent onset vpon them that stood about the kings standard, that, slaieng his standard-bearer sir Walter Blunt, and ouer-throwing the standard, they made slaughter of all those that stood about it ; as the earle of Stafford, that daie made by the king constable of the realme, and diuerse other.

The prince that daie holpe his father like a lustie yoong gentleman ; for although he was hurt in the face with an arrow, so that diuerse noble men, that were about him,

would haue conueied him foorth of the field, yet he would
not suffer them so to doo, least his departure from amongst
his men might happilie haue striken some feare into their
harts : and so, without regard of his hurt, he continued
with his men, & neuer ceassed either to fight where the
battell was most hot, or to incourage his men where it
seemed most need. This battell lasted three long houres,
with indifferent fortune on both parts, till at length, the
king, crieng, " saint George ! victorie ! " brake the arraie
of his enimies ; and aduentured so farre, that (as some
write) the earle Dowglas strake him downe, & at that,
instant slue sir Walter Blunt, and three other, apparelled
in the kings sute and clothing, saieng : " I maruell to see
so many kings thus suddenlie arise one in the necke of
an other." The king, in deed, was raised, & did that daie
manie a noble feat of armes for, as it is written, he slue
that daie with his owne hands six and thirtie persons
of his enimies. The other on his part, incouraged by his
dooings, fought valiantlie, and slue the lord Persie,
called sir Henrie Hotspurre. . . .

There was also taken the earle of Worcester, the procuror
and setter foorth of all this mischeefe, sir Richard Vernon,
and . . . diuerse other. There were slaine vpon the kings
part, beside the earle of Stafford, . . . sir Hugh Shorlie,
sir Iohn Clifton, . . . sir Robert Gausell, sir Walter
Blunt. . . . There died in all vpon the kings side sixteene
hundred, and foure thousand were greeuouslie wounded.
On the contrarie side were slaine, besides the lord Persie,
the most part of the knights and esquiers of the countie
of Chester, to the number of two hundred, besides yeomen
and footmen : in all there died of those that fought on
the Persies side, about fiue thousand. This battell was
fought on Marie Magdelene euen, being saturdaie. Upon
the mondaie folowing, the earle of Worcester, . . . and
sir Richard Vernon . . . were condemned and beheaded.
The earles head was sent to London, there to be set on
the bridge.

To conclude, the king's enimies were vanquished, and
put to flight ; in which flight, the earle of Dowglas, for
hast, falling from the crag of an hie mounteine, brake one
of his cullions, and was taken, and for his valiantnesse, of
the king frankelie and freelie deliuered.

SECOND PART OF KING HENRY THE FOURTH

[*H*. iii. 524] The earle of Northumberland was [I. i.]
now marching forward with great power, which he had
got thither, either to aid his sonne and brother (as was
thought) or at the least towards the king, to procure a
peace ; but the earle of Westmerland, and sir Robert
Waterton, knight, had got an armie on foot, and meant
to meet him. The earle of Northumberland, taking neither
of them to be his freend, turned suddenlie backe, and
withdrew himselfe into Warkewoorth castell.

[*H*. iii. 531] The French king had appointed [I. iii.]
one of the marshals of France, called Montmerancie, and the
master of his crosbowes, with twelue thousand men, to saile
into Wales to aid Owen Glendouer. They tooke shipping
at Brest, and, hauing the wind prosperous, landed at
Milford hauen, with an hundred and fourtie ships, as
Thomas Walsingham saith ; though *Euguerant de Monstrellet*
maketh mention but of an hundred and twentie. . . .

They departed towards the towne of Denbigh, where
they found Owen Glendouer abiding for their comming,
with ten thousand of his Welshmen. Here were the
Frenchmen ioifullie receiued of the Welsh rebels, and
so, when all things were prepared, they passed by
Glamorganshire towards Worcester, and there burnt the
suburbes : but, hearing of the kings approch, they
suddenlie returned towards Wales.

[*H*. iii. 530] [Northumberland] hearing that his [II. iii.]
counsell was bewraied, and his confederats brought to
confusion, through too much hast of the archbishop of
Yorke, with three hundred horsse got him to Berwike.
The king comming forward quickelie, wan the castell of
Warkewoorth. Wherevpon the earle of Northumberland,
not thinking himselfe in suertie at Berwike, fled with

the lord Berdolfe into Scotland, where they were receiued
of sir Dauid Fleming.

[*H*. iii. 536] The Welsh rebell Owen Glendouer [III. i.]
made an end of his wretched life in this tenth yeare of
king Henrie his reigne ; being driuen now in his latter
time (as we find recorded) to such miserie, that, in manner
despairing of all comfort, he fled into desert places and
solitarie caues ; where, being destitute of all releefe and
succour, dreading to shew his face to anie creature, and
finallie lacking meat to susteine nature, for meere hunger
and lacke of food, miserablie pined awaie and died.

[*H*. iii. 529–530] But at the same time, to [IV. i–ii.]
his further disquieting, there was a conspiracie put in
practise against him at home by the earle of Northumberland, who had conspired with Richard Scroope, archbishop
of Yorke, Thomas Mowbraie, earle marshall, sonne to
Thomas duke of Norfolke, (who for the quarrell betwixt
him and king Henrie had beene banished, as ye haue
heard), the lords Hastings, Fauconbridge, Berdolfe, and
diuerse others. It was appointed that they should meet
altogither with their whole power, vpon Yorkeswold, at a
daie assigned, and that the earle of Northumberland
should be cheefteine ; promising to bring with him a great
number of Scots. The archbishop, accompanied with the
earle marshall, deuised certeine articles of such matters,
as it was supposed that not onelie the commonaltie of the
Realme, but also the nobilitie found themselues greeued
with : which articles they shewed first vnto such of their
adherents as were neere about them, & after sent them
abroad to their freends further off ; assuring them that,
for redresse of such oppressions, they would shed the *last*
drop of blood in their bodies, if need were.

The archbishop, not meaning to staie after he saw
himselfe accompanied with a great number of men, that
came flocking to Yorke to take his part in this quarrell,
foorthwith discouered his enterprise ; causing the articles
aforesaid to be set vp in the publike streets of the citie of
Yorke, and vpon the gates of the monasteries, that ech
man might vnderstand the cause that mooued him to
rise in armes against the king : the reforming whereof
did not yet apperteine vnto him. Herevpon, knights,

esquires, gentlemen, yeomen, and other of the commons, as well of the citie townes and countries about, being allured either for desire of change, or else for desire to see a reformation in such things as were mentioned in the articles, assembled togither in great numbers ; and the archbishop, comming foorth amongst them clad in armor, incouraged, exhorted, and (by all means he could) pricked them foorth to take the enterprise in hand, and manfullie to continue in their begun purpose ; promising forgiuenesse of sinnes to all them, whose hap it was to die in the quarrell : and thus not onelie all the citizens of Yorke, but all other in the countries about, that were able to beare weapon, came to the archbishop, and the earle marshall. In deed, the respect that men had to the archbishop caused them to like the better of the cause, since the grauitie of his age, his integritie of life, and incomparable learning, with the reuerend aspect of his amiable personage, mooued all men to haue him in no small estimation.

The king, aduertised of these matters, meaning to preuent them, left his iournie into Wales, and marched with all speed towards the north parts. Also Rafe Neuill, earle of Westmerland, that was not farre off, togither with the lord Iohn of Lancaster the kings sonne, being informed of this rebellious attempt, assembled togither such power as they might make, and, togither with those which were appointed to attend on the said lord Iohn to defend the borders against the Scots, (as the lord Henrie Fitzhugh, the lord Rafe Eeuers, the lord Robert Umfreuill, & others,) made forward against the rebels ; and, comming into a plaine within the forrest of Galtree, caused their standards to be pitched downe in like sort as the archbishop had pitched his, ouer against them, being farre stronger in number of people than the other ; for (as some write) there were of the rebels at the least twentie thousand men.

When the earle of Westmerland perceiued the force of the aduersaries, and that they laie still and attempted not to come forward vpon him, he subtillie deuised how to quaile their purpose ; and foorthwith dispatched messengers vnto the archbishop to vnderstand the cause as it were of that great assemblie, and for what cause

(contrarie to the kings peace) they came in a[r]mour.
The archbishop answered, that he tooke nothing in hand
against the kings *peace*, but that whatsoeuer he did,
tended rather to aduance the peace and quiet of the
common-wealth, than otherwise ; and where he and his
companie were in armes, it was for feare of the king, to
whom he could haue no free accesse, by reason of such a
multitude of flatterers as were about him ; and therefore
he mainteined that his purpose to be good & profitable,
as well for the king himselfe, as for the realme, if men
were willing to vnderstand a truth : & herewith he shewed
foorth a scroll, in which the *articles* were written wherof
before ye haue heard.

The messengers, returning to the earle of Westmerland,
shewed him what they had heard & brought from the
archbishop. When he had read the articles, he shewed
in word and countenance outwardly that he *liked* of the
archbishops holie and vertuous intent and purpose ;
promising that he and his would prosecute the same in
assisting the archbishop, who, reioising hereat, gaue credit
to the earle, and persuaded the earle marshall (against his
will as it were) to go with him to a place appointed for
them to commune togither. Here, when they were met
with like number on either part, the articles were read
ouer, and, without anie more adoo, the earle of Westmerland and those that were with him agreed to doo their
best, to see that a reformation might be had, according
to the same.

The earle of Westmerland, vsing more policie than the
rest : " Well " (said he) " then our trauell is come to
the wished end ; and where our people haue beene long
in armour, let them depart home to their woonted trades
and occupations : in the meane time *let vs drinke togither*
in signe of agreement, that the people on both sides maie
see it, and know that it is true, that we be light at a point."
They had no sooner shaken hands togither, but that a
knight was sent streight waies from the archbishop, to
bring word to the people that there was peace concluded ;
commanding ech man to laie aside his armes, and to
resort home to their houses. The people, beholding such
tokens of peace, as shaking of hands, and drinking

togither of the lords in louing manner, they being alreadie wearied with the vnaccustomed trauell of warre, brake vp their field and returned homewards; but, in the meane time, whilest the people of the archbishops side withdrew awaie, the number of the contrarie part increased, according to order giuen by the earle of Westmerland; and yet the archbishop perceiued not that he was deceiued, vntill the earle of Westmerland arrested both him and the earle marshall, with diuerse other. Thus saith *Walsingham*.

[*H*. iii. 530] But others write somwhat otherwise of this matter; affirming that the earle of Westmerland, in deed, and the lord Rafe Eeuers, procured the archbishop and the earle marshall, to come to a communication with them, vpon a ground *iust* in the midwaie betwixt both the *armies ;* where the earle of Westmerland in talke declared to them how perilous an enterprise they had taken in hand, so to raise the people, and to mooue warre against the king; aduising them therefore to submit themselues without further delaie vnto the kings mercie, and his sonne the lord Iohn, who was present there in the field with banners spred, redie to trie the matter by dint of sword, if they refused this counsell: and therefore he willed them to remember themselues well; &, if they would not yeeld and craue the kings pardon, he bad them doo their best to defend themselues.

Herevpon as well the archbishop as the earle marshall submitted themselues vnto the king, and to his sonne the lord Iohn that was there present, and returned not to their armie. Wherevpon their troops scaled and fled their waies; but, being pursued, manie were taken, manie slaine, and manie spoiled of that that they had about them, & so permitted to go their waies. Howsoeuer the matter was handled, true it is that the archbishop, and the earle marshall were brought to Pomfret to the king, who in this meane while was aduanced thither with his power; and from thence he went to Yorke, whither the prisoners were also brought, and there beheaded the morrow after Whitsundaie in a place without the citie: that is to vnderstand, the archbishop himselfe, the earle marshall, sir Iohn Lampleie, and sir

William Plumpton. Unto all which persons, though indemnitie were promised, yet was the same to none of them at anie hand performed. . . .

At [Henry's] comming to Durham, the lord [IV. iii.] Hastings, the lord Fauconbridge, sir Iohn Colleuill of the Dale, and sir Iohn Griffith, being conuicted of the conspiracie, were there beheaded.

[*H.* iii. 540] [Henry] held his Christmas this yeare at Eltham, being *sore* vexed with *sick*nesse, so that it was thought sometime, that he had beene dead: notwithstanding it pleased God that he somwhat recouered his strength againe, and so passed that Christmasse with as much ioy as he might.

[*H.* iii. 534] *The earle of Northumberland,* [IV. iv.] *and the lord Bardolfe,* after they had beene in Wales, in France, and Flanders, to purchase aid against king Henrie, were returned backe into Scotland, and had remained there now for the space of a whole yeare: and, as their euill fortune would, whilest the king held a councell of the nobilitie at London, the said earle of Northumberland and lord Bardolfe, in a dismall houre, *with a great power of Scots,* returned into England; recouering diuerse of the earls castels and seigniories, for the people in great numbers resorted vnto them. Heerevpon, incouraged with hope of good successe, they entred into Yorkshire, & there began to destroie the countrie. At their comming to Threske, they published a proclamation, signifieng that they were come in comfort of the English nation, as to releeue the common-wealth; willing all such as loued the libertie of their countrie, to repaire vnto them, with their armor on their backes, and in defensible wise to assist them.

The king, aduertised hereof, caused a great armie to be assembled, and came forward with the same towards his enimies; but, yer the king came to Notingham, sir Thomas, or (as other copies haue) Rafe Rokesbie, *shiriffe of Yorkeshire,* assembled the forces of the countrie to resist the earle and his power; comming to Grimbaut brigs, beside Knaresbourgh, there to stop them the passage; but they, returning aside, got to Weatherbie, and so to Tadcaster, and finallie came forward vnto Bramham more,

neere to Haizelwood, where they chose their ground meet
to fight vpon. The shiriffe was as readie to giue battell
as the earle to receiue it, and so with a standard of S.
George spred, set fiercelie vpon the earle, who, vnder a
standard of his owne armes, incountred his aduersaries
with great manhood. There was a sore incounter and
cruell conflict betwixt the parties, but in the end the victorie
fell to the shiriffe. The lord Bardolfe was taken, but sore
wounded, so that he shortlie after died of the hurts. As
for the earle of Northumberland, he was slaine outright
. . . This battell was fought the nineteenth day of
Februarie.

[*H*. iii. 540] In this yeare, and vpon the twelfth
day of October, were three flouds in the Thames, the one
following vpon the other, & *no ebb*ing *betweene :* which
thing no man then liuing could remember the like to be
seene.

[*H*. iii. 541] During this [Henry's] last sicknesse, [IV. v.]
he caused his *crowne* (as some write) to be *set on* a
pillow at his beds head ; and suddenlie his pangs so sore
troubled him that he laie as though all his vitall spirits
had beene from him departed. Such as were about him,
thinking verelie that he had beene departed, couered his
face with a linnen cloth.

The prince, his sonne, being hereof aduertised, entered
into the chamber, tooke awaie the crowne, and departed.
The father, being suddenlie reuiued out of that trance,
quicklie perceiued the lacke of his crowne ; and, hauing
knowledge that the prince his sonne had taken it awaie,
caused him to come before his presence, requiring of him
what he meant so to misuse himselfe. The prince with a
good audacitie, answered : " Sir, to mine and all mens
iudgements you seemed dead in this world ; wherefore I,
as your next heire apparant, tooke that as mine owne, and
not as yours." " Well, faire sonne " (said the king with
a great sigh), " what right I had to it, *God know*eth."
" Well " (said the prince), " if you die king, I will haue
the garland and trust to keepe it with the sword against
all mine enimies, as you haue doone." Then said the
king, " I commit all to God, and remember you to doo
well." With that he turned himselfe in his bed, and

shortlie after departed to God in a chamber of the abbats of Westminster called Ierusalem, the twentith daie of March, in the yeare 1413, and in the yeare of his age 46 : when he had reigned thirteene yeares, fiue moneths, and od daies, in great perplexitie and little pleasure.

[*H*. iii. 540] In this fourteenth and last yeare of king Henries reigne, a councell was holden in the white friers in London ; at the which, among other things, order was taken for ships and gallies to be builded and made readie, and all other things necessarie to be prouided for a voiage which he meant to make into the holie land, there to recouer the citie of Ierusalem from the Infidels.

[*H*. iii. 541] We find, that he was taken with his last sickenesse, while he was making his praiers at saint Edwards shrine, there as it were to take his leaue, and so proceed foorth on his iournie : he was so suddenlie and greeuouslie taken that such as were about him, feared lest he would haue died presentlie ; wherfore to releeue him (if it were possible) they bare him into a chamber that was next at hand, belonging to the abbat of Westminster, where they laid him on a pallet before the fire, and vsed all remedies to reuiue him. At length, he recouered his speech, and, vnderstanding and perceiuing himselfe in a strange place which he knew not, he willed to know if the chamber had anie particular name ; wherevnto answer was made, that it was called Ierusalem. Then said the king : "*Lauds be* giuen *to* the father of heauen, for now I know that I shall die heere in this chamber ; according to the *prophesie* of me declared, that *I should* depart this life *in Ierusalem*."

[*H*. iii. 543] [Henry V] chose men of grauitie, [V. ii.] wit, and high policie, by whose wise counsell he might at all times rule to his honour and dignitie ; calling to mind how once, to hie offense of the king his father, he had with his fist striken the cheefe iustice for sending one of his minions (vpon desert) to prison : when the iustice stoutlie commanded himselfe also streict to ward, & he (then prince) obeied.

[*H*. iii. 543] He was crowned the ninth of [V. v.] Aprill, being Passion sundaie, which was a sore, ruggie, and tempestuous day, with wind, snow, and sleet ; that men greatlie maruelled thereat, making diuerse interpretations what the same might signifie. But this king euen at first appointing with himselfe, to shew that in his person princelie honors should change publike manners, he determined to put on him the shape of a new man. For whereas aforetime he had made himselfe a companion vnto misrulie mates of dissolute order and life, he now banished them all from his presence (but not vnrewarded or else vnpreferred); inhibiting them vpon a great paine, not once to approch, lodge, or soiourne within ten miles of his court or presence.

APPEARANCE AND CHARACTER OF HENRY IV

[*H*. iii. 541] This king was of a meane stature, well proportioned, and formallie compact; quicke and liuelie, and of a stout courage. In his latter daies he shewed himselfe so gentle, that he gat more loue amongst the nobles and people of this realme, than he had purchased malice and euill will in the beginning.

But yet to speake a truth, by his proceedings, after he had atteined to the crowne, what with such taxes, tallages, subsidies, and exactions as he was constreined to charge the people with; and what by punishing such as, mooued with disdeine to see him vsurpe the crowne (contrarie to the oth taken at his entring into this land, vpon his returne from exile), did at sundrie times rebell against him; he wan himselfe more hatred, than in all his life time (if it had beene longer by manie yeares than it was) had beene possible for him to haue weeded out & remooued.

HENRY V

[*The Famous Victories of Henry the fifth* along with Holinshed's Chronicles provided the plot of *Henry V*, in which Falstaff is dismissed and the riotous Prince Hal turned into a vigorous king. It is possible that a *Henry V* play, performed in 1595, may have provided Shakespeare with some hints for his dramatic treatment of the reign.]

[*H*. iii. 545] In the second yeare of his reigne, [I. i.] king Henrie called his high court of parlement, the last daie of Aprill, in the towne of Leicester; in which parlement manie profitable lawes were concluded, and manie petitions mooued were for that time deferred. Amongst which, one was, that a *bill* exhibited in the parlement holden at Westminster, *in the eleuenth yeare* of king Henrie the fourth (which by reason the king was then troubled with ciuill discord, came to none effect), might now with good deliberation be pondered, and brought to some good conclusion. The effect of which supplication was, that *the temporall lands* (deuoutlie *giuen*, and disordinatlie spent by religious, and other spirituall persons) should be seized into the kings hands; sith the same might suffice to *mainteine, to the honor* of the king, and defense of the realme, *fifteene earles, fifteene hundred knights, six thousand and two hundred esquiers*, and *a hundred almessehouses*, for *reliefe* onelie *of* the poore, impotent, and needie persons; *and the king* to haue cleerelie *to* his *coffers* twentie *thousand pounds :* with manie other prouisions and values of religious houses, which I passe ouer.

[*H*. iii. 545] This bill was much noted, and more feared, among the religious sort, whom suerlie it touched verie neere; and therefore to find remedie against it, they determined to assaie all waies to put by and ouerthrow this bill : wherein they thought best to trie if they might mooue the kings mood with some sharpe inuention, that he should not regard the importunate petitions of the commons. Wherevpon, on a daie in the parlement, Henrie Chichelie archbishop of Canturburie made a pithie oration, wherein he declared, how not onelie the duchies of Normandie and Aquitaine, with the counties of Aniou and Maine, and the countrie of Gascoigne, were by vndoubted title apperteining to the king, as to the lawfull and onelie heire of the same ; but also the whole realme of France, as heire to his great grandfather king Edward the third.

[*H*. iii. 545–546]   An attack was made against the   [I. ii.] surmised and false fained *law Salike*, which the Frenchmen alledge euer *against* the kings of England in *barre* of their iust title *to* the crowne of *France*.   The verie words of that supposed law are these :   " *In terram Salicam mulieres ne succedant ;* " that is to saie, " *I*nto the *Salike land* let not women *succeed.*"   *Which the French* glossers expound *to be the realme of France, and* that *this law* was made by king *Pharamond ;* whereas *yet their owne authors affirme, that the land Salike is in Germanie, betweene the* riuers *of Elbe and Sala ;* and that when *Charles the great* had ouercome *the Saxons,* he placed there *certeine French*men, which hauing *in disdeine* the *dishonest maners of the Germane women,* made a *law,* that the *females should* not succeed to any inheritance with*in that land, which at this daie is called Meisen :* so that, if this be true, this *law was not* made *for the realme of France, nor the French*men *possessed the land Salike, till foure hundred* and *one and twentie yeares after* the death *of Pharamond,* the *supposed* maker *of this* Salike *law ;* for this Pharamond deceassed *in the yeare* 426, *and Charles the great subdued the Saxons, and* placed *the French*men in those parts *beyond the riuer* of *Sala, in the yeare* 805.

Moreouer, it appeareth by *their* owne *writers,* that *king Pepine, which deposed Childerike,* claimed *the crowne of France, as heire generall,* for that he was *descended of Blithild, daughter to king Clothair* the first.   *Hugh Capet also, (who vsurped the crowne* vpon *Charles duke of Loraine, the sole heire male of the line and stocke of Charles the great,) to* make *his title* seeme true, and appeare good, *(though in* deed *it was* starke *naught,) conueied himselfe as heire to the ladie Lingard, daughter to* king *Charlemaine,*

sonne to Lewes the emperour, that was *son* to *Charles the
great.* *King Lewes also, the tenth,* (otherwise called saint
Lewes,) being verie *heire to the* said *vsurper* Hugh *Capet,
could* neuer be *satisfied in his conscience* how he might
iustlie keepe and possesse *the crowne of France, till* he was
persuaded and fullie instructed, *that queene Isabell his
grandmother was lineall*ie descended *of the ladie Ermengard,
daughter* and heire *to the* aboue named *Charles duke of
Loraine ; by the which marriage, the* bloud and *line of
Charles the great was* againe *vnited* and restored *to the
crowne* & scepter *of France : so that* more *cleere* than *the
sunne* it openlie *appear*eth, that the *title* of *king Pepin,*
the *claime* of *Hugh Capet,* the possession of *Lewes ;* yea,
and *the* French *kings to this daie,* are deriued and conueied
from *the* heire *female ;* though *they would,* vnder the colour
of such a fained *law, barre* the kings and princes of this
realme of England of their right and lawfull inheritance.

The archbishop further alledged out of *the booke of
Numbers* this saieng : " When a man *die*th without a
sonne, *let the inheritance descend to* his *daughter.*"

[*H.* iii. 546] Chichele hauing said sufficientlie for the
proofe of the kings just and lawfull title to the crowne of
France, he exhorted him to aduance foorth his banner to
fight for his *right,* to conquer his inheritance, to spare
neither *bloud, sword,* nor *fire ;* sith his warre was iust, his
cause good, and his claime true. And to the intent his
louing chapelins and obedient subiects *of the spiritualtie*
might shew themselues willing and desirous to aid his
maiestie, for the recouerie of his ancient right and true
inheritance, the archbishop declared that, in their spirituall
conuocation, they had granted to his *highnesse such a
summe* of monie, *as neuer* by no spirituall persons was to
any prince before those daies giuen or aduanced. . . .

When the archbishop had ended his prepared tale,
Rafe Neuill, earle of Westmerland, and as then lord
Warden *of* the *marches against Scot*land, vnderstanding that the king, vpon a couragious desire to recouer his
right in France, would suerlie take the wars in hand,
thought good to mooue the king to begin first with
Scotland; and therevpon declared how easie a matter it
should be to make a conquest there, and how greatlie

the same should further his wished purpose for the sub-
duing of the Frenchmen; concluding the summe of his
tale with this old saieng: that, "Who so *will France win,*
must *with Scotland first begin.*"

[*H*. iii. 545] Whilest in the Lent season the king
laie at Killingworth, there came to him *from* Charles
Dolphin of France certeine *ambassadors,* that brought
with them a barrell of Paris *balles;* which from their
maister they presented to him for a token that was taken
in verie ill part, as sent in *scorne,* to signifie, that it was
more meet for the king to passe the time with such
childish exercise, than to attempt any worthie exploit.

[*H*. iii. 548–549] When king Henrie had fullie [II. ii.]
furnished his nauie with men, munition, & other prouisions, perceiuing that his capteines misliked nothing so
much as delaie, determined his souldiors to go a ship-
boord and awaie. But see the hap! the night before the
daie appointed for their departure, he was crediblie
informed, that *Richard earle of Cambridge,* brother to
Edward duke of Yorke, and *Henrie lord Scroope of
Masham,* lord treasuror, with *Thomas Graie,* a knight *of
Northumberland,* being confederat togither, had conspired his death: wherefore he caused them to be apprehended. . . .

The said lord Scroope was in such fauour with the king,
that he admitted him sometime to be *his bedfellow;*
in whose fidelitie the king reposed such trust, that, when
anie priuat or publike councell was in hand, this lord had
much in the determination of it. For he represented so
great grauitie in his countenance, such modestie in behauiour, and so vertuous zeale to all godlinesse in his
talke, that whatsoeuer he said was thought for the most
part necessarie to be doone and followed. Also the
said sir Thomas Graie (as some write) was of the kings
priuie councell. . . .

These prisoners, vpon their examination, confessed,
that for a great summe of monie which they had receiued
of the French king, they intended verelie either to haue
deliuered the king aliue into the hands of his enimies, or
else to haue murthered him before he should arriue in the
duchie of Normandie. When king Henrie had heard all

things opened, which he desired to know, he caused all his nobilitie to come before his presence ; before whome he caused to be brought the offendors also, and to them said : " Hauing thus *conspired* the death and destruction of me, which am the head of the realme and gouernour of the people, it maie be (no doubt) but that you likewise haue sworne the confusion of all that are here with me, and also the *desolation* of your owne countrie. To what horror (O lord !) for any true English hart to consider, that such an execrable iniquitie should euer so bewrap you, as for pleasing of a forren enimie to imbrue your hands in your bloud, and to ruine your owne natiue soile. *Reuenge* herein *touching* my *person*, though I *seeke* not ; yet for the *safe*gard of you my deere freends, & for due preseruation of all sorts, I am by office to cause example to be shewed. *Get* ye *hence therefore*, ye *poore miserable wretches*, to the receiuing of *your* iust reward ; wherein *Gods* maiestie *giue you* grace *of his mercie, and repentance of your* heinous *offenses*." And so immediatlie they were had to execution.

This doone, the king, calling his lords againe afore him, said in words few and with good grace. Of his enterprises he recounted the honor and glorie, whereof they with him were to be partakers ; the great confidence he had in their noble minds, which could not but remember them of the famous feats that their ancestors aforetime in France had atchiued, whereof the due report for euer recorded remained yet in register. The great mercie of *God* that had *so gratiouslie* reuealed vnto him the *treason* at hand, whereby the true harts of those afore him made so eminent & apparant in his eie, as they might be right sure he would neuer forget it. The *doubt* of danger to be nothing in respect of the certeintie of honor that they should acquire ; wherein himselfe (as they saw) in person would be lord and leader through Gods grace. To whose maiestie, as cheeflie was knowne the equitie of his demand, euen so to his mercie, did he onelie recommend the successe of his trauels.

Diuerse write that Richard earle of Cambridge did not conspire with the lord Scroope & Thomas Graie for the murthering of king Henrie to please the French king withall, but onelie to the intent to exalt to the crowne

his brother in law Edmund earle of March as heire to
Lionell duke of Clarence : after the death of which earle of
March, (for diuerse secret impediments, not able to haue
issue,) the earle of Cambridge was sure that the crowne
should come to him by his wife, and to his children, of hir
begotten. And therefore (as was thought) he rather
confessed himselfe for need of monie to be corrupted by
the French king, than he would declare his inward mind,
and open his verie intent and secret purpose, which if it
were espied, he saw plainlie that the earle of March should
haue tasted of the same cuppe that he had drunken, and
what should haue come to his owne children he much
doubted. Therefore destitute of comfort & in despaire of
life to saue his children, he feined that tale ; desiring
rather to saue his succession than himselfe, which he did
in deed ; for his sonne Richard duke of Yorke not priuilie
but openlie claimed the crowne, and Edward his sonne
both claimed it, & gained it, as after it shall appeare.

PLANS FOR WAR WITH FRANCE

[*H*. iii. 548]   Henry first princelie appointing   [II. iv.]
to aduertise the French king of his comming, therefore
dispatched Antelope his pursueant at armes with letters to
him for restitution of that which he wrongfully withheld ;
contrarie to the lawes of God and man : the king further
declaring how sorie he was that he should be thus compelled for repeating of his right and iust title of inheritance,
to make warre to the destruction of christian people ;
but sithens he had offered peace which could not be
receiued, now, for fault of iustice, he was forced to take
armes. Neuerthelesse exhorted the French king, *in the
bowels of* Iesu Christ, to render him that which was his
owne ; whereby effusion of Christian bloud might be
auoided. These letters, cheeflie to this effect and purpose,
were written and dated from Hampton the fift of August.
When the same were presented to the French king, and by
his councell well perused, answer was made, that he would
take aduise, and prouide therein as time and place should
be conuenient : so the messenger licenced to depart at
his pleasure.

[*H*. iii. 547] The Dolphin, who had the gouernance of
the realme, bicause his father was fallen into his old disease
of frensie, sent for the dukes of Berrie and Alanson, and
all the other lords of the councell of France : by whose
aduise it was determined, that they should not onelie
prepare a sufficient armie to resist the king of England,
when so euer he arriued to inuade France, but also to
stuffe and furnish the townes on the frontiers and sea
coasts with conuenient garrisons of men.

[*H*. iii. 549] The French king, being aduertised that
king Henrie was arriued on that coast, sent in all hast the
lord de la Breth constable of France, the seneshall of
France, the lord Bouciqualt marshall of France, the
seneshall of Henault, the lord Lignie, with other ; which
fortified townes with men, victuals, and artillerie, on all
those frontiers towards the sea.

[*H*. iii. 547] Before the kings presence, [III. : Chorus.]
sitting in his throne imperiall, the archbishop of Burges
made an eloquent and a long oration, dissuading warre,
and praising peace ; offering to the king of England a
great summe of monie, with diuerse countries, being in
verie deed but base and poore, as a dowrie with the ladie
Catharine in mariage ; so that he would dissolue his
armie, and dismisse his soldiers, which he had gathered
and put in a readinesse.

[*H*. iii. 549–550] The duke of Glocester, to [III. ii.]
whome the order of the siege was committed, made three
mines vnder the ground ; and, approching to the wals
with his engins and ordinance, would not suffer them
within to take anie rest.

For although they with their countermining somwhat
disappointed the Englishmen, & came to fight with them
hand to hand with*in the mines,* so that they went no
further forward with that worke ; yet they were so inclosed
on ech side, as well by water as land, that succour they
saw could none come to them.

[*H*. iii. 550] The king, aduertised hereof, sent them
word, that, except they would surrender the towne to him
the morow next insuing, without anie condition, they
should spend no more time in talke about the matter.
But yet at length through the earnest sute of the French

lords, the king was contented to grant them truce vntill nine of the clocke the next sundaie, being the two and twentith of September; with condition, that, if in the meane time no rescue came, they should yeeld the towne at that houre, with their bodies and goods to stand at the kings pleasure. . . .

The lord Bacqueuill was sent vnto the French king, to declare in what point the towne stood. To whome the Dolphin answered, *that* the kings *power* was *not yet* assembled, in such number as was conuenient *to raise so great a siege.* This answer being brought vnto the capteins within the towne, they rendered it vp to the king of England, after that the third daie was expired; which was on the daie of saint Maurice, being the seuen and thirtith daie after the siege was first laid. The souldiors were ransomed, and the towne sacked, to the great gaine of the Englishmen. . . .

The king ordeined capteine to the towne his vncle the duke of Excester, who established his lieutenant there, one sir Iohn Fastolfe; with fifteene hundred men, or (as some haue) two thousand, and thirtie six knights. . . .

King Henrie, after the winning of Harflue, determined to haue proceeded further in the winning of other townes and fortresses; but, bicause the dead time of the winter approched, it was determined by aduise of his councell, that he should in all conuenient speed set forward, and march through the countrie towards Calis by land, least his returne as then homewards should of slanderous toongs be named a running awaie; and yet that iournie was adiudged perillous, by reason that the number of his people was much minished by the flix and other feuers, which sore vexed and brought to death aboue fifteene hundred persons of the armie: and this was the cause that his returne was the sooner appointed and concluded.

[*H.* iii. 552]   The French king, being at Rone,   [III. v.] and hearing that king Henrie was *passed the riuer* of Some, was much displeased therewith, and, assembling his councell to the number of fiue and thirtie, asked their aduise what was to be doone. There was amonst these fiue and thirtie, his sonne the Dolphin, calling himselfe king of Sicill; the dukes of Berrie and Britaine, the earle

of Pointeu the kings yoongest sonne, and other high
estates. At length thirtie of them agreed, that the
Englishmen should not depart vn*fought withall*, and fiue
were of a contrarie opinion, but the greater number ruled
the matter : and so Montioy king at armes was sent to the
king of England to defie him as the enimie of France, and
to tell him that he should shortlie haue battell.

[*H*. iii. 554] The noble men had deuised *a chariot*,
wherein they might triumphantlie conueie the king
captiue to the citie of Paris ; crieng to their soldiers :
" Haste you to the spoile, glorie and honor ! " little
weening (God wot) how soone their brags should be
blowne awaie.

[*H*. iii. 552.] The king of England, (hearing   [III. vi.]
that the Frenchmen approched, and that there was an
other riuer for him to passe with his armie by a bridge,
and doubting least, if the same bridge should be broken,
it would be greatlie to his hinderance,) appointed certeine
capteins with their bands, to go thither with all speed
before him, and to take possession thereof, and so to keepe
it, till his comming thither.

Those that were sent, finding the Frenchmen busie to
breake downe their bridge, assailed them so vigorouslie,
that they discomfited them, and tooke and slue them ;
and so the bridge was preserued till the king came, and
passed the riuer by the same with his whole armie. This
was on the two and twentith day of October.

[*H*. iii. 552] A souldiour took a pix out of a church,
for which he was apprehended, & the king not once
remooued till the box was restored, and the offendor
strangled.

[*H*. iii. 549] [Henry] caused proclamation to be made,
that no person should be so hardie, on paine of death,
either to take anie thing out of anie church that belonged
to the same ; or to hurt or doo anie violence either to
priests, women, or anie such as should be found without
weapon or armor, and not readie to make resistance.

[*H*. iii. 552] Yet in this great necessitie, the poore
people of the countrie were not spoiled, nor anie thing
taken of them without paiment. . . .

King Henrie aduisedlie answered : " Mine intent is to

doo as it pleaseth God : *I will not seeke* your maister at this time ; but, if he or his seeke me, I will meet with them, God willing. If anie of your nation attempt once to stop me in my iournie now towards Calis, at their ieopardie be it ; and yet wish I not anie of you so vnaduised, as to be the occasion that I die *your tawnie ground with your red bloud.*"

When he had thus answered the herald, he gaue him a princelie reward, and licence to depart.

[*H*. iii. 552] The cheefe leaders of the French host were these : the constable of France, the marshall, the admerall, the lord Rambures, maister of the crosbowes, and other of the French nobilitie ; which came and pitched downe their standards and banners in the countie of saint Paule, within the territorie of Agincourt: . . .

They were lodged euen in the waie by the which the Englishmen must needs passe towards Calis ; and all that night, after their comming thither, made great cheare, and were verie merie, pleasant, and full of game.

[*H*. iii. 552] [The French had] incamped not past two hundred and fiftie pases distant from the English.

[*H*. iii. 552] Fiers were made to giue light on euerie side, as there likewise were in the French host.

[*H*. iii. 554] As though they had beene sure of   [IV.] victorie made great triumph ; for the capteins had determined before how to diuide the spoile, and the soldiers the night before had plaid the Englishmen at dice.

[*H*. iii. 552] The Englishmen also for their parts were of good comfort, and nothing abashed of the matter ; and yet they were both hungrie, wearie, sore trauelled, and vexed with manie cold diseases. Howbeit, reconciling themselues with God by hoossell and shrift, requiring assistance at his hands that is the onelie giuer of victorie, they determined rather to die, than to yeeld, or flee.

[*H*. iii. 552] Order was taken by commande-   [IV. i.] ment from the king, after the armie was first set in battell arraie, that no noise or clamor should be made in the host ; so that, in marching foorth to this village, euerie man kept himselfe quiet.

[*H*. iii. 554] When the messenger was come backe to the French host, the men of warre put on their helmets,

and caused their trumpets to blow to the battell. They
thought themselues so sure of victorie, that diuerse of the
noble men made such hast towards the battell, that they
left manie of their seruants and men of warre behind them,
and some of them would not once staie for their standards :
as, amongst other, the duke of Brabant, when his standard
was not come, caused a baner to be taken from a trumpet
and fastened to a speare ; the which he commanded to be
borne before him in steed of his standard.

[*H.* iii. 552]   their armie (as some write)   [IV. i.]
[extended] to the number of threescore thousand horssemen, besides footmen, wagoners, and other.

[*H.* iii. 552]   Determined to make haste towards Calis,
and not to seeke for battell, except he were thereto constreined ; bicause that his armie by sicknesse was sore
diminished : in so much that he had but onelie two
thousand horssemen, and thirteene thousand archers,
bilmen, and of all sorts of other footmen.

[*H.* iii. 553]   It is said, that as he heard one of   [IV. i.]
the host vtter his wish to another thus : " I would to God
there were with vs now so manie good soldiers as are at
this houre within England ! " the king answered : " I
would not wish a man more here than I haue ; we are
indeed in comparison to the enimies but a few, but if God
of his clemencie doo fauour vs, and our iust cause, (as I
trust he will,) we shall speed well inough. But let no
man ascribe victorie to our owne strength and might, but
onelie to Gods assistance ; to whome I haue no doubt we
shall worthilie haue cause to giue thanks therefore. And
if so be that for our offenses sakes we shall be deliuered
into the hands of our enimies, the lesse number we be,
the lesse damage shall the realme of England susteine ;
but if we should fight in trust of multitude of men, and so
get the victorie, (our minds being prone to pride,) we
should thervpon peraduenture ascribe the victorie not so
much to the gift of God, as to our owne puissance, and
thereby prouoke his high indignation and displeasure
against vs : and if the enimie get the vpper hand, then
should our realme and countrie suffer more damage and
stand in further danger. But be you of good comfort,
and shew your selues valiant ! God and our iust quarrell

shall defend vs, and deliuer these our proud aduersaries
with all the multitude of them which you see (or at the
least the most of them) into our hands."

[*H*. iii. 554] Here we may not forget how the French,
thus in their iolitie, sent an herald to king Henrie, to
inquire what ransome he would offer. Wherevnto he
answered, that within two or three houres he hoped it
would so happen, that the Frenchmen should be glad to
common rather with the Englishmen for their ransoms,
than the English to take thought for their deliuerance ;
promising for his owne part, that his dead carcasse should
rather be a prize to the Frenchmen, than that his liuing
bodie should paie anie ransome.

[*H*. iii. 553] [The king] appointed a vaward, of the
which he made capteine, Edward duke of Yorke, who of
an haultie courage had desired that office.

[*H*. iii. 554] When the Frenchmen perceiued his intent,
they were suddenlie amazed and ran awaie like sheepe ;
without order or arraie. Which when the king perceiued,
he incouraged his men, and followed so quickelie vpon the
enimies, that they ran hither and thither, casting awaie
their armour : manie on their knees desired to haue their
liues saued.

[*H*. iii. 554] The Englishmen had taken a   [IV. vii.]
great number of prisoners, certeine Frenchmen on horssebacke, whereof were capteins Robinet of Borneuill, Rifflart
of Clamas, Isambert of Agincourt, and other men of
armes, to the number of six hundred horssemen, (which
were the first that fled,) hearing that the English tents
& pauilions were a good waie distant from the armie,
without anie sufficient gard to defend the same, either
vpon a couetous meaning to gain by the spoile, or vpon
a desire to be reuenged, entred vpon the kings campe ;
and there spoiled the hails, robbed the tents, brake vp
chests, and caried awaie caskets, and slue such seruants
as they found to make anie resistance. . . .

But when the outcrie of the lackies and boies, which
ran awaie for feare of the Frenchmen thus spoiling the
campe, came to the kings eares, he, (doubting least his
enimies should gather togither againe, and begin a new
field ; and mistrusting further that the prisoners would

be an aid to his enimies, or the verie enimies to their
takers in deed if they were suffered to liue,) contrarie to
his accustomed gentlenes, commanded by sound of
trumpet, that euerie man (vpon paine of death) should
incontinentlie slaie his prisoner.

[*H*. iii. 554–555] When this lamentable slaughter [IV.]
was ended, the Englishmen disposed themselues in order
of battell, readie to abide a new field, and also to
inuade, and newlie set on, their enimies : with great
force they assailed the earles of Marle and Fauconbridge,
and the lords of Louraie, and of Thine, with six hundred
men of armes ; who had all that daie kept togither, but
now slaine and beaten downe out of hand.

[*H*. iii. 555] Some write, that the king, perceiuing his
enimies in one part to assemble togither, as though they
meant to giue a new battell for preseruation of the
prisoners, sent to them an herald, commanding them
either to depart out of his sight, or else to come forward
at once and giue battell : promising herewith, that, if
they did offer to fight agine, not onelie those prisoners
which his people alreadie had taken, but also so manie of
them as, in this new conflict, which they thus attempted,
should fall into his hands, should die the death without
redemption.

The Frenchmen fearing the sentence of so terrible a
decree, without further delaie parted out of the field.

[*H*. iii. 555] In the morning, Montioie king at armes
and foure other French heralds came to the K., to know the
number of prisoners, and to desire buriall for the dead.
Before he made them answer (to vnderstand what they
would saie) he demanded of them whie they made to him
that request ; considering that he knew not whether the
victorie was his or theirs ? When Montioie by true and
iust confession had cleered that doubt to the high praise
of the king, he desired of Montioie to vnderstand the name
of the castell neere adioining : when they had told him
that it was called Agincourt, he said, "*Then* shall *this*
conflict be *call*ed *the* battell *of Agincourt.*"

[*H*. iii. 552] The daie following was the fiue and
twentith of October in the yeare 1415; being then
fridaie, and the feast of Crispine and Crispinian: a day

faire and fortunate to the English, but most sorrowfull
and vnluckie to the French.

[*H.* iii. 555] [The King] feasted the French officers of
armes that daie, and granted them their request; which
busilie sought through the field for such as were slaine.
But the Englishmen suffered them not to go alone, for
they searched with them, & found manie hurt, but not in
ieopardie of their liues; whom they tooke prisoners, and
brought them to their tents.

[*H.* 554] The king that daie shewed himselfe a valiant
knight, albeit almost felled by the duke of Alanson; yet
with plaine strength he slue two of the dukes companie,
and felled the duke himselfe; whome, when he would
haue yelded, the kings gard (contrarie to his mind) slue
out of hand.

[*H.* iii. 555] There were taken prisoners: [IV. viii.]
Charles duke of Orleance, nephue to the French *king*; *Iohn
duke of Burbon*; the *lord Bouciqualt, one of the marshals
of France* (he after died in England); *with a number of
other lords, knights, and esquiers,* at the least *fifteene
hundred, besides* the *common* people. There were *slaine*
in all of the *French* part to the *number of ten thousand*
men; whereof were *princes* and noble men *bearing baners
one hundred twentie* and *six*; *to these, of knights, esquiers,
and gentlemen,* so manie as made vp the number of *eight
thousand and foure hundred* (*of the which fiue hundred were
dubbed knights* the night before the battell): *so as, of the*
meaner sort, not past *sixteene hundred.* Amongst those
of the nobilitie that were slaine, these were the cheefest:
Charles lord *de la Breth, high constable of France*; *Iaques
of Chatilon, lord of Dampier, admerall of France*; *the lord
Rambures, master of the crossbowes*; *sir Guischard Dolphin,
great master of France*; *Iohn duke of Alanson*; *Anthonie
duke of Brabant, brother to the duke of Burgognie*; *Edward
duke of Bar*; the earle of Neuers, an other brother to the
duke of Burgognie; with the *erles of Marle, Vaudemont,
Beaumont, Grandpree, Roussie, Fauconberge, Fois, and
Lestrake*; beside a great number of lords and barons
of name.

Of Englishmen, there died at this battell, *Edward duke
of Yorke*; *the earle of Suffolke*; *sir Richard Kikelie*; **and**

Dauie Gamme, esquier ; and, of all other, not aboue *fiue and twentie* persons.

[*H.* iii. 555] And so, about foure of the clocke in the after noone, the king, when he saw no apperance of enimies, caused the retreit to be blowen ; and, gathering his armie togither, gaue thanks to almightie God for so happie a victorie ; causing his prelats and chapleins to sing this psalme : " In exitu Israel de Aegypto ; " and commanded euerie man to kneele downe on the ground at this verse : " *Non nobis,* Domine, non nobis, sed nomini tuo da gloriam." Which doone, he caused *Te Deum,* with certeine anthems to be soong ; giuing laud and praise to God, without boasting of his owne force or anie humane power.

[*H.* iii. 555] When the king of England had well refreshed himselfe, and his souldiers, (that had taken the spoile of such as were slaine,) he, with his prisoners, in good order, returned to his towne of Calis.

[*H.* iii. 556] After that the king of England had [V.] refreshed himselfe, and his people at Calis. . . . the six daie of Nouember, he with all his prisoners tooke shipping, and the same daie landed at Douer. . . . In this passage, the seas were so rough and troublous, that two ships belonging to sir Iohn Cornewall, lord Fanhope, were driuen into Zeland ; howbeit, nothing was lost, nor any person perisht.

[*H.* iii. 556] The maior of London, and the aldermen, apparelled in orient grained scarlet, and foure hundred commoners clad in beautifull murrie, (well mounted, and trimlie horssed, with rich collars, & great chaines,) met the king on Blackheath ; reioising at his returne : and the clergie of London, with rich crosses, sumptuous copes, and massie censers, receiued him at saint Thomas of Waterings with solemne procession.

The king, like a graue and sober personage, and as one remembring from whom all victories are sent, seemed little to regard such vaine pompe and shewes as were in triumphant sort deuised for his welcomming home from so prosperous a iournie : in so much that he would not suffer his helmet to be caried with him, whereby might haue appeared to the people the blowes and dints that were to be seene in the same ; neither would he suffer anie ditties

to be made and soong by minstrels of his glorious victorie,
for that he would wholie haue the praise and thanks
altogither giuen to God.

[*H.* iii. 572] There came to him eftsoones [V. ii.]
ambassadours from the French king and the duke of
Burgognie to mooue him to peace. The king, minding
not to be reputed for a destroier of the countrie, which he
coueted to preserue, or for a causer of christian bloud still
to be spilt in his quarell, began so to incline and giue
eare vnto their sute and humble request, that at length,
(after often sending to and fro), and that the bishop of
Arras, and other men of honor had beene with him, and
likewise the earle of Warwike, and the bishop of Rochester
had beene with the duke of Burgognie, they both finallie
agreed vpon certeine articles ; so that the French king
and his commons would thereto assent.

Now was the French king and the queene with their
daughter Katharine at Trois in Champaigne ; gouerned
and ordered by them, which so much fauoured the duke
of Burgognie, that they would not, for anie earthlie good,
once hinder or pull backe one iot of such articles as the
same duke should seeke to preferre. And therefore what
needeth manie words ? a truce tripartite was accorded
betweene the two kings and the duke, and their countries ;
and order taken that the king of England should send, in
the companie of the duke of Burgognie, his ambassadours
vnto Trios in Champaigne ; sufficientlie authorised to
treat and conclude of so great matter. The king of
England, being in good hope that all his affaires should
take good successe as he could wish or desire, sent to the
duke of Burgognie, his vncle the duke of Excester, the
earle of Salisburie, the bishop of Elie, the lord Fanhope,
the lord Fitz Hugh, sir Iohn Robsert, and sir Philip Hall,
with diuerse doctors, to the number of fiue hundred horsse ;
which in the companie of the duke of Burgognie came to
the citie of Trois the eleuenth of March. The king, the
queene, and the ladie Katharine them receiued, and hartilie
welcomed ; shewing great signes and tokens of loue and
amitie.

After a few daies they fell to councell, in which at
length it was concluded, that king Henrie of England

should come to Trois, and marie the ladie Katharine ; and the king hir father after his death should make him heire of his realme, crowne, and dignitie. It was also agreed, that king Henrie, during his father in lawes life, should in his steed haue the whole gouernement of the realme of France, as regent thereof : with manie other couenants and articles, as after shall appeere.

[*H*. iii. 569] Mistrusting that the duke of Burgognie was the verie *let* and stop of his desires, [the King] said vnto him before his departure : " Coosine, we will haue your kings daughter, and *all* things that we demand with hir, or we will driue your king and you out of his realme."

[*H*. iii. 572] Accompanied with his brethren the dukes of Clarence and Glocester, the earles of Warwike, Salisburie, Huntington. . . .

The two kings and their councell assembled togither diuerse daies ; wherein the first concluded agreement was in diuerse points altered and brought to a certeinetie, according to the effect aboue mentioned.

[*H*. iii. 573] 1 First, it is accorded betweene our father and vs, that forsomuch as by the bond of matrimonie made for the good of the peace betweene vs and our most deere beloued Katharine, daughter of our said father, & of our most deere moother Isabell his wife, the same Charles and Isabell beene made our father and moother : therefore them as our father and moother we shall haue and worship, as it fitteth and seemeth so worthie a prince and princesse to be worshipped, principallie before all other temporall persons of the world.

[*H*. iii. 574] 25 Also *that* our said father, during his life, *shall name*, call, and *write* vs *in French in this* maner : *Nostre treschier filz Henry roy d'Engleterre heretere de France. And in Latine* in this maner : *Præclarissimus filius noster Henricus rex Angliæ & hæres Franciæ.*

[*H*. iii. 572] [Henry] went to visit the French king, the queene, and the ladie Katharine, whome he found in saint Peters church, where there was a verie ioious meeting betwixt them ; (and this was on the twentith daie of Maie ;) and there the king of England and the ladie Katharine were affianced.

[*H*. iii. 572] The kings sware for their parts to obserue

all the couenants of this league and agreement. Likewise
the duke of Burgognie, and a great number of other princes
and nobles which were present, receiued an oth.

[*H*. iii. 583] This Henrie was a king, of life without
spot ; a prince whome all men loued, and of none disdained ; a capteine against whome fortune neuer frowned,
nor mischance once spurned ; whose people him so seuere
a iusticer both loued and obeied, (and so humane withall,)
that he left no offense vnpunished, nor freendship vnrewarded ; a terrour to rebels, and suppressour of sedition ;
his vertues notable, his qualities most praise-worthie.

In strength and nimblenesse of bodie from his youth
few to him comparable ; for in wrestling, leaping, and
running, no man well able to compare. In casting of great
iron barres and heauie stones he excelled commonlie all
men ; neuer shrinking at cold, nor slothfull for heat ; and,
when he most laboured, his head commonlie vncouered ;
no more wearie of harnesse than a light cloake ; verie
valiantlie abiding at needs both hunger and thirst ; so
manfull of mind as neuer seene to quinch at a wound, or
to smart at the paine ; to turne his nose from euil sauour,
or to close his eies from smoke or dust ; no man more
moderate in eating and drinking, with diet not delicate,
but rather more meet for men of warre, than for princes or
tender stomachs. Euerie honest person was permitted
to come to him, sitting at meale ; where either secretlie or
openlie to declare his mind. High and weightie causes, as
well betweene men of warre and other, he would gladlie
heare ; and either determined them himselfe, or else for
end committed them to others. He slept verie little, but
that verie soundlie, in so much that when his soldiers soong
at nights, or minstrels plaied, he then slept fastest ; of
courage inuincible, of purpose vnmutable ; so wisehardie
alwaies, as feare was banist from him ; at euerie alarum
he first in armor, and formost in ordering. In time of
warre such was his prouidence, bountie and hap, as he had
true intelligence, not onelie what his enimies did, but what
they said and intended : of his deuises and purposes, few,
before the thing was at the point to be done, should be
made priuie.

He had such knowledge in ordering and guiding an

armie, with such a gift to incourage his people, that the
Frenchmen had constant opinion he could neuer be
vanquished in battell. Such wit, such prudence, and such
policie withall, that he neuer enterprised any thing, before
he had fullie debated and forecast all the maine chances
that might happen ; which doone, with all diligence and
courage, he set his purpose forward. What policie he had
in finding present remedies for sudden mischeeues, and
what engines in sauing himselfe and his people in sharpe
distresses, were it not that by his acts they did plainlie
appeare, hard were it by words to make them credible.
Wantonnesse of life and thirst in auarice had he quite
quenched in him ; vertues in deed in such an estate of
souereigntie, youth, and power, as verie rare, so right
commendable in the highest degree. So staied of mind
and countenance beside, that neuer iolie or triumphant
for victorie, nor sad or damped for losse or misfortune.
For bountifulnesse and liberalitie, no man more free,
gentle, and franke, in bestowing rewards to all persons,
according to their deserts : for his saieng was, that he
neuer desired monie to keepe, but to giue and spend.

Although that storie properlie serues not for theme of
praise or dispraise, yet what in breuitie may well be
remembred, in truth would not be forgotten by sloth ;
were it but onlie to remaine as a spectacle for magnanimite
to haue alwaies in eie, and for incouragement to nobles
in honourable enterprises. Knowen be it therefore, of
person and forme was this prince rightlie representing his
heroicall affects ; of stature and proportion tall and manlie,
rather leane than grose, somewhat long necked, and blacke
haired, of countenance amiable ; eloquent and graue was
his speech, and of great grace and power to persuade : for
conclusion, a maiestie was he that both liued & died a
paterne in princehood, a lode-starre in honour, and
mirrour of magnificence ; the more highlie exalted in his
life, the more deepelie lamented at his death, and famous
to the world alwaie.

HENRY VI. PART I

[Holinshed is freely used in all three parts of *Henry VI*, although the borrowing must have been made largely by other dramatists than Shakespeare. The First Part, which treats Holinshed's narrative most boldly and is thought by most critics to contain only a small percentage of lines written by Shakespeare, first appeared in the Folio of 1623, but the Second Part had been issued in 1594 as *The first part of the Contention betwixt the two famous Houses of Yorke and Lancaster*, while the Third Part appeared as *The True Tragedie of Richard, Duke of Yorke* in 1595. In the whole of these plays there is a less determined effort to keep to the main lines of history than there is in Shakespeare's later and independent efforts.]

[*H*. iii. 585] And suerlie the death of this king [I. i.] Charles caused alterations in France. For a great maniè of the nobilitie, which before, either for feare of the English puissance, or for the loue of this king Charles, (whose authoritie they followed,) held on the English part, did now reuolt to the Dolphin ; with all indeuour to driue the English nation out of the French territories. Whereto they were the more earnestlie bent, and thought it a thing of greater facilitie, because of king Henries yoong yeares ; whome (because he was a child) they esteemed not, but with one consent reuolted from their sworne fealtie.

[*H*. iii. 612–613] But heere is one cheefe point to be noted, that either the disdeine amongst the cheefe peeres of the realme of England, (as yee haue heard,) or the negligence of the kings councell, (which did not foresee dangers to come,) was the losse of the whole dominion of France, betweene the riuers of Somme and Marne ; and, in especiall, of the noble citie of Paris. For where before, there were sent ouer thousands for defense of the holds and fortresses, now were sent hundreds, yea, and scores ; some rascals, and some not able to draw a bowe, or carrie a bill.

[*H*. iii. 585] *The Dolphin*, which lay the same time in the citie of Poitiers, after his fathers deceasse, caused himselfe to be proclamed *king of France*, by the name of *Charles* the seuenth; and, in good hope to recouer his patrimonie, with an haultie courage preparing war. assembled a great armie; and first the warre began by light skirmishes, but after it grew into maine battels.

Betweene *twentie and three* and twentie *thousand* men, . . . fought with the *lord Talbot* (who had with him not past *six thousand* men) neere vnto a village in Beausse called Pataie: at which battell the charge was giuen by the French so vpon a sudden, that the Englishmen had not *leisure* to put themselues in araie, after they had put vp their *stakes* before their *archers*; so that there was no remedie but to fight at aduenture. This battell continued by the space of *three* long *houres*; for the Englishmen, though they were ouerpressed with multitude of their enimies, yet they neuer fled backe one foot, till their capteine the lord Talbot was sore wounded at the *backe*, and so taken.

Then their hearts began to faint, and they fled ; in which flight were slaine about twelue hundred, and fortie taken, of whome the lord Talbot, the lord Scales, the lord Hungerford, & sir Thomas Rampston were cheefe. . . . From this battell departed without anie stroke stricken sir Iohn Fastolfe ; the same yeare for his valiantnesse elected into the order of the garter.

[*H.* iii. 583] The dukes of Bedford and Glocester, & the earles of Salisburie and Warwike, [had gone to the death-bed of Henry V.]

Now, when he saw them pensife for his sicknesse and great danger of life wherein he presentlie laie, he, with manie graue, courteous, and pithie words, recomforted them the best he could ; and therewith exhorted them to be trustie and faithfull vnto his sonne, and to see that he might be well and vertuouslie brought vp. And, as concerning the rule and gouernance of his realms, during the minoritie and yoong yeares of his said sonne, he willed them to ioine togither in freendlie loue and concord, keeping continuall peace and amitie with the duke of Burgognie ; and neuer to make treatie with Charles that called himselfe Dolphin of Vienne, by the which anie part, either of the crowne of France, or of the duches of

Normandie and Guien, may be lessened or diminished;
and further, that the duke of Orleance and the other
princes should still remaine prisoners, till his sonne came
to lawfull age; least, returning home againe, they might
kindle more fire in one daie than might be quenched in
three.

He further aduised them, that if they thought it
necessarie, that it should be good to haue his brother
Humfreie duke of Glocester to be protector of England,
during the nonage of his sonne, and his brother the duke
of Bedford, with the helpe of the duke of Burgognie, to
rule and to be regent of France; commanding him with
fire and sword to persecute the Dolphin, till he had
either brought him to reason and obeisance, or else to
driue and expell him out of the realme of France. . . .

The noble men present promised to obserue his precepts,
and to performe his desires; but their hearts were so
pensife, and replenished with sorrow, that one could not
for weeping behold an other.

[*H*. iii. 585] The custodie of this yoong prince was
appointed to Thomas duke of Excester, & to Henrie
Beauford bishop of Winchester.

[*H*. iii. 591] My said lord of Winchester, without the
aduise and assent of my said lord of Glocester, or of the
kings councell, purposed and disposed him to set hand
on the kings person, and to haue remooued him from
Eltham, the place that he was in, to Windsor, to the intent
to put him in governance as him list.

THE SIEGE OF ORLEANS

[*H*. iii. 599]   After the siege had continued full   [I. ii.]
three weekes, the bastard of Orleance issued out of the
gate of the bridge, and fought with the Englishmen; but
they receiued him with so fierce and terrible strokes, that
he was with all his companie compelled to retire and flee
backe into the citie. But the Englishmen followed so
fast, in killing and taking of their enimies, that they
entered with them. The bulworke of the bridge, with
a great tower standing at the end of the same, was taken
incontinentlie by the Englishmen, who behaued them-

selues right valiantlie vnder the conduct of their couragious
capteine, as at this assault, so in diuerse skirmishes against
the French : partlie to keepe possession of that which
Henrie the fift had by his magnanimitie & puissance
atchiued, as also to inlarge the same. . . .

In this conflict, manie Frenchmen were taken, but more
were slaine ; and the keeping of the tower and bulworke
was committed to William Glasdale esquier.   By the
taking of this bridge the passage was stopped, that neither
men nor vittels could go or come by that waie.

[*H*. iii. 600]   In time of this siege at Orleance (French
stories saie), the first weeke of March 1428, vnto Charles
the Dolphin, at Chinon, as he was in verie great care
and studie how to wrestle against the English nation,
by one Robert Badricourt, capteine of Vacouleur, (made
after marshall of France by the Dolphins creation,) was
caried a yoong wench of an eighteene yeeres old, called
Ione Arc, by name of hir father (a sorie *sheepheard*) Iames
of Arc, and Isabell hir mother ; brought vp poorelie in
their trade of keeping cattell ; borne at Domprin (therefore reported by *Bale*, Ione Domprin) vpon Meuse in
Lorraine, within the diocesse of Thoule.   Of fauour was
she counted likesome, of person stronglie made and manlie,
of courage great, hardie, and stout withall : an vnder-
stander of counsels though she were not at them ; great
semblance of chastitie both of bodie and behauiour ; the
name of Iesus in hir mouth about all hir businesses ;
humble, obedient ; and fasting diuerse daies in the weeke.
A person (as their bookes make hir) raised vp by power
diuine, onelie for succour to the French estate then deepelie
in distresse ; in whome, for planting a credit the rather,
first the companie that toward the Dolphin did conduct
hir, through places all dangerous, as holden by the English,
(where she neuer was afore,) all the waie and by nightertale
safelie did she lead : then at the Dolphins sending by
hir assignement, from *saint Katharins church* of Fierbois
in Touraine, (where she neuer had beene and knew not,)
in a secret place there among *old iron*, appointed she hir
sword to be sought out and brought hir, (that *with fiue*
floure delices was grauen on both sides,) wherewith she
fought and did manie slaughters by hir owne hands.

On warfar rode she in armour cap a pie & mustered as a
man ; before hir an ensigne all white, wherein was Iesus
Christ painted with a floure delice in his hand.

Unto the Dolphin into his gallerie when first she was
brought ; and he, shadowing himselfe *behind*, setting other
gaie lords before him to trie hir cunning, from all the
companie, with a salutation, (that indeed marz all the
matter,) she pickt him out alone ; who therevpon had
hir to the end of the gallerie, where she held him an houre
in secret and priuate *talke*, that of his priuie chamber
was thought *verie long*, and therefore would haue broken
it off ; but he made them a signe to let hir saie on.   In
which (among other), as likelie it was, she set out vnto
him the singular feats (for sooth) giuen hir to vnderstand
by reuelation diuine, that in vertue of that sword shee
should atchiue ; which were, how with honor and victorie
shee would raise the siege at Orleance, set him in state of
the crowne of France, and driue the English out of the
countrie, thereby he to inioie the kingdome alone.   Heerevpon he hartened at full, appointed hir a sufficient armie
with absolute power to lead them, and they obedientlie
to doo as she bad them.   Then fell she to worke, and
first defeated, indeed, the siege at Orleance ; by and by
incouraged him to crowne himselfe king of France at
Reims, that a little before from the English she had woone.
Thus after pursued she manie bold enterprises to our
great displeasure a two yeare togither : for the time she
kept in state vntill she were taken and for heresie and
witcherie burned ; as in particularities hereafter followeth.

[*H*. iii. 590]   There fell a great diuision in the [I. iii.]
realme of England ; which of a sparkle was like to haue
grown to a great flame.   For whether the bishop of
Winchester, called Henrie Beaufort, (sonne of Iohn duke
of Lancaster by his third wife,) enuied the authoritie of
Humfreie duke of Glocester, protectour of the realme ;
or whether the duke disdained at the riches and pompous
estate of the bishop ; sure it is that the whole realme was
troubled with them and their partakers.

Charges against Winchester

[*H*. iii. 591] 1 First, whereas he, being protectour, and defendour of this land, desired the Tower to be opened to him, and to lodge him therein, Richard Wooduile esquier (hauing at that time the charge of the keeping of the Tower) refused his desire; and kept the same Tower against him vndulie and against reason, by the commandement of my said lord of Winchester.

[*H*. iii. 591] 3 Item, that where my said lord of Glocester, (to whome of all persons that should be in the land, by the waie of nature and birth, it belongeth to see the gouernance of the kings person,) informed of the said vndue purpose of my said lord of Winchester, (declared in the article next abouesaid,) and, in letting thereof, determining to haue gone to Eltham vnto the king to haue prouided as the cause required; my said lord of Winchester, vntrulie, and against the kings peace, to the intent to trouble my said lord of Glocester going to the king, purposing his death, in case that he had gone that waie, set men of armes and archers at the end of London bridge next Suthworke; and, in forebarring of the kings high waie, let draw the chaine of the stoupes there, and set vp pipes and hurdles in manner and forme of bulworks; and set men in chambers, cellars, & windowes, with bowes and arrowes and other weapons, to the intent to bring finall destruction to my said lord of Glocester's person, as well as of those that then should come with him.

[*H*. iii. 591] 4 Item, my said lord of Glocester saith and affirmeth, that our souereigne lord, his brother, that was king Henrie the fift, told him on a time, (when our souereigne lord, being prince, was lodged in the palace of Westminster, in the great chamber,) by the noise of a spaniell, there was on a night a man spied and taken behind a tapet of the said chamber; the which man was deliuered to the earle of Arundell to be examined vpon the cause of his being there at that time; the which so examined, at that time confessed that he was there by the stirring and procuring of my said lord of Winchester; ordeined to haue slaine the said prince there in his bed:

wherefore the said earle of Arundell let sacke him foorthwith, and drowned him in the Thames.

THE FRENCH WAR

[*H.* iii. 606] Amongst other of the cheefest [I. iv.] *prisoners*, that valiant capteine, *Poton de Santrails*, was one; who without delaie was *exchanged* for the lord Talbot, before taken prisoner at the battell of Pataie.

[*H.* iii. 599] Bedford appointed the earle of Suffolke to be his lieutenant and capteine of the siege; and ioined with him the lord Scales, the lord Talbot, sir Iohn Fastolfe, and diuerse other right valiant capteins.

[*H.* iii. 599] In the *tower* that was taken at the bridge end (as before you haue heard) there was an high chamber, hauing a *grate* full of *barres* of *iron*, by the which a man might looke all the length of the bridge into the *citie*; at which grate manie of the cheefe capteins stood manie times, viewing the citie, and deuising in what place it was best to giue the assault. They within the citie well perceiued this tooting hole, and laid a *peece of ordinance* directlie against the window.

It so chanced, that the nine and fiftith daie after the siege was laid, the earle of Salisburie, sir Thomas Gargraue, and William Glasdale, with diuerse other went into the said tower, and so into the high chamber, and looked out at the grate; and, within a short space, the sonne of the maister-gunner, perceiuing men looking out at the window, tooke his match, (as his father had taught him; who was gone downe to dinner,) and fired the gun; the shot whereof brake and shiuered the iron barres of the grate, so that one of the same bars strake the earl so violentlie on the head, that it stroke awaie one of his eies, and the side of his cheeke. Sir Thomas Gargraue was likewise stricken, and died within two daies.

[*H.* iii. 600–601] [Joan] roade from Poictiers to Blois, and there found men of warre, vittels, and munition, readie to be conueied to Orleance.

Heere was it knowne that the Englishmen kept not so diligent watch as they had been accustomed to doo, and therefore this maid (with other French capteins) comming forward in the dead time of the night, and in a great raine and *thunder*, entred into the citie with all their vittels, artillerie, and other necessarie prouisions. The next daie the Englishmen boldlie assaulted the towne, but the Frenchmen defended the walles, so as no great feat worthie of memorie chanced that daie betwixt them, though the Frenchmen were amazed at the valiant attempt of the Englishmen : whervpon the bastard of Orleance gaue knowledge to the duke of Alanson, in what danger the towne stood without his present helpe ; who, comming within two leagues of the citie, gaue knowledge to them within, that they should be readie the next daie to receiue him.

[*H*. iii. 598] [The English] withdrew without [II. i.] any tarriance into the castell, which standeth at the gate of saint Vincent, whereof was constable Thomas Gower esquier ; whither also fled manie Englishmen ; so as for vrging of the enimie, prease of the number, and lacke of vittels, they could not haue indured long : wherfore they priuilie sent a messenger to the lord Talbot, which then laie at Alanson, certifieng him in how hard a case they were. The lord Talbot, hearing these newes, like a carefull capteine, in all hast assembled togither about seuen hundred men ; & in the euening departed from Alanson, so as in the morning he came to a castell called Guierch, two miles from Mans, and there staied a while, till he had sent out Matthew Gough, as an espiall, to vnderstand how the Frenchmen demeaned themselues.

Matthew Gough so well sped his businesse, that priuile in the night he came into the castell, where he learned that the Frenchmen verie negligentlie vsed themselues, without taking heed to their watch, as though they had beene out of all danger : which well vnderstood, he returned againe, and within a mile of the citie met the lord Talbot, and the lord Scales, and opened vnto them all things, according to his credence. The lords then, to make hast in the matter, (bicause the daie approched,) with all speed possible came to the posterne gate ; and, alighting from their horsses, about six of the clocke in the morning, they issued out of the castell, crieng, " *saint George ! Talbot !* "

The Frenchmen, being thus suddenlie taken, were sore amazed ; in so much that some of them, being not out of their beds, got vp *in their shirts*, and lept *ouer the walles*. Other ran naked out of the gates to saue their liues, leauing all their apparell, horsses, armour, and riches behind them : none was hurt but such as resisted.

[*H*. iii. 597] Lord Talbot, being both of noble birth, and of haultie courage, after his comming into France, obteined so manie glorious victories of his enimies, that his onelie name was & yet is dreadfull to the French nation ; and much renowmed amongst all other people.

[*H*. iii. 598] This earle was the man at that [II. ii.] time, by whose wit, strength, and policie, the English name was much fearefull and terrible to the French nation ; which of himselfe might both appoint, command, and doo all things in manner at his pleasure ; in whose power (as it appeared after his death) a great part of the conquest consisted : for, suerlie, he was a man both painefull, diligent, and readie to withstand all dangerous chances that were at hand, prompt in counsell, and of courage inuincible ; so that in no one man, men put more trust ; nor any singular person wan the harts so much of all men.

[*H*. iii. 612] The duke of Yorke, perceiuing [II. iii.] his euill will, openlie dissembled that which he inwardlie minded, either of them working things to the others displeasure ; till, through malice and diuision betweene them, at length by mortall warre they were both consumed, with almost all their whole lines and ofspring.

[*H*. iii. 589–590] During the same season, [II. v.] Edmund Mortimer, the last earle of March of that name, (which long time had beene restreined from his libertie, and finallie waxed lame,) deceassed without issue ; whose inheritance descended to the lord Richard Plantagenet, sonne and heire to Richard earle of Cambridge, beheaded (as before yee haue heard) at the towne of Southampton.

[*H*. iii. 590] The citizens of London were [III. i.] faine to keepe dailie and nightlie watches, *and to shut* vp their *shops, for feare* of that which was doubted to haue insued of [the factious lords'] assembling of people about them.

[*H*. iii. 595] The said lord of Winchester should haue

these words that follow vnto my said lord of Glocester :
" My lord of Glocester, I haue conceiued to my great
heauinesse, that yee should haue receiued by diuerse
reports, that I should haue purposed and imagined against
your person, honor, and estate, in diuers maners ; for
the which yee haue taken against me great displeasure :
Sir, I take God to my witnesse, that what reports so euer
haue beene to you of me, (peraduenture of such as haue
had no great affection to me, God forgiue it them !) I
neuer imagined, ne purposed anie thing that might be
hindering or preiudice to your person, honor, or estate ;
and therefore I praie you, that yee be vnto me good lord
from this time foorth : for, by my will, I gaue neuer
other occasion, nor purpose not to doo hereafter, by the
grace of God." The which words so by him said, it was
decreed by the same arbitrators, that my lord of Glocester
should answer and saie : " Faire vncle, sith yee declare
you such a man as yee saie, I am right glad that it is so,
and for such a man I take you." And when this was
doone, it was decreed by the same arbitrators, that
euerie each of my lord of Glocester, and Winchester,
should take either other by the hand, in the presence of
the king and all the parlement, in signe and token of
good loue & accord ; the which was doone, and the parlement adiorned till after Easter.

[H. iii. 595] But, when the great fier of this dissention,
betweene these two noble personages, was thus by the
arbitrators (to their knowledge and iudgement) vtterlie
quenched out, and laid vnder boord, all other controuersies
betweene other lords, (taking part with the one partie or
the other), were appeased, and brought to concord ; so
that for ioy the king caused a solemne fest to be kept
on Whitsundaie ; on which daie he created Richard
Plantagenet, sonne and heire to the erle of Cambridge,
(whome his father at Southampton had put to death,
as before yee haue heard,) duke of Yorke ; not foreseeing
that this preferment should be his destruction, nor that
his seed should of his generation be the extreame end and
finall conclusion.

[H. iii. 581] This yeare, at Windsore, on the daie of
saint Nicholas, in December, the queene was deliuered of

a sonne named Henrie; whose godfathers were Iohn duke of Bedford, and Henrie bishop of Winchester, and Iaquet, or (as the Frenchmen called hir) Iaqueline, of Bauier, countesse of Holland, was his godmother. The king, being certified hereof, as he laie at seige before Meaux, gaue God thanks; in that it had pleased his diuine prouidence to send him a sonne, which might succeed in his crowne and scepter. But, when he heard reported the place of his natiuitie, were it that he [was] warned by some prophesie, or had some foreknowledge, or else iudged himselfe of his sonnes fortune, he said vnto the lord Fitz Hugh, his trustie chamberleine, these words: "My lord, I *Henrie, borne at Monmouth*, shall small time reigne, & much get; *and Henrie, borne at Windsore*, shall long reigne, and *all loose :* but, as God will, so be it."

[*H*. iii. 619-620]   Sir Francis the Arragonois, [III. ii.] hearing of [the fall of Evreux], apparelled six strong fellowes, like men of the countrie, with sacks and baskets, as cariers of corne and vittels; and sent them to the castell of Cornill, in the which diuerse Englishmen were kept as prisoners; and he, with an ambush of Englishmen, laie in a vallie nigh to the fortresse.

The six counterfet husbandmen entered the castell vnsuspected, and streight came to the chamber of the capteine, & laieng hands on him, gaue knowledge to them that laie in ambush to come to their aid. The which suddenlie made foorth, and entered the castell, slue and tooke all the Frenchmen, and set the Englishmen at libertie.

[*H*. iii. 618]   Philip, duke of Burgognie, [III. iii.] partlie mooued in conscience to make amends to Charles duke of Orleance (as yet prisoner in England) for the death of duke Lewes his father, whome duke Iohn, father to this duke Philip, cruellie murthered in the citie of Paris; and partlie intending the aduancement of his neece, the ladie Marie, daughter to Adolfe duke of Cleue, (by the which aliance, he trusted, that all old rancor should ceasse,) contriued waies to haue the said duke of Orleance set at libertie, vpon promise by him made to take the said ladie Marie vnto wife. This duke had beene prisoner in England euer since the battell was fought at Agincourt, vpon the daie of Crispine and Crispinian, in the yeare

1415, and was set now at libertie in the moneth of Nouember, in the yeare 1440; paieng for his ransome foure hundred thousand crownes, though other saie but three hundred thousand.

The cause whie he was deteined so long in captiuitie, was to pleasure thereby the duke of Burgognie: for, so long as the duke of Burgognie continued faithfull to the king of England, it was not thought necessarie to suffer the duke of Orleance to be ransomed, least vpon his deliuerance he would not ceasse to seeke meanes to be reuenged vpon the duke of Burgognie, for the old grudge and displeasure betwixt their two families; and therefore such ransome was demanded for him as he was neuer able to pay. But, after the duke of Burgognie had broken his promise, and was turned to the French part, the councell of the king of England deuised how to deliuer the duke of Orleance, that thereby they might displeasure the duke of Burgognie. Which thing the duke of Burgognie perceiuing, doubted what might follow if he were deliuered without his knowledge, and therefore to his great cost practised his deliuerance, paid his ransome, and ioined with him amitie and aliance by mariage of his neece.

[*H. iii. 623*] About this season, Iohn, the [III. iv.] valiant *lord Talbot*, for his approued prowesse and wis-dome, as well in England as in France, both in peace & warre so well tried, was *created earle of Shrewesburie*; and with a companie of three thousand men sent againe into Normandie, for the better defense of the same.

[*H. iii. 606*] There were in his companie of [IV. i.] his owne nation, his vncle the cardinall of Winchester, the cardinall and archbishop of Yorke, the dukes of Bedford, Yorke, and Norffolke, the earles of Warwike, Salisburie, Oxenford, Huntington, Ormond, Mortaigne, and Suffolke.

He was crowned king of France, in our ladie church of Paris, by the cardinall of Winchester: the bishop of Paris not being contented that the cardinal should doo such an high ceremonie in his church and iurisdiction.

[*H. iii. 611*] The duke of Burgognie, to set a veile before the king of Englands eies, sent Thoison Dore his cheefe herald to king Henrie with letters; excusing the matter by way of information, that he was constreined to enter in this league with K. Charles, by the dailie outcries, complaints, and lamentations of his people, alledging against him that he was the onlie cause of the long continuance of the wars, to the vtter impouerishing of his owne people, and the whole nation of France. . . .

. . . The superscription of this letter was thus: " To the high and mightie prince, Henrie, by the grace of God, *king* of England, his welbeloued cousine." Neither naming him king of France, nor his souereigne lord, according as (euer before that time) he was accustomed to doo. This letter was much maruelled at of the councell, after they had throughlie considered all the contents thereof, & they could not but be much disquieted; so far foorth that diuerse of them stomaked so muche the vntruth of the duke, that they could not temper their passions, but openlie called him traitor.

[*H.* iii. 619] In the beginning of this twentith yeare, Richard duke of Yorke, regent of France, and gouernour of Normandie, determined to inuade the territories of his enimies both by sundrie armies, and in seuerall places, and therevpon without delaie of time he sent the lord of Willoughbie with a great crue of soldiers to destroie the countrie of Amiens; and Iohn lord Talbot was appointed to besiege the towne of Diepe; and the regent himselfe, accompanied with Edmund duke of Summerset, set forward into the duchie of Aniou. . . .

The dukes of Yorke and Summerset . . . entered into Aniou and Maine, and there destroied townes, and spoiled the people, and with great preies and prisoners repaired againe into Normandie.

[*H.* iii. 640] [The French] retired in good order into the place which they had trenched, diched, and fortified with ordinance. The earle, aduertised how the siege was remoued, hasted forward towards his enimies, doubting most least they would haue beene quite fled and gone before his comming. But they, fearing the displeasure of the French king (who was not far off) if they should haue fled, abode the earles comming, and so receiued him: who though he first with manfull courage, and sore fighting wan the entrie of their campe, yet at length they compassed him about, and shooting him through the

thigh with an handgun, slue his horsse, and finallie killed
him lieng on the ground ; whome they durst neuer looke
in the face, while he stood on his feet.

[*H*.iii.640] It was said, that after [Talbot] [IV.v.-vi.]
perceiued there was no remedie, but present losse of the
battell, he counselled his sonne, the lord Lisle, to saue
himselfe by flight, sith the same could not redound to
enie great reproch in him, this being the first iournie in
which he had beene present. Manie words he vsed to
persuade him to haue saued his life ; but nature so
wrought in the son, that neither desire of life, nor feare of
death, could either cause him to shrinke, or conueie himselfe out of the danger, and so there manfullie ended his
life with his said father.

[*H*. iii. 611] Motion was made among Sigis- [V. i.]
mund the emperour and other christen kings . . . that,
sith such horror of bloudshed betweene the two nations
continuallie so lamentablie raged in France, some media-
tion might be made for accord.

[*H*. iii. 611] The cardinall of S. Crosse . . . declared
to the three parties the innumerable mischeefes, that had
followed to the whole state of the christian common-
wealth by their continuall dissention and dailie discord ;
exhorting them, for the honour of God, & for the loue
which they ought to beare towards the aduancement of his
faith and true religion, to conforme themselues to reason,
and to laie aside all rancor, malice and displeasure ; so
that, in concluding *a godlie peace*, they might receiue
profit and quietnesse heere in this world, and of God an
euerlasting reward in heauen.

[*H*. iii. 623–624] In this yeare died in Guien the
countesse of Comings, to whome the French king and also
the earle of Arminacke pretended to be heire, in so much
that the earle entred into all the lands of the said ladie.
And bicause he knew the French king would not take the
matter well, to haue a Rouland for an Oliuer he sent
solemne ambassadours to the king of England, *offer*ing
him *his daughter in mariage*, with promise to be bound
(beside great summes of monie, which he would giue with
hir) to deliuer into the king of Englands hands all such
castels and townes, as he or his ancestors deteined from

him within anie part of the duchie of Aquitaine, either
by conquest of his progenitors, or by gift and deliuerie of
anie French king ; and further to aid the same king with
monie for the recouerie of other cities, within the same
duchie, from the French king ; or from anie other person
that against king Henrie vniustlie kept, and wrongfullie
withheld them.

This offer seemed so profitable and also honorable to
king Henrie and the realme, that the *ambassadours* were
well heard, honourablie receiued, and with rewards sent
home into their countrie. After whome were sent, for the
conclusion of the marriage, into Guien, sir Edward Hull,
sir Robert Ros, and Iohn Grafton, deane of S. Seuerines ;
the which (as all the chronographers agree) both concluded the mariage, and by proxie affied the yoong ladie.

[*H.* iii. 613] The citie of Paris [was] brought [V. ii.]
into possession of Charles the French king, through the
vntrue demeanour of the citizens, who, contrarie to their
oths, and promised allegiance, like false and inconstant
people, so reuolted from the English.

[*H.* iii. 624] England was vnquieted. . . . [V. iii.]
and France by spoile, slaughter, and burning sore defaced ;
(a mischeefe in all places much lamented ;) therefore, to
agree the two puissant kings, all the princes of christendom
trauelled so effectuouslie by their oratours and ambassadours, that a diet was appointed to be kept at the citie
of Tours in Touraine ; where for the king of England
appeared William de la Poole earle of Suffolke.

[*H.* iii. 624] In treating of this truce, the earle of
Suffolke, aduenturing somewhat vpon his commission,
without the assent of his associats, imagined that the
next waie to come to a perfect peace was to contriue a
mariage betweene the French kings kinsewoman, the
ladie Margaret, daughter to Reiner duke of Aniou, and
his souereigne lord king Henrie.

THE CONFESSION OF JOAN

[*H.* iii. 604--605] The lord regent, by Peter [V. iv.]
Chauchon bishop of Beauuois, (in whose diocesse [Joan]
was taken,) caused hir life and beleefe, after order of law,

to be inquired vpon and examined. Wherein found
though a virgin, yet first, shamefullie reiecting hir sex
abominablie in acts and apparell, to haue counterfeit
mankind, and then, all damnablie faithlesse, to be a
pernicious instrument to hostilitie and bloudshed in
diuelish witchcraft and sorcerie, sentence accordinglie was
pronounced against hir. Howbeit, vpon humble confession of hir iniquities with a counterfeit contrition
pretending a carefull sorow for the same, execution spared
and all mollified into this, that from thencefoorth she
should cast off hir vnnaturall wearing of mans abilliments,
and keepe hir to garments of hir owne kind, abiure hir
pernicious practises of sorcerie and witcherie, and haue
life and leasure in perpetuall prison to bewaile hir mis-
deeds. Which to performe (according to the maner of
abiuration) a solemne oth verie gladlie she tooke.

But herein (God helpe vs !) she fullie afore possest of
the feend, not able to hold her in anie towardnesse of
grace, falling streight waie into hir former abominations,
(and yet seeking to eetch out life as long as she might,)
stake not (though the shift were shamefull) to confesse hir
selfe a *strumpet*, and (vnmaried as she was) to be *with
child*. For triall, the lord regents lenitie gaue hir nine
moneths staie, at the end wherof she (found herein as
false as wicked in the rest, an eight daies after, vpon a
further definitiue sentence declared against hir to be relapse
and a renouncer of hir oth and repentance) was therevpon
deliuered ouer to secular power, and so executed by
consumption of fire in the old market place at Rone, in
the selfe same steed where now saint Michaels church
stands : hir ashes afterward without the towne wals
shaken into the wind. Now recounting altogither, hir
pastorall bringing vp, rude, without any vertuous instruc-
tion, hir campestrall conuersation with wicked spirits,
whome, in hir first salutation to Charles the Dolphin, she
vttered to be our Ladie, saint Katharine, and saint Anne,
that in this behalfe came and gaue hir commandements from
God hir maker, as she kept hir fathers lambs in the fields . . .

These matters may verie rightfullie denounce vnto all
the world hir execrable abhominations, and well iustifie
the iudgement she had, and the execution she was put

to for the same. A thing yet (God wot) verie smallie shadowed and lesse holpen by the verie trauell of the Dolphin, whose dignitie abroad foulie spotted in this point, that, contrarie to the holie degree of a right christen prince (as he called himselfe), for maintenance of his quarels in warre would not reuerence to prophane his sacred estate, as dealing in diuelish practises with misbeleeuers and witches.

[*H.* iii. 611] The Englishmen would that king Charles should haue nothing but what it pleased the king of England, and that not as dutie, but as a benefit by him of his meere liberalitie giuen and distributed. The Frenchmen, on the other part, would that K. Charles should haue the kingdome franklie and freelie, and that the king of England should leaue the name, armes, and title of the king of France, and to be content with the dukedomes of Aquitaine and Normandie, and to forsake Paris, and all the townes which they possessed in France, betweene the riuers of Some and Loire ; being no parcell of the duchie of Normandie. To be breefe, the demands of all parts were betweene them so farre out of square, as hope of concord there was none at all.

[*H.* iii. 624] The earle of Suffolke with his [V. v.] companie returned into England, where he forgat not to declare what an honourable truce he had taken, out of the which there was a great hope that a finall peace might grow the sooner for that honorable mariage, which he had concluded ; omitting nothing that might extoll and set foorth the personage of the ladie, or the nobilitie of hir kinred.

But although this mariage pleased the king and diuerse of his councell, yet Humfrie duke of Glocester protector of the realme was much against it ; alledging that it should be both contrarie to the lawes of God, and dishonorable to the prince, if he should breake that promise and contract of mariage, made by ambassadours sufficientlie thereto instructed, with the daughter of the earle of Arminacke, vpon conditions both to him and his realme, as much profitable as honorable. But the dukes words could not be heard, for the earles dooings were onelie liked and allowed.

HENRY VI. PART II

MARGARET AND HENRY

[*H*. iii. 625] [Suffolk and his company] came to [I. i.]
the *citie* of *Tours* in Touraine, where they were honorablie
receiued both of *the* French *king* and of the king of *Sicill*.
The marquesse of Suffolke, as procurator to king Henrie,
espoused the said ladie in the church of saint Martins. At
the which mariage were present the father and mother
of the bride; the French king himselfe, which was vncle
to the husband; and the French queene also, which was
aunt to the wife. There were also *the Dukes of Orleance*,
of *Calabre*, of *Alanson*, and of *Britaine*, *seauen earles*,
twelue barons, *twentie bishops*, beside knights and gentlemen. When the feast, triumph, bankets and iusts
were ended, the ladie was deliuered to the marquesse,
who in great estate conueied hir through Normandie vnto
Diepe, and so transported hir into England, where she
landed at Portesmouth in the moneth of Aprill.

[*H*. iii. 625] Upon the thirtith of Maie next following,
she was crowned queene of this realme of England at
Westminster, with all the solemnitie thereto apperteining.

[*H*. iii. 624] One thing seemed to be a great hinderance to [peace]; which was, bicause the king of England
occupied a great part of the duchie of Aniou, and the
whole countie of Maine, apperteining (as was alledged)
to king Reiner.

The earle of Suffolke (I cannot saie), either corrupted
with bribes, or too much affectioned to this vnprofitable
mariage, condescended, that *the duchie of Aniou and the
countie of Maine* should *be* deliuered *to the king* the
brides *father*; demanding for hir mariage neither penie
nor farthing; as who would saie, that this new affinitie
passed all riches, and excelled both gold and pretious
stones.

[*H*. iii. 625] During the time of the truce, Richard
duke of Yorke and diuerse other capteins repaired into
England ; both to visit their wiues, children, and freends,
and also to consult what should be doone, if the truce
ended.

[*H*. iii. 625] [Suffolk] with his wife and manie honorable personages of men and women richlie adorned both
with apparell & iewels, hauing with them manie costlie
chariots and gorgeous horslitters, sailed into France, for
the conueiance of the nominated queene into the realme
of England. For King Reiner hir father, for all his long
stile, had too short a pursse to send his daughter honorablie
to the king hir spouse.

[*H*. iii. 629] [There] began a new rebellion in Ireland ;
but Richard duke of Yorke, being sent thither to appease
the same, so asswaged the furie of the wild and sauage
people there, that he wan him such fauor amongst them,
as could neuer be separated from him and his linage ;
which in the sequele of this historie may more plainelie
appeare.

The Attack on Gloucester

[*H*. iii. 627] Diuerse articles were laid against [I. iii.]
him in open councell, and in especiall one : That he had
caused men, adiudged to die, to be put to other execution,
than the law of the land assigned. Surelie the duke, verie
well learned in the law ciuill, detesting malefactors, and
punishing offenses in seueritie of iustice, gat him hatred of
such as feared condign reward for their wicked dooings.

[*H*. iii. 625] A parlement was called, in the which it
was especiallie concluded, that by good foresight Normandie
might be so furnished for defense before the end of the
truce, that the French king should take no aduantage
through want of timelie prouision : for it was knowne,
that, if a peace were not concluded, the French king did
prepare to imploie his whole puissance to make open warre.
Heerevpon monie was granted, an armie leuied, and the
duke of Summerset appointed to be regent of Normandie,
and the duke of Yorke thereof discharged. . . .

I have seene in a register booke belonging sometime to

the abbeie of saint Albons, that the duke of York was
established regent of France, after the deceasse of the
duke of Bedford, to continue in that office for the tearme
of fiue yeares ; which being expired, he returned home,
and was ioifullie receiued of the king with thanks for his
good seruice, as he had full well deserued in time of that
his gouernement : and, further, that now, when a new
regent was to be chosen and sent ouer, to abide vpon
safegard of the countries beyond the seas as yet subiect
to the English dominion, the said duke of *Yorke* was
eftsoones (as a *man* most *meet* to supplie that roome)
appointed to go ouer again, as *regent of France*, with all
his former allowances.

But the duke of Summerset, still maligning the duke of
Yorkes aduancement, as he had sought to hinder his
dispatch at the first when he was sent ouer to be regent,
(as before yee haue heard,) he likewise now wrought so,
that the king reuoked his grant made to the duke of
Yorke for enioieng of that office the terme of other fiue
yeeres, and, with helpe of William marquesse of Suffolke,
obteined that grant for himselfe.

[*H*. iii. 612]   Although the duke of Yorke was worthie
(both for birth and courage) of this honor and preferment, yet so disdeined of Edmund duke of Summerset,
(being cousine to the king,) that by all meanes possible he
sought his hinderance, as one glad of his losse, and sorie
of his well dooing : by reason whereof, yer the duke of
Yorke could get his dispatch, Paris and diuerse other of
the cheefest places in France were gotten by the French
king.

[*H*. iii. 622–623]   Diuers secret attempts were   [I. iv.]
aduanced forward this season, against this noble man
Humfreie duke of Glocester, a far off, which, in conclusion,
came so neere, that they beereft him both of life and land ;
as shall hereafter more plainelie appeere.

For, first, this yeare, dame Eleanor Cobham, wife to the
said duke, was accused of treason ; for that she by sorcerie
and inchantment intended to destroie the king, to the
intent to aduance hir husband vnto the crowne. . . .
At the same season were arrested, arreigned, and adiudged
giltie, as aiders to the duchesse, Thomas Southwell priest,

and canon of S. Stephans at Westminster, Iohn Hun priest, Roger Bolingbrooke a cunning necromancer (as it was said), and Margerie Iordeine, surnamed the witch of Eie.

The matter laid against them was, for that they (at the request of the said duchesse) had deuised an image of wax, representing the king, which by their sorcerie by little and little consumed ; intending thereby in conclusion to waste and destroie the kings person.

[H. iii. 627] Richard, duke of Yorke, (being [II. ii.] greatlie alied by his wife to the chiefe peeres and potentates of the realme, beside his owne progenie,) perceiuing the king to be no ruler, but the whole burthen of the realme to rest in direction of the queene, & the duke of Suffolke, began secretlie to allure his friends of the nobilitie ; and priuilie declared vnto them his title and right to the crowne, and likewise did he to certeine wise gouernours of diuerse cities and townes. Which attempt was so politikelie handled, and so secretlie kept, that prouision to his purpose was readie, before his purpose was openlie published ; and his friends opened themselues, yer the contrarie part could them espie : for in conclusion all shortlie in mischiefe burst out, as ye may hereafter heare.

York's Claim

[H. iii. 657] *Edward the third* had issue, *Edward prince of Wales* ; *William of Hatfield*, his *second* sonne ; *Lionell the third, duke of Clarence* ; *Iohn of Gant*, fourth, *duke of Lancaster* ; *Edmund* of *Langlie, fift, duke of Yorke* ; *Thomas of Woodstoke, sixt, duke of Glocester* ; and *William of Windsor, seauenth.*

The said *Edward* prince of Wales, which *died* in the life time of *his father*, had issue *Richard*, which succeeded *Edward the third* his grandsire ; Richard died without issue ; *William of Hatfield*, the second sonne of Edward the third, *died without* issue ; Lionell *the third sonne* of Edward the third, *duke of Clarence, had issue Philip* his *daughter* and heire, which was coupled in matrimonie vnto *Edmund Mortimer earle of March*, and *had issue Roger* Mortimer *earle of March*, hir sonne and heire ; which *Roger had issue Edmund* erle of March, Roger

Roger Mortimer, *Anne, Elianor;* which Edmund, and
Elianor died without issue. And the said *Anne* coupled
in matrimonie to *Richard earle of Cambridge,* the *sonne*
of *Edmund* of *Langleie,* the *fift sonne* of *Edward the
third,* and had issue Richard Plantagenet, commonlie
called duke of Yorke. . . . To the which Richard duke
of Yorke, as sonne to Anne, daughter *to Roger* Mortimer
earle of March, sonne and heire of the said *Philip, daughter*
and heire of the said *Lionell,* the third sonne of king Edward
the third, the right, title, dignitie roiall, and estate of the
crownes of the realmes of England and France, and the
lordship of Ireland, perteineth and belongeth afore anie
issue of the said Iohn of Gant, the fourth sonne of the
same king Edward.

The Punishment of the Duchess of Gloucester.

[*H.* iii. 623] [The Duchess of Gloucester] was   [II. iii.]
examined in saint Stephans chappell before the bishop
of Canturburie, and there by examination conuict, and
iudged to doo open penance in three open places within
the citie of London. . . . and after that adiudged to perpetuall imprisonment *in the Ile of Man,* vnder the keeping
of *sir Thomas Stanlie* knight.

Margerie Iordeine was *burnt in Smithfield,* and Roger
Bolingbrooke was drawne to Tiborne, and hanged and
quartered ; taking vpon his death that there was neuer
anie such thing by them imagined. Iohn Hun had his
pardon, and Southwell died in the Tower the night before
his execution.

[*H.* iii. 626] [The Queen] disdaining that hir husband
should be ruled rather than rule, could not abide that the
duke of Glocester should doo all things concerning the
order of weightie affaires, least it might be said, that she
had neither wit nor stomach, which would permit and
suffer hir husband, being of most perfect age, like a
yoong *pupill,* to be gouerned by the direction of an other
man. Although this toy entered first into hir braine
thorough hir owne imagination, yet she was pricked forward
to the matter both by such of hir husbands counsell, as of
long time had borne malice to the duke for his plainnesse

vsed in declaring their vntruth (as partlie ye haue heard),
and also by counsell from king Reiner hir father ; aduising
that she and the king should take vpon them the rule of
the realme, and not to be kept vnder, as wards and
mastered orphanes.

What needeth manie words ? The queene, persuaded
by these meanes, first of all excluded the duke of Glocester
from all rule and gouernance.

GLOUCESTER'S ARREST

[*H*. iii. 627] But, to auoid danger of tumult that [III. i.]
might be raised, if a prince so well beloued of the people
should be openlie executed, his enimies determined to
worke their feats in his destruction, yer he should haue
anie warning. For effecting whereof, a parlement was
summoned to be kept at Berrie ; whither resorted all the
peeres of the realme, and amongst them the duke of
Glocester, which on the second daie of the session was
by the lord Beaumont, then high constable of England,
(accompanied with the duke of Buckingham, and others,)
arrested, apprehended, and put in ward, and all his
seruants sequestred from him, and thirtie two of the cheefe
of his retinue were sent to diuerse prisons, to the great
admiration of the people.

[*H*. iii. 627] Oft times it hapneth that a man, in
quenching of smoke, burneth his fingers in the fire : so
the queene, in casting how to keepe hir husband in honor,
and hir selfe in authoritie, in making awaie of this noble
man, brought that to passe, which she had most cause to
haue feared ; which was the deposing of hir husband, &
the decaie of the house of Lancaster, which of likelihood
had not chanced if this duke had liued : for then durst
not the duke of Yorke haue attempted to set foorth his
title to the crowne, as he afterwards did, to the great
trouble of the realme, and destruction of king Henrie, and
of many other noble men beside.

[*H*. iii. 627] Although the duke sufficientlie answered
to all things against him obiected ; yet, because his death
was determined, his wisedome and innocencie nothing
auailed. . . . .

The duke, the night after he was thus committed to prison, being the foure and twentith of Februarie, was found dead in his bed, and his bodie shewed to the lords and commons as though he had died of a palsie, or of an imposteme.

But all indifferent persons (as saith *Hall*) might well vnderstand that he died of some violent death. Some iudged him to be *strangled*, some affirme that an hot spit was put in at his fundament, other write that he was smouldered betweene two featherbeds; and some haue affirmed that he died of verie greefe, for that he might not come openlie to his answer.

JACK CADE

[*H*. iii. 632] Those that fauoured the duke of Yorke, and wished the crowne vpon his head, for that (as they iudged) he had more right thereto than he that ware it, procured a ccmmotion in Kent on this manner. A certeine yoong man, of a goodlie stature and right pregnant of wit, was intised to take vpon him the name *of Iohn Mortimer*, coosine to the duke of Yorke; (although his name was *Iohn Cade*, or, of some, Iohn Mend-all, an Irishman, as *Polychronicon* saith ;) and not for a small policie, thinking by that surname, that those which fauoured the house of the earle of March would be assistant to him.

THE CHARGES AGAINST SUFFOLK

[*H*. iii. 631] [The Commons] began to make [III. ii.] exclamation against the duke of Suffolke, charging him to be the onelie cause of the deliuerie of Aniou and Maine, the cheefe procuror of the duke of Glocester's death, the verie occasion of the losse of Normandie, the swallower vp of the kings treasure, the remoouer of good and vertuous councellours from about the prince, and the aduancer of vicious persons, and of such as by their dooings shewed themselues apparant aduersaries to the common-wealth.

The queene hereat, doubting not onelie the dukes destruction, but also hir owne confusion, caused the parlement, before begun at the Blackfriers, to be adiourned to

Leicester; thinking there, by force and rigor of law, to suppresse and subdue all the malice and euill will conceiued against the duke & hir. At which place few of the nobilitie would appeare: wherefore it was againe adiourned to Westminster, where was a full appearance. In the which session the commons of the nether house put vp to the king and the lords manie articles of treason, misprision, and euill demeanor, against the duke of Suffolke.

[*H.* iii. 632] The parlement was adiourned to Leicester, whither came the king and queene in great estate, and with them the duke of Suffolke, as cheefe councellour. The commons of the lower house, not forgetting their old grudge, besought the king, that such persons, as assented to the release of Aniou, and deliuerance of Maine, might be dulie punished. . . . When the king perceiued that there was no remedie to appease the peoples furie by anie colourable waies, shortlie to pacifie so long an hatred, he first sequestred the lord Saie, (being treasuror of England,) and other the dukes adherents, from their offices and roomes; and after banished the duke of Suffolke, as the abhorred tode and common noiance of the whole realme, for tearme of fiue yeares: meaning by this exile to appease the malice of the people for the time, and after (when the matter should be forgotten) to reuoke him home againe.

SUFFOLK'S DEATH

[*H.* iii. 632] But Gods iustice would not [IV. i.] that so vngratious a person should so escape; for, when he shipped in Suffolke, intending to transport himselfe ouer into France, he was incountered with a ship of warre, apperteining to the duke of Excester, constable of the Tower of London, called the Nicholas of the Tower. The capteine of that barke with small fight entered into the dukes ship, and, perceiuing his person present, brought him to Douer road, and there, on the one side of a cock bote, caused his head to be striken off, and left his bodie with the head lieng there on the sands. Which corps, being there found by a chapleine of his was conueied to Wingfield college in Suffolke, and there buried.

THE REBELS

[*H*. iii. 430] [The rebels] began to shew proofe [IV. ii.]
of those things which they had before conceiued in their
minds, beheading all such men of law, iustices, and iurors,
as they might catch, and laie hands vpon, without respect
of pitie, or remorse of conscience : alledging that the land
could neuer enioy hir natiue and true libertie, till all those
sorts of people were dispatched out of the waie.

JACK CADE

[*H*. iii. 437] Now the time was come appointed to
them by God, in which they might (if they would) cast off
the yoke of bondage, & recouer libertie. He counselled
them therefore to remember themselues, and to take good
hearts vnto them, that, after the manner of a good
husband that tilleth his ground, and riddeth out thereof
such euill weeds as choke and destroie the good corne,
they might destroie first the great lords of the realme,
and after the iudges and lawiers, questmoongers, and all
other whom they vndertooke to be against the commons ;
for so might they procure peace and suertie to themselues
in time to come, if, dispatching out of the waie the great
men, there should be an equalitie in libertie, no difference
in degrees of nobilitie, but a like dignitie and equall
authoritie in all things brought in among them.

[*H*. iii. 634] The queene (that bare rule), [IV. iv.]
being of his retrait aduertised, sent *sir Humfreie Stafford*
knight, and William his brother, with manie other
gentlemen, to follow the Kentishmen, thinking that they
had fled : but they were deceiued, for at the first skirmish
both the Staffords were slaine, & all their companie
discomfited.

[*H*. iii. 634] Iacke Cade, vpon victorie against the
Staffords, apparelled himselfe in sir Humfreies brigandine
set full of guilt nailes, and so in some glorie returned againe
toward London : diuerse idle and vagarant persons, out
of Sussex, Surrie and other places, still increasing his
number.

[*H*. iii. 632–633] [Cade] sent vnto the king an humble

supplication, affirming that his comming was not against his grace, but against such of his councellours, as were louers of themselues, and oppressors of the poore commonaltie ; flatterers of the king, and enimies to his honor ; suckers of his purse, and robbers of his subiects ; parciall to their freends, and extreame to their enimies ; thorough bribes corrupted, and for indifferencie dooing nothing.

[*H*. iii. 634] [Cade] came againe to the plaine of Blackheath, & there stronglie incamped himselfe ; to whome were sent from the king, the archbishop of Canturburie, and Humfreie duke of Buckingham, to common with him of his greefes and requests.

These lords found him sober in talke, wise in reasoning, arrogant in hart, and stiffe in opinion ; as who that by no means would grant to dissolue his armie, except the king in person would come to him, and assent to the things he would require. The K., vpon the presumptuous answers & requests of this villanous rebell, begining asmuch to doubt his owne meniall seruants, as his vnknowen subiects, (which spared not to speake, that the capteins cause was profitable for the common-wealth,) departed in all hast to the castell of Killingworth in Warwikeshire, leauing onlie behind him the lord Scales to keepe the Tower of London. The Kentish capteine, being aduertised of the kings absence, came first into Southwarke, and there lodged at the white hart, prohibiting to all his retinue, murder, rape, and robberie ; by which colour of well meaning he the more allured to him the harts of the common people.

[*H*. iii. 634] The maior and other the [IV. v.] magistrates of London perceiuing themselues neither to be sure of goods, nor of life well warranted, determined to repell and keepe out of their citie such a mischieuous caitife and his wicked companie. And, to be the better able so to doo, they made the lord Scales, and that renowmed capteine Matthew Gough, priuie both of their intent and enterprise ; beseeching them of their helpe and furtherance therein. The lord Scales promised them his aid, with shooting off the artillerie in the Tower ; and Matthew Gough was by him appointed to assist the maior and Londoners in all that he might.

[*H*. iii. 634] [Cade] entred into London, cut the ropes of the draw bridge, & strooke his sword on London stone ; saieng : "*Now is Mortimer lord of this citie !* "

[*H*. iii. 635] [The townsfolk] tooke vpon them [IV. vii.] in the night to keepe the bridge, and would not suffer the Kentishmen once to approch. The rebels, who neuer soundlie slept for feare of sudden assaults, hearing that the bridge was thus kept, ran with great hast to open that passage, where betweene both parties was a fierce and cruell fight.

Matthew Gough, perceiuing the rebels to stand to their tackling more manfullie than he thought they would haue doone, aduised his companie not to aduance anie further toward *Southwarke*, till the daie appeared ; that they might see where the place of ieopardie rested, and so to prouide for the same : but this little auailed. For the rebels with their multitude droue back the citizens from the stoops at the bridge foot to the draw bridge, & began to set fire in diuerse houses. . . . Yet the capteins, not sparing, fought on the bridge all the night valiantlie : but, in conclusion, the rebels gat the draw bridge, and drowned manie ; and slue Iohn Sutton alderman, and Robert Heisand, a hardie citizen, with manie other, beside Matthew Gough, a man of great wit and much experience in feats of chiualrie, the which in continuall warres had spent his time in seruice of the king and his father.

[*H*. iii. 431] [The rebels marched to Gaunt's] house of the Sauoie, to the which, in beautie and statelinesse of building, with all maner of princelie furniture, there was not any other in the realme comparable ; which, in despite of the duke (whome they called traitor,) they set on fire, and by all waies and means indeuoured vtterlie to destroie it. . . .

Now after that these wicked people had thus destroied the duke of Lancasters house, and done what they could deuise to his reproch, they went to the temple ; and burnt the men of lawes lodgings, with their bookes, writings, and all that they might lay hand vpon.

[*H*. iii. 430] The common vplandish people. . . . purposed to *burne* and destroie *all records*, euidences, court-rolles, and other muniments, that, the remembrance of

ancient matters being remooued out of mind, their land-
lords might not haue whereby to chalenge anie right at
their hands.

[*H.* iii. 632] [Cade declared] if either by force or policie
they might get the king and queene into their hands, he
would cause them to be honourablie vsed, and take such
order for the punishing and reforming of the misdeamean-
ours of their bad councellours, that neither *fifteens* should
hereafter be demanded, nor once anie impositions or taxes
be spoken of. . . .

[He] caused sir Iames Fines, lord Saie, and treasuror of
England, to be brought to the Guildhall, and there to be
arreigned ; who, being before the kings iustices put to
answer, desired to be tried by his peeres, for the longer
delaie of his life. The capteine, perceiuing his dilatorie
plee, by force tooke him from the officers, and brought
him to the standard in Cheape, and there (before his
confession ended) caused his head to be striken off, and
pitched it vpon an high pole, which was openlie *borne
before* him *thorough the streets.*

[He] went to Mile end, and there apprehended sir
Iames Cromer, then shiriffe of Kent, and sonne in law
to the said lord Saie ; causing him likewise (without
confession or excuse heard) to be beheaded, and his head
to be fixed on a pole ; and with these two heads this
bloudie wretch entred into the citie againe, and as it were
in a spite caused them in euerie street to kisse togither,
to the great detestation of all the beholders.

[*H.* iii. 635] [The battle] indured in doubtfull wise on
the bridge, till nine of the clocke in the morning : for
somtime, the Londoners were beaten backe to saint Magnus
corner : and suddenlie againe, the rebels were repelled to
the stoops in Southwarke, so that both parts being faint
and wearie, agreed to leaue off from fighting till the next
daie ; vpon condition, that neither Londoners should pass
into Southwarke, nor Kentishmen into London.

[*H.* iii. 635] The archbishop of Canturburie, being
chancellor of England and as then for his suertie lieng
within the Tower, called to him the bishop of Winchester,
who for some safegard laie then at Haliwell. These two
prelats, seeing the furie of the Kentish people, by their

late repulse, to be somewhat asswaged, passed by the riuer of Thames from the Tower into Southwarke; bringing with them, vnder the kings great seale, a generall pardon vnto all the offendors, and caused the same to be openlie published. The poore people were so glad of this pardon, and so readie to receiue it, that, without bidding farewell to their capteine, they withdrew themselues the same night euerie man towards his home. . . .

But Iacke Cade, despairing of succours, and fearing the reward of his lewd dealings, put all his pillage and goods that he had robbed into a barge, and sent it to Rochester by water, and himselfe went by land, and would haue entred into the castle of Quinborow with a few men that were left about him; but he was there let of his purpose: wherefore he, disguised in strange attire, priuilie fled into the wood countrie beside Lewes in Sussex, hoping so to scape. The capteine & his people being thus departed, not long after proclamations were made in diuerse places of Kent, Sussex, and Southerie, that, whosoeuer could take the foresaid capteine aliue or dead, should haue a thousand markes for his trauell.

[*H*. iii. 635–636] The king himselfe came [IV. ix.] into Kent, and there sat in iudgement vpon the offendors; and, if he had not mingled his iustice with mercy, more than fiue hundred by rigor of law had beene iustlie put to execution. Yet he, punishing onelie the stubborne heads, & disordered ringleaders, pardoned the ignorant and simple persons, to the great reioising of all his subiects.

York comes from Ireland

[*H*. iii. 637] The duke of Yorke, pretending (as yee haue heard) a right to the crowne, as heire to Lionell duke of Clarence, came this yeare out of Ireland vnto London, in the parlement time, there to consult with his special freends: as Iohn duke of Northfolke, Richard earle of Salisburie, and the lord Richard, his sonne, (which after was earle of Warwike,) Thomas Courtneie earle of Deuonshire, & Edward Brooke lord Cobham. After long deliberation and aduise taken, it was thought expedient to keepe their cheefe purpose secret; and that the duke should raise an armie of men, vnder a pretext to remooue diuerse councellors about the king, and to reuenge the manifest iniuries doone to the common-wealth by the same rulers. Of the which, as principall, the duke of Summerset was namelie accused, both for that he was greatlie hated of the commons for the losse of Normandie; and for that it was well knowne, that he would be alto-gither against the duke of Yorke in his chalenge to be made (when time serued) to the crowne.

[*H*. iii. 637] [York] assembled a great hoast, [V. i.] to the number of ten thousand able men, in the marches of Wales; publishing openlie that the cause of this his gathering of people was for the publike wealth of the realme. The king, much astonied at the matter, by aduise of his councell raised a great power, and marched forward toward the duke. But he, being thereof aduertised, turned out of that way, which by espials he vnderstood that the king held, and made streight toward London; and, hauing knowledge that he might not be suffered to passe through the citie, he crossed ouer the Thames at Kingston bridge, and so kept on towards Kent, where he knew that he had both freends & wellwillers, and there on Burnt heath, a mile from Dertford, and twelue miles from London, he imbattelled, and incamped himselfe verie stronglie, inuironing his field with artillerie and trenches. The king hereof aduertised, brought his armie with all diligence vnto Blackeheath, and there pight his tents.

Whilest both these armies laie thus imbattelled, the king sent the bishop of Winchester, and Thomas Bourchier, bishop of Elie, Richard Wooduile, lord Riuers, and Richard Andrew, the keeper of his priuie seale, to the duke: both to know the cause of so great a commotion, and also to make a concord; if the requests of the duke and his companie seemed consonant to reason. The duke, hearing the message of the bishops: answered that his comming was neither to damnifie the king in honour, nor in person, neither yet anie good man; but his intent was, to remooue from him certeine euill disposed persons of his councell, bloud-succours of the nobilitie, pollers of the cleargie, and oppressours of the poore people.

Amongst these, he cheeflie named Edmund duke of
Summerset, whome if the king would commit to ward,
to answer such articles as against him in open parlement
should be both proponed and proued, he promised not
onelie to dissolue his armie, but also offered himselfe
(like an obedient subiect) to come to the kings presence,
and to doo him true and faithfull seruice, according to
his loiall and bounden dutie.

[*H*. iii. 639] It was so agreed vpon by aduise, for the
auoiding of bloudshed, and pacifieng of the duke and his
people, that the duke of Summerset was committed to
ward, as some say ; or else commanded to keepe himselfe
priuie in his owne house for a time. . . .

The duke of Yorke, the first of March, dissolued his
armie, brake vp his campe, and came to the kings tent,
where contrarie to his expectation, & against promise
made by the king (as other write) he found the duke of
Summerset going at large and set *at libertie*, whome the
duke of Yorke boldlie accused of treason, briberie, oppression, and manie other crimes. The duke of Summerset
not onelie made answer to the dukes obiections, but also
accused him of high *treason* ; affirming, that he with his
fautors and complices had consulted togither, how to
come by the scepter and regall crowne of this realme.

[*H*. iii. 639] Whilest the councell treated of sauing or
dispatching of this duke of Yorke, a rumor sprang through
London, that Edward earle of March, sonne and heire
apparant to the said duke, with a great armie of Marchmen,
was comming toward London ; which tidings sore appalled
the queene and the whole councell.

HENRY VI. Part III

The Victory of York

[*H*. iii. 655]   Maister *Edward Hall* in his chronicle [I. i.]
maketh mention of an oration, which the duke of Yorke
vttered, sitting in *the regall seat*, there in the chamber of
the peeres, either at this his first comming in amongst
them, or else at some one time after : the which we haue
thought good also to set downe ; though *Iohn Whetham-
sted*, the abbat of saint Albons, who liued in those daies,
and by all likelihood was there present at the parlement,
maketh no further recitall of anie words, which the duke
should vtter at that time in that his booke of records,
where he intreateth of this matter.   But for the oration
(as maister *Hall* hath written thereof) we find as followeth :
During the time (saith he) of this parlement, the duke of
Yorke with a bold countenance entered into the chamber
of the peeres, and sat downe in the throne roiall, vnder the
cloth of estate, (which is the kings peculiar seat,) and, in
the presence of the nobilitie, as well spirituall as temporall
(after a pause made), he began to declare his title to
the crowne, in this forme and order as insueth.

[*H*. iii. 645]   [The Queen] could attempt nothing
against him neere to London ; because the duke was in
more estimation there, than either the king hir husband,
or hir selfe.

[*H*. iii. 657]   After long debating of the matter, and
deliberate consultation amongst the peeres, prelats, and
commons ; vpon the vigill of All saints, it was condescended : for so much as king Henrie had beene taken
as king by the space of thirtie and eight yeares and more,
that he should inioy the name and title of king, and haue
possession of the realme during his naturall life.   And,
if he either died, or resigned, or forfeited the same, by
breaking or going against anie point of this concord,

then the said crowne & authoritie roiall should immediatlie be deuoluted and come to the duke of Yorke, if he then liued ; or else to the next heire of his linage.

[*H.* iii. 658] Item, the said Richard duke of Yorke, shall promit and bind him by his solemne oth, in maner and forme as followeth :

" In the name of God, Amen : I, Richard duke of Yorke, promise and sweare by the faith and truth that I owe to almightie God, that I shall neuer consent, procure, or stirre, directlie or indirectlie, in priuie or apert, neither (as much as in me is) shall suffer to be doone, consented, procured, or stirred, anie thing that may sound to the abridgement of the naturall life of king Henrie the sixt, or to the hurt or diminishing of his reigne or dignitie roiall, by violence, or anie other waie, against his freedome or libertie."

[*H.* iii. 659] Vpon the saturdaie next insuing, Richard duke of Yorke was by sound of trumpet solemnelie proclamed heire apparant to the crowne of England, and protectour of the realme.

[*H.* iii. 659] The duke of Yorke, well knowing that the queene would spurne against all this, caused both hir and hir sonne to be sent for by the king. But she, as woont rather to rule, than to be ruled, and thereto counselled by the dukes of Excester and Summerset, not onelie denied to come, but also assembled a great armie ; intending to take the king by fine force out of the lords hands.

[*H.* iii. 659] [York] assigned the duke of Nor- [I. ii.] ffolke, and erle of Warwike, his trustie freends, to be about the king, while he, with the earles of Salisburie and Rutland, and a conuenient number, departed out of London the second daie of December, northward ; and appointed the earle of March his eldest sonne to follow him with all his power. The duke came to his castell of Sandall beside Wakefield on Christmasse eeuen, & there began to make muster of his tenants and freends.

[*H.* iii. 653] The people of [Kent] and other parts were altogither bent in their [the Yorkists] fauor ; and no lesse addicted to doo them seruice both with bodie and goods, than the Irishmen seemed to be at their receiuing of the said duke of Yorke, and his yoonger sonne Edmund earle of Rutland ; whom they so highlie honoured, that they offered to liue and die in their quarrell. . . .

But it is to be read in a late writer, that the commons of Kent . . . sent priuilie messengers to Calis to the foresaid erles ; beseeching them in all hast possible to come to their succour. Wherevpon the said earles sent ouer into Kent the lord Fauconbridge, to know if their deeds would accord with their words : so that anon the people of Kent, and the other shires adioining, resorted to the said lord Fauconbridge in great number.

[*H.* iii. 659] [The Queen] determined to cope with him yer his succour were come.

Now she, hauing in hir companie the prince hir sonne, the dukes of Excester and Summerset, the earle of Deuon-shire, the lord Clifford, the lord Ros, and in effect all the lords of the north parts, with eighteene thousand men, or (as some write) two and twentie thousand, marched from Yorke to Wakefield, and bad base to the duke, euen before his castell gates.

THE DEFEAT OF YORK

[*H.* iii. 659] [York] fought manfullie, yet was he within half an houre slaine and dead, and his whole armie discomfited : with him died of his trustie freends, his two bastard vncles, sir Iohn and sir Hugh Mortimer, sir Dauie Hall, sir Hugh Hastings, sir Thomas Neuill, William and Thomas Aparre, both brethren ; and two thousand and eight hundred others, whereof manie were yoong gentlemen, and heires of great parentage in the south parts : whose kin reuenged their deaths within foure moneths next, as after shall appeare.

[*H.* iii. 659] After this victorie by the queene, the earle of Salisburie and all the prisoners were sent to Pomfret, and there beheaded ; whose heads (togither with the duke of Yorkes head) were conueied to Yorke, and there set on poles ouer the gate of the citie, in despite of them and their linage.

[*H.* iii. 660] Newes was brought to [Edward] [II. i.] that Iasper earle of Penbroke, halfe brother to king Henrie,

and Iames Butler, earle of Ormund and Wilshire, had
assembled a great number of Welsh and Irish people to take
him : he, herewith quickned, retired backe and met with
his enimies in a faire plaine neere to Mortimers crosse,
not far from Hereford east, on Candle masse daie in the
morning. At which time the sunne (as some write)
appeared to the earle of March like three sunnes, and
suddenlie ioined altogither in one. Upon which sight
he tooke such courage, that he, fiercelie setting on his
enimies, put them to flight : and for this cause men
imagined that he gaue the sunne in his full brightnesse
for his badge or cognisance.

[*H*. iii. 661]   True report came not onelie to the queene,
but also to the citie ; that the earle of March, hauing
vanquished the earles of Penbroke and Wilshire, had met
with the earle of Warwike (after this last battell at saint
Albons) at Chipping Norton by Cotsold ; and that they
with both their powers were comming toward London.

[*H*. iii. 660]   Now after that the noble men and other
were fled, and the king left in maner alone without anie
power of men to gard his person, he was counselled by an
esquier called Thomas Hoo, a man well languaged, and
well seene in the lawes, to send some conuenient messenger
to the northerne lords, aduertising them, that he would
now gladlie come vnto them, (whome he knew to be his
verie freends, and had assembled themselues togither for
his seruice), to the end he might remaine with them, as
before he had remained vnder the gouernement of the
southerne lords.

[*H*. iii. 661]   The duches of Yorke, seeing hir husband
and sonne slaine, and not knowing what should succeed
of hir eldest sonnes chance, sent hir two yonger sonnes,
George and Richard, ouer the sea, to the citie of Utrecht
in Almaine, where they were of Philip duke of Burgognie
well receiued ; and so remained there, till their brother
Edward had got the crowne and gouernement of the
realme.

[*H*. iii. 660]   [The Queen] caused the king to dub hir
sonne prince Edward, knight ; with thirtie other persons,
which the day before fought on hir side against his part.

[*H*. iii. 664]   The bastard of Salisburie, brother   [II. iii.]

to the earle of Warwike, a valiant yoong gentleman, and
of great audacitie [was slain].

When the earle of Warwike was informed hereof, like
a man desperat, he mounted on his hacknie, and hasted
puffing and blowing to king Edward, saieng ; " Sir, I praie
God haue mercie of their soules, which in the beginning of
your enterprise haue lost their liues ! And bicause I see
no succors of the world but in God, I remit the vengeance
to him our creator and redeemer." With that he alighted
downe, and slue his horse with his sword, saieng : " Let
him flee that will, for suerlie I will tarrie with him that
will tarrie with me " : and kissed the crosse of his sword
as it were for a vow to the promise.

[*H*. iii. 664] King Edward, perceiuing the courage of
his trustie friend the earle of Warwike, made proclamation,
that all men which were afraid to fight should depart : and,
to all those that tarried the battell, he promised great
rewards ; with addition, that anie souldier which voluntarilie would abide, and afterwards, either in or before
the fight should seeme to flee or turne his backe, then he
that could kill him should haue a great reward and double
wages.

[*H*. iii. 665] King Henrie, after he heard of [II. v.]
the irrecouerable losse of his armie, departed incontinentlie
with his wife and sonne to the towne of Berwike ; and,
leauing the duke of Summerset there, went into Scotland,
and, comming to the king of Scots, required of him and
his councell, aid and comfort.

[*H*. iii. 664] The lord Clifford, either for heat [II. vi.]
or paine, putting off his gorget, suddenlie with an arrow
(as some saie, without an head) was stricken into the
throte, and immediatlie rendred his spirit.

[*H*. iii. 665] [Edward] caused the heads of his
father, the earle of Salisburie, and other his freends, to
be taken from the gates, and to be buried with their
bodies : and there he caused the earle of Deuonshire, and
three other, to be beheaded, and set their heads in the
same place.

[*H*. iii. 665] [He] returned, after the maner and
fashion of a triumphant conquerour, with great pompe
vnto London ; where, according to the old custome of

the realme, he called a great assemblie of persons of all
degrees ; and the nine & twentith daie of Iune was at
Westminster with solemnitie *crowned* and annointed
king. . . .

Also, after this, he created his two yoonger brethren
dukes ; that is to saie, lord George, duke of Clarence,
lord Richard, duke of Glocester.

[*H.* iii. 627] Some thinke that the name and title of
Glocester hath beene vnluckie to diuerse, which for their
honours haue beene erected by creation of princes to that
stile and dignitie ; as Thomas Spenser, Thomas of Woodstoke, sonne to king Edward the third, and this duke
Humfreie : which three persons by miserable death finished
their daies ; and after them king Richard the third also,
duke of Glocester, in ciuill warre slaine.

[*H.* iii. 667] Whether he was past all feare ;   [III. i.]
or that hee was not well established in his wits and perfect
mind ; or for that he could not long keepe himselfe
secret, [Henry] in *disguised* atire boldlie entred into
England.

He was no sooner entred, but he was knowne and taken
of one Cantlow, and brought toward the king ; whom the
earle of Warwike met on the way by the kings commandement, and brought him through London to the Tower, &
there he was laid in sure hold.

The Suit of Elizabeth Gray

[*H.* iii. 726] There came to make a sute by [III. ii.]
petition to the king dame Elizabeth Greie, which was after
his queene, at that time a widow, borne of noble bloud
by hir mother, duches of Bedford yer she maried the lord
Wooduile, hir father.

Howbeit, this dame Elizabeth hir selfe, being in seruice
with queene Margaret, wife vnto king Henrie the sixt, was
maried vnto one Iohn Greie, an esquier, whome king
Henrie made knight vpon the field that he had on Barnet
heath by saint Albons, against king Edward.   But litle
while inioied he that knighthood : for he was at the same
field slaine. . . . this poore ladie made humble sute
vnto the king, that she might be restored vnto such

small lands as hir late husband had giuen her in iointure.

[*H*. iii. 668] The king being on hunting in the forrest of Wichwood besides Stonistratford, came for his recreation to the manor of Grafton, where the duchesse of Bedford then soiourned, wife to sir Richard Wooduile lord Riuers; on whome was then attendant a daughter of hirs, called the ladie Elizabeth Graie, widow of sir Iohn Graie knight, slaine at the last battell of saint Albons. . . .

This widow, hauing a sute to the king for such lands as hir husband had giuen hir in iointure, so kindled the kings affection towards hir, that he not onelie fauoured hir sute, but more hir person; for she was a woman of a more formall countenance than of excellent beautie; and yet both of such beautie and fauour, that, with hir sober demeanour, sweete looks, and comelie smiling, (neither too wanton, nor too bashfull,) besides hir pleasant toong and trim wit, she so allured and made subiect vnto hir the heart of that great prince, that, after she had denied him to be his paramour, (with so good maner, and words so well set as better could not be deuised,) he finallie resolued with himselfe to marrie hir; not asking counsell of anie man, till they might perceiue it was no bootie to aduise him to the contrarie of that his concluded purpose.

[*H*. iii. 726] Whome when the king beheld, and heard hir speake, as she was both faire and of a goodlie fauour, moderate of stature, well made and verie wise: he not onelie pitied hir, but also waxed inamoured of hir. And, taking hir afterward secretlie aside, began to enter in talking more familiarlie. Whose appetite when she perceiued, she vertuouslie denied him.

But that did she so wiselie, and with so good maner, and words so well set, that she rather kindled his desire than quenched it. And, finallie, after manie a meeting, much wooing, and many great promises, she well espied the kings affection toward hir so greatlie increased, that she durst somewhat the more boldlie saie hir mind; as to him whose hart she perceiued more feruentlie set, than to fall off for a word. And, in conclusion, she shewed him plaine, that, as she wist hir selfe *too* simple *to be* his wife, so thought she hir selfe *too good to be* his *concubine*. The king, much maruelling at hir constancie, (as he that had not been woont elsewhere to be so stiffelie said naie,) so much esteemed hir continencie and chastitie, that he set hir vertue in the steed of possession and riches : and thus, taking counsell of his desire, determined in all possible hast to marie her.

Now after he was thus appointed, and had betweene them twaine insured hir ; then asked he counsell of his other freends, and that in such maner, as they might then perceiue it booted not greatlie to say naie.

[*H.* iii 665] [Henry] sent his wife, and his   [III. iii.] sonne into France to king Reiner hir father ; trusting by his aid and succour to assemble an armie, and once againe to recouer his right and dignitie : but he in the meane time made his aboad in Scotland, to see what waie his friends in England would studie for his restitution.

The queene, being in France, did obteine of the yoong French king, then Lewes the eleuenth, that all hir husbands friends, and those of the Lancastriall band, might safelie and suerlie haue resort into anie part of the realme of France : prohibiting all other of the contrarie faction anie accesse or repaire into that countrie.

[*H.* iii. 667] It was thought meet by [Edward] and those of his councell, that a marriage were prouided for him in some conuenient place ; and therefore was the earle of Warwike sent ouer into France, to demand the ladie Bona, daughter to Lewes duke of Sauoie, and sister to the ladie Carlot, then queene of France ; which Bona was at that time in the French court.

The earle of Warwike, comming to the French king, then lieng at Tours, was of him honourablie receiued, and right courteouslie interteined. His message was so well liked, and his request thought so honourable for the aduancement of the ladie Bona, that hir sister queene Carlot obteined both the good will of the king hir husband, and also of hir sister the foresaid ladie : so that the matrimonie on that side was cleerelie assented to, and the erle of Dampmartine appointed (with others) to saile into England, for the full finishing of the same.

[*H.* iii. 665] The earle of Oxford far striken in age, and

his sonne and heire the lord Awbreie Veer, either through
malice of their enimies, or for that they had offended the
king, were both, with diuerse of their councellours,
attainted, and put to execution ; which caused Iohn earle
of Oxord euer after to rebell.

[*H*. iii. 661] Incontinentlie was Edward earle of March,
sonne and heire to Richard duke of Yorke, by the lords
in the said councell assembled, named, elected, and
admitted for king and gouernour of the realme.

On which daie, the people of the earles part being in their
muster in S. Iohns field, and a great number of the
substantiall citizens there assembled to behold their order,
the lord Fauconbridge, who tooke the musters, wiselie
anon declared to the people the offenses and breaches of
the late agreement, committed by king Henrie the sixt ;
and demanded of the people, whether they would haue
him to rule and reigne anie longer ouer them ? To whome
they with whole voice answered : " Naie, naie ! " Then
he asked them, if they would serue, loue, honour, and obeie
the erle of March, as their onlie king and souereigne lord ?
To which question they answered : " Yea, yea ! " crieng,
" King Edward ! " with manie great showts & clapping
of hands in assent and gladnesse of the same.

The lords were shortlie aduertised of the louing consent
which the commons frankelie and freelie had giuen. Whervpon, incontinentlie, they all with a conuenient number
of the most substantiall commons repaired to the erle at
Bainards castell ; making iust and true report of their
election and admission, and the louing assent of the
commons.

[*H*. iii. 663] After that this prince Edward earle of
March had taken vpon him the gouernement of this
realme of England (as before ye haue heard), the morow
next insuing, being the fourth of March, he rode to the
church of saint Paule, and there offered ; and, after
Te Deum soong, with great solemnitie he was conueied to
Westminster, and there set in the hall with the scepter
roiall in his hand : whereto people in great numbers
assembled. His claime to the crowne was declared to be
by two maner of waies ; the first, as sonne and heire to
duke Richard his father, right inheritor to the same ; the

second, by authoritie of parlement, and forfeiture committed by king Henrie. Wherevpon it was againe demanded of the commons, if they would admit and take the said erle as their prince and souereigne lord ; which all with one voice cried : " Yea, yea ! "

[*H*. iii. 668] The French king was not well pleased to be thus dallied with; but he shortlie (to appease the greefe of his wife and hir sister the ladie Bona) married the said ladie Bona to the duke of Millan.

Now when the earle of Warwike had knowledge by letters sent to him out of England from his trustie friends, that king Edward had gotten him a new wife, he was not a little troubled in his mind ; for that he tooke it his credence thereby was greatlie minished, and his honour much stained, namelie, in the court of France ; for that it might be iudged he came rather like as espiall, to mooue a thing neuer minded, and to treat a marriage determined before not to take effect. Suerlie he thought himselfe euill vsed, that when he had brought the matter to his purposed intent and wished conclusion, then to haue it quaile on his part ; so as all men might thinke at the least wise, that his prince made small account of him, to send him on such a sleeuelesse errand.

All men for the most part agree, that this marriage was the onlie cause, why the earle of Warwike conceiued an hatred against king Edward, whome he so much before fauoured.

WARWICK AND THE KING

[*H*. iii. 674–675] When queene Margaret, that soiourned with duke Reiner hir father, heard tell that the earle of Warwike was come to the French court, with all diligence shee came to Ambois to see him, with hir onelie sonne prince Edward.

With her also came Iasper earle of Penbroke, and Iohn earle of Oxford, which, after diuerse imprisonments latelie escaped, fled out of England into France, and came by fortune to this assemblie. These persons, after intreatie had of their affaires, determined by meanes of the French king to conclude a league and amitie betweene them. And first to begin withall, for the sure foundation of their

new intreatie, Edward prince of Wales wedded Anne
second daughter to the earle of Warwike, which ladie
came with hir mother into France. After which mariage,
the duke and the earles tooke a solemne oth, that they
should neuer leaue the warre, till either king Henrie the
sixt, or his sonne prince Edward, were restored to the
crowne: and that the queene and the prince should
depute and appoint the duke and the earle to be gouernors
& conseruators of the common wealth till time the prince
were come to estate. . . .

The French king lent both ships, men, and monie vnto
queene Margaret, and to hir partakers; and appointed
the bastard of Burbon, admerall of France, with a great
nauie, to defend them against the nauie of the duke of
Burgognie; which he laid at the mouth of the riuer Saine,
readie to incounter them, being of greater force than both
the French nauie and the English fleet.

[*H*. iii. 671] The earle of Warwike, being a [IV. i.]
far casting prince, perceiued somewhat in the duke of
Clarence, whereby he iudged that he bare no great will
towards the king his brother; and therevpon, feeling his
minde by such talke as he of purpose ministred, vnderstood how he was bent, and so wan him to his purpose.

[*H*. iii. 671–672] [The] duke of Clarence, being come
to Calis with the earle of Warwike, after he had sworne
on the sacrament to keepe his promise and pact made
with the said earle whole and inuiolate, he married the
ladie Isabell, eldest daughter to the earle, in our ladies
church there.

[*H*. iii. 672] King Edward, hauing perfect knowledge
of all the dooings of the earle of Warwike, and of his
brother the duke of Clarence, was by diuerse letters
certified of the great armie of the northerne men, with all
speed comming toward London; and therefore in great
hast he sent to William lord Herbert, whom (as yee haue
heard) he had created earle of Penbroke; requiring him
without delaie to raise his power, and incounter with the
northerne men. . . .

And, to assist him with archers, was appointed Humfrie
lord Stafford of Southwike, named but not created earle of
Deuonshire by the king; in hope that he would serue

valiantlie in that iournie : he had with him eight hundred archers.

[*H*. iii. 675]   It is almost not to be beleeued,   [IV. ii.] how manie thousands men of warre at the first tidings of the earles [Warwick's] landing resorted vnto him.

[*H*. iii. 675]   He made proclamation in the   [IV. iii.] name of king Henrie the sixt, vpon high paines commanding and charging all men able to bear armor, to prepare themselues to fight against Edward duke of Yorke, which contrarie to right had vsurped the crowne.

[*H*. iii. 673]   [Edward] assembled his power, and was comming toward the earle, who, being aduertised thereof, sent to the duke of Clarence, requiring him to come and ioine with him.   The duke, being not farre off, with all speed repaired to the earle, and so they ioined their powers togither, and vpon secret knowledge had, that the king (bicause they were entered into termes by waie of communication to haue a peace) tooke small heed to himselfe, nothing doubting anie outward attempt of his enimies.

The earle of Warwike, intending not to leese such opportunitie of aduantage, in the dead of the night, with an elect companie of men of warre, (as secretlie as was possible,) set on the kings field, killing them that kept the watch, and, yer the king was ware, (for he thought of nothing lesse than of that which then hapned,) at a place called Wolnie, foure miles from Warwike, he was taken prisoner and brought to the castell of Warwike.   And, to the intent his friends should not know what was become of him, the earle caused him by secret iournies in the night to be conueied to Middleham castell in Yorkeshire ; and there to be kept vnder the custodie of the archbishop of Yorke, and other his freends in those parties.

[*H*. iii. 677]   [Edward's] freends went to   [IV. iv.] diuerse sanctuaries, and amongst other his wife queene Elizabeth tooke *sanctuarie* at Westminster, and there, in great penurie, forsaken of all hir friends, was deliuered of a faire son called Edward.

[*H*. iii. 673]   King Edward, being thus in   [IV. v.] capitiuitie, spake euer faire to the archbishop, and to his other keepers, so that he had leaue diuerse daies to go hunt. . . .

Now, on a daie, vpon a plaine, when he was thus abrode, there met with him sir William Stanleie, sir Thomas a Borough, and diuers other of his friends, with such a great band of men, that neither his keepers would, nor once durst, moue him to returne vnto prison againe. Some haue thought that his keepers were corrupted with monie, or faire promises, and therfore suffred him thus to scape out of danger.

[*H*. iii. 675] Accompanied with the duke of Glocester his brother, the lord Hastings his chamberlaine, (which had maried the earles sister, and yet was euer true to the king his maister,) and the lord Scales, brother to the queene, [Edward] departed into Lincolneshire. And, bicause he vnderstood that all the realme was vp against him, and some part of the earle of Warwiks power was within halfe a daies iournie of him, following the aduise of his counsell, with all hast possible, he passed the Washes in great ieopardie, & comming to Lin found there an English ship, and two hulkes of Holland, readie (as fortune would) to make saile.

Wherevpon he, with his brother the duke of Glocester, the lord Scales, and diuerse other his trustie friends, entered into the ship. The lord Hastings taried a while after, exhorting all his acquaintance, that of necessitie should tarie behind, to shew themselues openlie as friends to king Henrie for their owne safegard, but hartilie required them in secret to continue faithfull to king Edward. This persuasion declared, he entered the ship with the other, and so they departed; being in number in that one ship and two hulkes, about seuen or eight hundred persons, hauing no furniture of appareli or other necessarie things with them, sauing apparell for warre.

[*H*. iii. 677] On the fiue and twentith day of [IV. vi.] the said moneth, the duke of Clarence, accompanied with the earles of Warwike and Shrewesburie, the lord Strange, and other lords and gentlemen, some for feare, and some for loue, and some onelie to gaze at the wauering world, went to the Tower, and from thense brought king Henrie, apparelled in a long gowne of blew veluet, through London to the church of saint Paule; the people on euerie side the streets reioising and crieng, "God saue the king ! " as though ech thing had succeeded as they would haue had it : and, when he had offered (as kings vse to doo), he was conueied to the bishops palace, where he kept his household like a king.

[H. iii. 677–678] When king Henrie had thus readepted and eftsoons gotten his regall power and authoritie, he called his high court of parlement, to begin the six and twentith day of Nouember, at Westminster ; in the which king Edward was adiudged a traitor to the countrie, and an vsurper of the realme. *His goods* were *confiscat* and forfeited. . . .

The crownes of the realmes of England and France were by authoritie of the same parlement intailed to king Henrie the sixt, and to his heires male ; and, for default of such heires, to remaine to George duke of Clarence, & to his heires male : and, further, the said duke was inabled to be next heire to his father Richard duke of Yorke, and to take from him all his landes and dignities, as though he had beene his eldest sonne at the time of his death.

[H. iii. 678] When queene Margaret vnderstood by hir husbands letters, that the victorie was gotten by their freends, she with hir sonne prince Edward and hir traine entered their ships, to take their voiage into England : but the winter was so sharpe, the weather so stormie, and the wind so contrarie, that she was faine to take land againe, and to deferre hir iournie till another season.

[H. iii. 678] Jasper earle of Penbroke went into Wales, to visit his lands in Penbrokeshire, where he found lord Henrie, sonne to his brother Edmund earle of Richmond, hauing not full ten yeares of age ; he being kept in maner like a captiue, but honorablie brought vp by the ladie Herbert, late wife to William earle of Penbroke. . . .

The earle of Penbroke tooke this child, being his nephue, out of the custodie of the ladie Herbert, and at his returne brought the child with him to London to king Henrie the sixt ; whome when the king had a good while beheld, he said to such princes as were with him : " Lo, suerlie this is he, to whom both we and our aduersaries, leauing the possession of all things, shall hereafter giue roome and place." So this holie man shewed before the chance that should happen, that this earle Henrie, so

ordeined by God, should in time to come (as he did indeed)
haue and inioy the kingdome and whole rule of this realme
of England.

[*H*. iii. 693] [Pembroke] was conueied to Tinbie, where
he got ships, and with his nephue, the lord Henrie earle of
Richmond, sailed into Britaine, where, of the duke, they
were courteouslie interteined ; with assurance made, that
no creature should doo them anie wrong or iniurie within
his dominions.

[*H*. iii.] [The Duke of Burgundy] would not   [IV. vii.]
consent openlie to aid king Edward ; but yet secretlie
vnder hand by others he lent vnto him fiftie thousand
florens of the crosse of S. Andrew, and further caused
foure great ships to be appointed for him in the hauen of
de Veere, otherwise called Camphire in Zeland, which
in those daies was free for all men to come vnto, and the
duke hired for him fourteene ships of the Easterlings well
appointed, & for the more suertie tooke a bond of them
to serue him trulie, till he were landed in England, and
fifteene daies after.

[*H*. iii. 680] There came to [Edward] sir Thomas
Burgh, & sir Thomas Montgomerie, with their aids ;
which caused him at their first comming to make proclamation in his owne name, to wit, of K. Edward the fourth :
boldlie affirming to him, that they would serue no man
but a king.

[*H*. iii. 693] Iohn earle of Oxford, which   [V. iii.]
after Barnet field both manfullie and valiantlie kept saint
Michaels mount in Cornewall, either for lacke of aid, or
persuaded by his friends, gaue vp the mount, and yeelded
himselfe to king Edward (his life onelie saued), which to
him was granted.   But, to be out of all doutfull imaginations, king Edward also sent him ouer the sea to the castell
of Hammes, where, by the space of twelue yeeres, hee was
in strong prison shut vp and warilie looked to.

PRINCE EDWARD'S DEATH

[*H*. iii. 688] After the field was ended, proclamation
was made, that whosoeuer could bring foorth prince
Edward aliue or dead, should haue an annuitie of a

hundred pounds during his life, and the princes life to be
saued, if he were brought foorth aliue. Sir Richard
Crofts, nothing mistrusting the kings promise, brought
foorth his prisoner prince Edward, being a faire and
well proportioned yoong gentleman; whom when king
Edward had well aduised, he demanded of him, how he
durst so presumptuouslie enter into his realme with
banner displaied?

Wherevnto the prince boldlie answered, saieng: "To
recouer my fathers kingdome & heritage, from his father
and grandfather to him, and from him after him to me,
lineallie descended." At which words king Edward said
nothing, but with his hand thrust him from him, or (as
some saie) stroke him with his gantlet; whom, incontinentlie, George duke of Clarence, Richard duke of Glocester,
Thomas Greie marquesse Dorcet, and William lord
Hastings, that stood by, suddenlie murthered.

MURDER OF HENRY

[*H*. iii. 690] In the Tower . . . Richard duke of
Glocester, (as the constant fame ran,) . . . (to the intent
that his brother king Edward might reigne in more
suertie) murthered the said king Henrie with a dagger.

RICHARD III

[Various points of connection have been traced between Richard III and other plays on the same subject, such as Legge's *Ricardus Tertius* and the anonymous *True Tragedie of Richard III*, but the outline in the chronicler seems to have been Shakespeare's prime authority. The play was a popular one, as is amply proved by the seven editions of the text issued from 1597 to 1623.]

[*H*. iii. 712] Some wise men . . . thinke that [I. i.] [Richard] long time in king Edwards life forethought to be king ; in case that the king his brother (whose life he looked that *euill diet* should shorten) should happen to deceasse (as in deed he did) while his children were yoong. And they deeme, that for this intent he was glad of his brothers death the duke of Clarence, whose life must needs haue hindered him so intending ; whether the same duke of Clarence had kept him true to his nephue the yoong king, or enterprised to be king himselfe.

[*H*. iii. 703] [The death of Clarence] rose of a foolish *prophesie, which* was, *that*, after K. Edward, one should reigne, whose first letter of his name should be a *G*. Wherewith the king and queene were sore troubled, and began to conceiue a greeuous grudge against this duke, and could not be in quiet till they had brought him to his end. And, as the diuell is woont to incumber the minds of men which delite in such diuelish fantasies, they said afterward, that that prophesie lost not his effect, when, after king Edward, Glocester vsurped his kingdome.

[*H*. iii. 690–691] The *dead* corps [of Henry], on [I. ii.] the Ascension euen, was conueied with billes and glaues pompouslie (if you will call that a funerall pompe) from the Tower to the church of saint Paule, and there, laid on a beire or coffen bare faced, the same in presence of the beholders did *bleed*: where it rested the space of one whole daie. From thense he was caried to the Black-friers, and bled there likewise : and, on the next daie after, it was conueied in a boat, without priest or clerke, torch or taper, singing or saieng, vnto the monasterie of Chertseie, distant from London fifteene miles, and there was it first buried.

[*H.* iii. 716] The duke of Glocester bare him in open sight so reuerentlie to the prince, with all semblance of lowlinesse, that, from the great obloquie in which he was so late before, he was suddenlie fallen in so great trust, that at the councell next assembled he was made the onelie man, chosen and thought most meet to be protector of the king and his realme ; so that (were it destinie or were it follie) the lambe was betaken to the woolfe to keepe.

[*H.* iii. 703] Finallie the duke [of Clarence] [I. iv.] was cast into the Tower, and therewith adiudged for a traitor, and priuilie *drown*ed in a *butt* of *malmesie*, the eleuenth of March, in the beginning of the seuententh yeare of the kings reigne.

[*H.* iii. 713] King Edward, in his life, albeit [II. i.] that this dissention betweene his freends somewhat irked him ; yet in his good health he somewhat the lesse regarded it : bicause he thought, whatsoeuer businesse should fall betweene them, himselfe should alwaie be able to rule both the parties.

But, in his last sicknesse, when he perceiued his naturall strength so sore infeebled, that he despaired all recouerie, then he, considering the youth of his children, albeit he nothing lesse mistrusted than that that hapned, yet well foreseeing that manie harmes might grow by their debate, while the youth of his children should lacke discretion of themselues, & good counsell of their freends, of which either partie should counsell for their owne commoditie, & rather by plesant aduise to win themselues fauour, than by profitable aduertisement to doo the children good, he called some of them before him that were at variance, and in especiall the lord marquesse Dorset, the queenes sonne by hir first husband.

So did he also William the lord Hastings, a noble man, then lord chamberleine, against whome the queene speciallie grudged, for the great fauour the king bare him : and also for that she thought him secretlie familiar with

the king in wanton companie. Hir kinred also bare him
sore, as well for that the king had made him capteine of
Calis, (which office the lord Riuers, brother to the queene,
clamed of the kings former promise,) as for diuerse other
great gifts which he receiued, that they looked for.

[*H*. iii. 714] And therewithall the king, no longer
induring to sit vp, laid him downe on his right side, his
face towards them : and none was there present that could
refraine from weeping.

But the lords, recomforting him with as good words as
they could, and answering for the time as they thought to
stand with his pleasure, there in his presence, as by their
words appeared, ech forgaue other, and ioined their hands
togither ; when (as it after appeared by their deeds) their
hearts were farre asunder.

[*H*. iii. 703] Although king Edward were consenting to
[Clarence's] death, yet he much did both lament his
infortunate chance, & repent his sudden execution : insomuch that when anie person sued to him for the
pardon of malefactors condemned to death, he would
accustomablie saie, & openlie speake : " Oh infortunate
brother, for whose life not one would make sute ! "

[*H*. iii. 714–715] As soone as the king was [II. ii.]
departed, the noble prince his sonne drew toward London ;
which at the time of his deceasse kept his houshold at
Ludlow in Wales. . . .

To the gouernance and ordering of this yoong prince, at
his sending thither, was there appointed sir Anthonie
Wooduile, lord Riuers, and brother vnto the queene ; a
right honourable man, as valiant of hand as politike in
counsell. Adioined were there vnto him other of the same
partie ; and in effect euerie one as he was neerest of kin
vnto the queene, so was he planted next about the prince.
That drift by the queene not vnwiselie deuised, whereby
hir bloud might of youth be rooted into the princes fauour,
the duke of Glocester turned vnto their destruction ; and
vpon that ground set the foundation of all his vnhappie
building. For whome soeuer he perceiued either at
variance with them, or bearing himselfe their fauour, he
brake vnto them, some by mouth, & some by writing. . . .

With these words and writings, and such other, the

duke of Glocester soone set on fire them that were of
themselues easie to kindle, &, in especiall, twaine, Henry
duke of Buckingham, and William lord Hastings, then
chamberleine ; both men of honour & of great power : the
one by long succession from his ancestrie, the other by his
office and the kings fauour. These two, not bearing ech
to other so much loue, as hatred both vnto the queenes
part, in this point accorded togither with the duke of
Glocester ; that they would vtterlie remoue from the kings
companie all his mothers freends, vnder the name of
their enimies.

Upon this concluded the duke of Glocester, vnderstanding that the lords, which at that time were about the
king, intended to bring him vp to his coronation accompanied with such power of their freends, that it should be
hard for him to bring his purpose to passe, without the
gathering and great assemblie of people and in maner of
open warre, whereof the end (he wist) was doubtfull ; and
in which, the king being on their side, his part should haue
the face and name of a rebellion : he secretlie therfore by
diuers means caused the queene to be persuaded and
brought in the mind, that it neither were need, and also
should be ieopardous, the king to come vp strong.

For whereas now euerie lord loued other, and none other
thing studied vpon, but about the coronation and honor
of the king ; if the lords of hir kindred should assemble in
the kings name much people, they should giue the lords,
betwixt whome and them had beene sometime debate, to
feare and suspect, least they should gather this people,
not for the kings safegard, (whome no man impugned,)
but for their destruction ; hauing more regard to their old
variance, than their new attonement. For which cause
they should assemble on the other partie much people
againe for their defense, (whose power she wist well far
stretched,) and thus should all the realme fall on a rore.
And of all the hurt that thereof should insue, (which was
likelie not to be little, and the most harme there like to
fall where she least would,) all the world would put hir
and hir kindered in the wight, and saie that they had
vnwiselie and vntrulie also broken the amitie & peace, that
the king hir husband so prudentlie made, betweene his

kin and hirs in his death bed, and which the other partie faithfullie obserued.

The queene, being in this wise persuaded, such word sent vnto hir sonne, and vnto hir brother, being about the king, and ouer that the duke of Glocester himselfe and other lords, the chiefe of his bend, wrote vnto the king so reuerentlie, and to the queenes freends there so louinglie, that they, nothing earthlie mistrusting, brought the king vp in great hast, not in good speed, with a sober companie.

[*H.* iii. 721] Began there, here and there [II. iii.] abouts, some maner of muttering among the people, as though all should not long be well, though they neither wist what they feared, nor wherefore : were it, that, *before* such great things, *mens* hearts of a secret *instinct* of nature misgiue them; as the sea without the wind *swell*eth of himselfe sometime *before a* tempest.

[*H.* iii. 715] Now was the king in his waie to [II. iv.] London gone from *Northampton,* when these dukes of Glocester and Buckingham came thither; where remained behind the lord Riuers the kings vncle, intending on the *morrow* to follow the king, and to be with him *at Stonie Stratford,* certeine miles thence, earlie, yer he departed.

[*H.* iii. 715] The duke of Glocester tooke vpon himselfe the order and gouernance of the yoong king, whome with much honor and humble reuerence he conueied vpward towards the citie. But, anon, the tidings of this matter came hastilie to the queene a little before the midnight following, and that in the sorest wise : that the king hir son was taken, hir brother, hir sonne, & hir other freends arrested, and sent, no man wist whither, to be doone with God wot what. . . .

Now came there one in likewise not long after midnight from the lord chamberleine, to doctor Rotheram the archbishop of Yorke, then chancellor of England, to his place not farre from Westminster. And for that he shewed his seruants that he had tidings of so great importance, that his maister gaue him in charge, not to forbeare his rest, they letted not to wake him, nor he to admit this messenger in, to his bed side. Of whom he heard that these dukes were gone back with the kings grace from Stonie Stratford vnto Northampton. " Notwithstanding,

sir" (quoth he) "my lord sendeth your lordship word, that
there is no feare: for he assureth you that all shall be
well." "I assure him" (quoth the archbishop) "be it as
well as it will, it will neuer be so well as we haue seene it."

[*H*. iii. 715] [Richard] *sent* the *lord Riuers*, and the
lord Richard, *with sir Thomas Vaughan*, into the north
countrie, into diuerse places to *prison*; and afterward all
to Pomfret, where they were in conclusion beheaded. . . .

[The Queen] in great fright & heauinesse, bewailing
hir childes reigne, hir freends mischance, and hir owne
infortune, damning the time that euer she dissuaded the
gathering of power about the king, gat hir selfe in all the
hast possible with hir yoonger soone and hir daughters
out of the palace of Westminster, (in which she then laie,)
in*to* the *sanctuarie*; lodging hir selfe and hir companie
there in the abbats place. . . .

[The archbishop] caused in all the hast all his seruants
to be called vp, and so, with his owne houshold about
him, and euerie man weaponed, he tooke the great seale
with him, and came yet before daie vnto the queene.
About whom he found much heauinesse, rumble, hast,
and businesse ; cariage and conueiance of hir stuffe into
sanctuarie ; chests, coffers, packs, fardels, trussed all on
mens backs ; no man vnoccupied, some lading, some
going, some discharging, some comming for more, some
breaking downe the walles to bring in the next waie, and
some yet drew to them that holpe to carrie a wrong
waie. . . .

The queene hir selfe sate alone alow on the rushes all desolate and dismaid, whome the archbishop comforted in best
manner he could ; shewing hir that he trusted the matter
was nothing so sore as she tooke it for, and that he was
put in good hope and out of feare by the message sent him
from the lord chamberleine. " Ah, wo woorth him ! "
(quoth she) " for he is one of them that laboreth to destroie
me and my bloud." " Madame " (quoth he) " be yee of
good cheere, for I assure you, if they crowne anie other
king than your sonne, whome they now haue with them,
we shall on the morow crowne his brother, whome you
haue here with you. And here is the great seale, which
in likewise as that noble prince your husband deliuered it

vnto me ; so here I deliuer it vnto you, to the vse and
behoofe of your sonne : " and therewith he betooke hir
the great seale, and departed home againe, yet in the
dawning of the daie.

[*H*. iii. 716]   When the king approched neere   [III. i.]
to the citie, Edmund Shaw, goldsmith, then maior, with
William White, and Iohn Matthew, shiriffes, and all the
other aldermen in scarlet, with fiue hundred horsse of the
citizens, in violet, receiued him reuerentlie at Harnesie ;
and riding from thence accompanied him into the citie,
which he entered the fourth daie of Maie, the first and
last yeare of his reigne.

RICHARD'S SPEECH

[*H*. iii. 717]   " Wherefore me thinketh it were   [III. i.]
not worst to send vnto the queene, for the redresse of
this matter, some honorable trustie man, such as both
tendereth the kings weale and the honour of his councell,
and is also in fauour and credence with hir.   For all which
considerations, none seemeth more meetlie, than our
reuerend father here present, my *lord cardinall*, who may
in this matter doo most good of anie man, if it please him
to take the paine."

   " And if she be percase so *obstinate*, and so preciselie
set vpon hir owne will, that neither his wise and faithfull
aduertisement can not mooue hir, nor anie mans reason
content hir ; then shall we, by mine aduise, by the kings
authoritie, fetch him out of that prison, and bring him
to his noble presence, in whose continuall companie he
shall be so well cherished and so honorablie intreated,
that all the world shall to our honour and hir reproch
perceiue, that it was onelie malice, frowardnesse, or follie,
that caused hir to keepe him there."

ROTHERHAM'S SPEECH

[*H*. iii. 717]   " God forbid that anie man should, for
anie thing earthlie, enterprise to breake the immunitie &
libertie of the sacred sanctuarie, that hath beene the safegard of so manie a good mans life.   And I trust " (quoth

he) " with Gods grace, we shall not need it. But, for anie maner need, I would not we should doo it."

BUCKINGHAM'S SPEECH

[*H*. iii. 718] " As farre foorth as reason will, which is not fullie so farre foorth, as may serue to let vs of the fetching foorth of this noble man to his honor and wealth, out of that place, in which he neither is, nor can be, a sanctuarie man. . . .

" But where a man is by lawfull means in perill, there needeth he the tuition of some speciall priuilege ; which is the onelie ground and cause of all sanctuaries.

" From which necessitie, this noble prince is farre, whose loue to his king, nature and kinred prooueth ; whose innocencie to all the world, his tender youth prooueth ; and so sanctuarie, as for him, neither none he needeth, nor also none can haue. Men come not to sanctuarie, as they come to baptisme, to require it by their godfathers ; he must aske it himselfe that must haue it. And reason, sith no man hath cause to haue it, but whose conscience of his owne fault maketh him fain need to require it. What will then hath yonder babe, which, and if he had discretion to require it, if need were, I dare say would now be right angrie with them that keepe him there ? . . .

" And verelie, *I haue often heard of sanctuarie men, but I neuer heard earst of sanctuarie children.*"

[*H*. iii. 719] It was agreed that, if he were not deliuered, he should be fetched. Howbeit, they thought it all best, in the auoiding of all maner of rumor, that the lord cardinall should first assaie to get him with hir good will.

Wherevpon all the councell came vnto the Starre chamber at Westminster ; and the lord cardinall, leauing the protector with the councell in the Starchamber, departed into the sanctuarie to the queene, with diuers other lords with him. . . .

[*H*. iii. 721] When the lord cardinall, and these other lords with him, had receiued this yoong duke, they brought him into the Star chamber, where the protector tooke him in his armes and kissed him with these words :

" Now welcome, my lord, euen with all my verie heart ! "
And he said in that of likelihood as he thought.   Therevpon, foorthwith they brought him vnto the king his
brother into the bishops palace at Paules, and from thense
thorough the citie honourablie into the Tower, out of the
which after that daie they neuer came abroad. . . .

When the protector had both the children in his hands,
he opened himselfe more boldlie, both to certeine other
men, and also cheeflie to the duke of Buckingham.
Although I know that manie thought that this duke was
priuie to all the protectors counsell, euen from the beginning ; and some of the protectors freends said, that
the duke was the first moouer of the protector to this
matter ; sending a priuie messenger vnto him, streict
after king Edwards death.

But others againe, which knew better the subtill wit
of the protector, denie that he euer opened his enterprise
to the duke, vntill he had brought to passe the things
before rehearsed.   But when he had imprisoned the
queenes kinsfolks, & gotten both hir sonnes into his
owne hands, then he opened the rest of his purpose with
lesse feare to them whome he thought meet for the matter,
and speciallie to the duke, who being woone to his purpose, he thought his strength more than halfe increased.

[H. iii. 722]   The protector and the duke of Buckingham made verie good semblance vnto the lord Hastings,
and kept him much in companie.   And vndoubtedlie the
protector loued him well, and loth was to haue lost him,
sauing for feare least his life should haue quailed their
purpose.

For which cause he mooued Catesbie to prooue with
some words cast out a *farre off*, whether he could thinke
it possible to win the lord Hastings vnto their part.

[H. iii. 721].   It was agreed, that the protector should
haue the dukes aid to make him king. . . . and that the
protector should grant him the quiet possession of the
earldome of Hereford, which he claimed as his inheritance,
and could neuer obteine it in king Edwards time.

Besides these requests of the duke, the protector, of
his owne mind, promised him a great quantitie of the
kings treasure, and of his houshold stuffe. . . .

They went about to prepare for the corona- [III. ii.]
tion of the yoong king, as they would haue it seeme.
And that they might turne both the eies and minds of
men from perceiuing of their drifts other-where, the lords,
being sent for from all parts of the realme, came thicke
to that solemnitie. But the protector and the duke,
after that they had sent the lord cardinall, the archbishop of Yorke, then lord chancellor, the bishop of Elie,
the lord Stanleie, and the lord Hastings, then lord chamberleine, with manie other noble men, to common &
deuise about the coronation in one place, as fast were
they in an other place, contriuing the contrarie, and to
make the protector king.

[H. iii. 722] The lord Stanleie, (that was after earle of
Derbie,) wiselie mistrusted it, and said vnto the lord Hastings, that he much misliked these *two* seuerall *councels*.
" For while we " (quoth he) " talke of one matter in the
tone place, little wot we wherof they talke in the tother
place."

" My lord " (quoth the lord Hastings) " on my life,
neuer doubt you : for while one man is there, which is
neuer thense, neuer can there be thing once mooued, that
should sound amisse toward me, but it should be in mine
eares yer it were well out of their mouths." This ment
he by Catesbie, which was of his neere secret councell,
and whome he verie familiarlie vsed, and in his most
weightie matters put no man in so speciall trust ; reckon-
ing himselfe to no man so liefe, sith he well wist there
was no man so much to him beholden as was this Catesbie,
which was a man well learned in the lawes of this land,
and, by the speciall fauour of the lord chamberlaine, in
good authoritie, and much rule bare in all the countie of
Leicester, where the lord chamberlains power cheefelie
laie.

But suerlie great pitie was it, that he had not had either
more truth, or lesse wit. For his dissimulation onelie
kept all that mischeefe vp. In whome if the lord Hastings
had not put so speciall trust, the lord Stanleie & he had
departed with diuerse other lords, and broken all the
danse ; for manie ill signes that he saw, which he now
construes all to the best. So suerlie thought he, that

there could be none harm toward him in that councell intended, where Catesbie was.

[*H*. iii. 723] The selfe night next before his death, the lord Stanleie sent a trustie messenger vnto Hastings at midnight in all the hast, requiring him to rise and ride awaie with him, for he was disposed vtterlie no longer to bide, he had so fearfull a *dreame* ; in which him thought that **a** *boare* with his tuskes so *rased* them both by the heads, that the bloud ran about both their shoulders. And, forsomuch as the protector gaue the boare for his cognisance, this dreame made so fearefull an impression in his heart, that he was throughlie determined no longer to tarie, but had his horsse readie, if the lord Hastings would go with him, to ride so farre yet the same night, that they should be out of *danger* yer daie.

" Ha, good Lord ! " (quoth the lord Hastings to this messenger) " leaneth my lord thy maister so much to such trifles, and hath such faith in dreames, which either his owne feare fantasieth, or doo rise in the nights rest by reason of his daies thought ? Tell him it is plaine witchcraft to beleeue in such dreames, which if they were tokens of things to come, why thinketh he not that we might be as likelie to make them true by our going, if we were caught & brought backe, as freends faile fliers ; for then had the boare a cause likelie to rase vs with his tusks, as folke that fled for some falsehood. . . . And therefore go to thy maister (man) and commend me to him, & praie him be merie & haue no feare : for I insure him I am as sure of the man that he woteth of, as I am of mine owne hand." " God send grace, sir ! " (quoth the messenger) and went his waie.

[*H*. iii. 723] Upon the verie Tower wharfe, so neare the place where his head was off soone after, there met he with one Hastings, *a purseuant* of his owne name. And, at their meeting in that place, he was put in remembrance of another time, in which it had happened them before to meet in like manner togither in the same place. At which other time the lord chamberleine had beene accused vnto king Edward by the lord Riuers, the queenes brother, in such wise, as he was for the while (but it lasted not long) farre fallen into the kings indignation,

& stood in great feare of himselfe. And, forsomuch as he
now met this purseuant in the same place, that ieopardie
so well passed, it gaue him great pleasure to talke with
him thereof; with whom he had before talked thereof in
the same place, while he was therein.

And therefore he said: "Ha, Hastings! art thou
remembred when I met thee here once with an heauie
heart?" "Yea, my lord" (quoth he) "that remember
I well, and thanked be God, they gat no good, nor you
no harme thereby." "Thou wouldest say so" (quoth he)
"if thou knewest as much as I know, which few know
else as yet, and mo shall shortlie." That meant he by
the lords of the queenes kinred that were taken before,
and should that daie be beheaded at Pomfret: which he
well wist, but nothing ware that the ax hung ouer his
owne head. "In faith, man" (quoth he) "I was neuer
so sorie, nor neuer stood in so great dread in my life, as
I did when thou and I met here. And, lo, how the world
is turned! now stand mine enimies in the danger, (as
thou maiest hap to heare more hereafter,) and I neuer in
my life so merrie, nor neuer in so great suertie!"

[*H.* iii. 723] A knight [came] vnto him, as it were of
courtesie, to accompanie him to the councell, but of truth
sent by the protector to hast him thitherwards; with
whome he was of secret confederacie in that purpose:
a meane man at that time, and now of great authoritie.

This knight (I say) when it happened the lord chamberleine by the waie to staie his horsse, & common a while
with a priest whom he met in the Tower street, brake his
tale, and said merilie to him: "What, my lord, I pray
you come on, whereto talke you so long with that priest?
you haue no need of a priest yet": and therwith he
laughed vpon him, as though he would say, "Ye shall
haue soone." But so little wist the tother what he ment,
and so little mistrusted, that he was neuer merier, nor
neuer so full of good hope in his life; which selfe thing
is oft seene a signe of change.

[*H.* iii. 725] Now was it so deuised by the [III. iii.]
protector and his councell, that the selfe daie, in which
the lord chamberleine was beheaded in the Tower of
London, and about the selfe same houre, was there (not

without his assent) beheaded at Pomfret, the foreremembred lords & knights that were taken from the king at Northampton and Stonie Stratford. Which thing was doone in the presence, and by the order, of sir Richard Ratcliffe, knight; whose seruice the protector speciallie vsed in that councell, and in the execution of such lawlesse enterprises; as a man that had beene long secret with him, hauing experience of the world, and a shrewd wit, short & rude in speech, rough and boisterous of behauior, bold in mischiefe, as far from pitie as from all feare of God.

This knight bringing them out of the prison to the scaffold, and shewing to the people about that they were traitors, (not suffering them to declare & speake their innocencie, least their words might haue inclined men to pitie them, and to hate the protector and his part,) caused them hastilie, without iudgement, processe, or maner of order to be beheaded; and without other earthlie gilt, but onelie that they were good men, too true to the king, and too nigh to the queene.

[H. iii. 722–723] Manie lords assembled in   [III. iv.] the Tower, and there sat in councell, deuising the honourable solemnitie *of the* kings *coronation*; of which the time appointed then so neere approched, that the pageants and subtilties were in making daie & night at Westminster, and much vittels killed therfore, that afterward was cast awaie. These lords so sitting togither communing of this matter, the protector came in amongst them, first about nine of the clocke, saluting them courteouslie, and excusing himselfe that he had beene from them so long; saieng merilie that he had beene a sleeper that daie.

After a little talking with them, he said vnto the bishop of Elie: "My lord, you haue verie *good strawberies at your garden in Holborn*, I require you let vs haue a messe of them." "Gladlie, *my lord*" (quoth he) "would God I had some better thing as readie to your pleasure as that!" And therewithall in all the hast he sent his seruant for a messe of strawberies. The protector set the lords fast in communing, & therevpon, praieng them to spare him for a little while, departed thense. And soone after one houre, betweene ten & eleuen, he returned into

the chamber amongst them, all changed, with a woonderfull soure angrie countenance, knitting the browes,
frowning, and fretting and gnawing on his lips: and so
sat him downe in his place.

All the lords were much dismaid, and sore maruelled at
this maner of sudden change, and what thing should him
aile. Then, when he had sitten still a while, thus he
began: "What were they worthie to haue that compasse
and imagine the destruction of me, being so neere of
bloud vnto the king, and protector of his roiall person
and his realme?" At this question, all the lords sat sore
astonied, musing much by whome this question should be
meant, of which euerie man wist himselfe cleere. Then
the lord chamberlaine (as he that for the loue betweene
them thought he might be boldest with him) answered
and said, that they were worthie to be punished as
heinous traitors, whatsoeuer they were. And all the
other affirmed the same. "That is" (quoth he) "yonder
sorceresse my brothers wife, and other with hir" (meaning
the queene.)

At these words manie of the other lords were greatlie
abashed, that fauoured hir. But the lord Hastings was
in his mind better content, that it was mooued by hir,
than by anie other whome he loued better: albeit his
heart somewhat grudged, that he was not afore made of
councell in this matter, as he was of the taking of hir
kinred, and of their putting to death, which were by his
assent before deuised to be beheaded at Pomfret this
selfe same daie; in which he was not ware that it was by
other deuised, that he himselfe should be beheaded the
same daie at London. Then said the protector: "Ye
shall all see in what wise that sorceresse, and that other
witch of hir councell, Shores wife, with their affinitie, haue,
by their sorcerie and *witchcraft*, wasted my bodie." And
therwith he plucked vp his dublet sleeue to his elbow,
vpon his left arme, where he shewed a weerish *withered
arme*, and small; as it was neuer other.

Herevpon euerie mans mind sore misgaue them, well
perceiuing that this matter was but a quarell. For they
well wist that the queene was too wise to go about anie
such follie. And also, if she would, yet would she, of all

folke least, make Shores wife of hir counsell; whome of all women she most hated, as that concubine whome the king hir husband had most loued. And also, no man was there present, but well knew that his arme was euer such since his birth. Naithlesse, the lord chamberlaine (which from the death of king Edward kept Shores wife, on whome he somewhat doted in the kings life, sauing, as it is said, he that while forbare hir of reuerence toward the king, or else of a certeine kind of fidelitie to his freend) answered and said: "Certeinelie, my lord, if they haue so heinouslie doone, they be worthie heinous punishment."

"What" (quoth the protector) "thou seruest me, I weene, with 'ifs' and with 'ands': I tell thee they haue so doone, and that I will make good on thy bodie, traitor!" and therewith, as in a great anger, he clapped his fist vpon the boord a great rap. At which token one cried, "Treason!" without the chamber. Therewith a doore clapped, and in come there rushing men in harnesse, as manie as the chamber might hold. And anon the protector said to the lord Hastings: "I arrest thee, traitor!" "What me, my lord?" (quoth he.) "Yea, thee, traitor!" quoth the protector. . . .

Then were they all quickelie bestowed in diuerse chambers, except the lord chamberleine, whome the protector bad speed and shriue him apace, "for, by saint Paule" (quoth he) "I will not to dinner till I see thy head off!" It booted him not to aske whie, but heauilie he tooke a priest at aduenture, and made *a short shrift* for a longer would not be suffered, the protector made so much hast to dinner, which he might not go to, vntill this were doone, for sauing of his oth.

[*H*. iii. 723] So was he brought foorth to the greene beside the chappell within the Tower; and his head laid downe vpon a long log of timber, and there striken off.

[*H*. iii. 723–724] Now flew the fame of this [III. v.] lords death swiftlie through the citie, and so foorth further about, like a wind in euerie mans eare. But the protector, immediatlie after dinner, intending to set some colour vpon the matter, sent in all the hast for manie substantiall men out of the citie into the Tower.

Now, at their comming, himselfe with the duke of

Buckingham stood harnessed in old ill faring briganders, such as no man should weene, that they would vouchsafe to haue put vpon their backs, except that some sudden necessitie had constreined them. And then the protector shewed them, that the lord chamberleine, and other of his conspiracie, had contriued to haue suddenlie destroied him, and the duke, there the same day in the councell. And what they intended further, was as yet not well knowne. Of which their treason he neuer had knowledge before ten of the clocke the same forenoone; which sudden feare draue them to put on for their defense such harnesse as came next to hand. And so had God holpen them, that the mischiefe turned vpon them that would haue doone it. And this he required them to report.

Euerie man answered him *faire,* as though no man mistrusted the matter, which of truth no man beleeued.

[*H.* iii. 735] Foorthwith was the prince and his brother both shut vp, & all other remooued from them; onelie one (called Blacke Will, or William Slaughter) excepted, set to serue them and see them sure.

[*H.* iii. 724] [The indictment of Hastings] [III. vi.] made within two houres after that he was beheaded, and it was so curiouslie indicted, & so faire written in parchment, *in* so well *a set hand,* and therewith of it selfe so long a processe, that euerie child might well perceiue that it was prepared before. For all the time, betweene his death and the proclaming, could scant haue sufficed vnto the bare writing alone, all had it bene but in paper, and scribled foorth in hast at aduenture. So that, vpon the proclaming thereof, one that was schoolemaister of Powles, of chance standing by, and comparing the shortnesse of the time with the length of the matter, said vnto them that stood about him : " Here is a gaie goodlie cast, foule cast awaie for hast." And a merchant answered him, that it was written by prophesie.

BUCKINGHAM'S SPEECH

[*H.* iii. 729] " The kings greedie appetite [III. vii.] was insatiable, and euerie where ouer all the realme intollerable.

"For no woman was there anie where, yoong or old, rich or poore, whome he set his eie vpon, in whome he anie thing liked, either person or fauour, speech, pase, or countenance, but, without anie feare of God, or respect of his honour, murmur or grudge of the world, he would importunelie pursue his appetite, and haue hir, to the great destruction of manie a good woman, and great dolor to their husbands. . . . And all were it that, with this and other importable dealing, the realme was in euerie part annoied, yet speciallie yee heere, the citizens of this noble citie, as well for that amongest you is most plentie of all such things as minister matter to such iniuries, as for that you were neerest at hand ; sith that neere heere abouts was commonlie his most abiding."

The Plot

[*H.* iii. 725–726] Now was all the labor and studie in the deuise of some conuenient pretext, for which the people should be content to depose the prince, and accept the protector for king. In which diuerse things they deuised. But the cheefe thing & the weightiest of all that inuention rested in this, that they should alledge bastardie, either in king Edward himselfe, or in his children, or both. So that he should seeme disabled to inherit the crowne by the duke of Yorke, and the prince by him.

To laie bastardie in king Edward sounded openlie to the rebuke of the protectors owne mother, which was mother to them both ; for in that point could be no other color, but to pretend that his owne mother was an adultresse ; which, notwithstanding, to further this purpose, he letted not. But neuerthelesse he would that point should be lesse and more fauourablie handled : not euen fullie plaine and directlie, but that the matter should be touched aslope, craftilie ; as though men spared in that point to speake all the truth, for feare of his displeasure. But the other point, concerning the bastardie that they deuised to surmize in king Edwards children, that would he should be openlie declared and inforced to the vttermost.

[*H.* iii. 730–731] When the duke had said, and looked that the people, whome he hoped that the maior had framed before, should, after this proposition made, haue cried, "King Richard, king Richard!" all was husht and mute, and not one word answered therevnto. . . .

When the maior saw this he, with other partners of that councell drew about the duke, and said that the people had not beene accustomed there *to be spoken vnto, but by the recorder*, which is the mouth of the citie, and happilie to him they will answer. With that the recorder, called Fitz William, a sad man, & an honest, which was so new come into that office, that he neuer had spoken to the people before, and loth was with that matter to begin, notwithstanding, thervnto commanded by the maior, made rehearsall to the commons of that the duke had twise rehearsed to them himselfe.

But the recorder so tempered his tale, that he shewed euerie thing as the dukes words, and no part his owne. But all this nothing no change made in the people, which alwaie after one stood as they had beene men amazed. . . .

The people began to whisper among themselues secretly, that the voice was neither lowd nor distinct, but as it were the sound of a swarme of bees ; till at the last, in the nether end of the hall, an ambushment of the dukes seruants, and one Nashfield, and other belonging to the protector, with some prentisses and lads that thrust into the hall amongst the prease, began suddenlie at mens backes to crie out, as lowd as their throtes would giue : "King Richard, king Richard ! " and threw vp their caps in token of ioy. And they, that stood before, cast backe their heads, maruelling thereof, but nothing they said. Now when the duke and the maior saw this maner, they wiselie turned it to their purpose, and said it was a goodlie crie, & a ioifull, to heare euerie man with one voice, no man saieng naie.

"Wherefore, friends " (quoth the duke) "sith we perceiue it is all your whole minds to haue this noble man for your king, (whereof we shall make his grace so effectuall report, that we doubt not but it shall redound vnto your great weale and commoditie,) we require ye, that ye to morrow go with vs, and we with you, vnto his noble grace, to make our humble request vnto him in maner

before remembred." And therewith the lords came
downe, and the companie dissolued and departed. . . .

The maior with all the aldermen, and chiefe commoners
of the citie, in their best maner apparelled, assembling
themselues togither, resorted vnto Bainards castell, where
the protector laie. To which place repaired also, (according to their appointment,) the duke of Buckingham, and
diuerse noble men with him, beside manie knights and
other gentlemen. And therevpon the duke sent word
vnto the lord protector, of the being there of a great and
honourable companie, to mooue a great matter vnto his
grace. Wherevpon the protector made difficultie to come
out vnto them, but if he first knew some part of their
errand, as though he doubted and partlie mistrusted the
comming of such a number vnto him so suddenlie, without
anie warning, or knowledge whether they came for good
or harme.

Then the duke, when he had shewed this to the maior
and other, that they might thereby see how little the
protector looked for this matter, they sent vnto him by
the messenger such louing message againe, and therewith
so humblie besought him, to vouchsafe that they might
resort to his presence to propose their intent, of which they
would vnto none other person anie part disclose ; that at
the last he came foorth of his chamber, and yet not downe
vnto them, but stood aboue in a gallerie ouer them where
they might see him, and speake to him, as though he
would not yet come too neere them till he wist what they
ment. . . .

And therevpon the duke of Buckingham first made
humble petition vnto him on the behalfe of them all, that
his grace would pardon them, and licence them to propose
vnto his grace the intent of their comming, without his
displeasure ; without which pardon obteined, they durst
not be bold to mooue him of that matter.

In which albeit they ment as much honor to his grace, as
wealth to all the realme beside, yet were they not sure
how his grace would take it ; whome they would in no
wise offend. Then the protector (as he was verie gentle of
himselfe, and also longed sore to wit what they ment)
gaue him leaue to propose what him liked ; verelie trusting

(for the good mind that he bare them all) none of them anie thing would intend vnto himward, wherewith he ought to bee greeued. When the duke had this leaue and pardon to speake, then waxed he bold to shew him their intent and purpose, with all the causes moouing them therevnto (as ye before haue heard); and finallie to beseech his grace, that it would like him, of his accustomed goodnesse and zeale vnto the realme, now with his eie of pitie to behold the long continued distresse and decaie of the same, and to set his gratious hands to redresse and amendment thereof.

All which he might well doo, by taking vpon him the crowne and gouernance of this realme, according to his right and title lawfullie descended vnto him; and to the laud of God, profit of the land, & vnto his noble grace so much the more honour, and lesse paine, in that, that neuer prince reigned vpon anie people, that were so glad to liue vnder his obeisance, as the people of this realme vnder his. When the protector had heard the proposition, he looked verie strangelie thereat, and answered: that all were it that he partlie knew the things by them alledged to be true, yet such entire loue he bare vnto king Edward and his children, & so much more regarded his honour in other realmes about, than the crowne of anie one, (of which he was neuer desirous,) that he could not find in his hart in this point to incline to their desire.

Notwithstanding, he not onlie pardoned them the motion that they made him, but also thanked them for the loue and hartie fauour they bare him; praieng them for his sake to giue and beare the same to the prince.

[*H*. iii. 751] [Richard] procured a common [IV. ii.] rumor (but he would not haue the author knowne) to be published and spred abroad among the common people, that the queene was dead; to the intent that she, taking some conceit of this strange fame, should fall into some sudden sicknesse or greeuous maladie: and to prooue, if afterwards she should fortune by that or anie other waies to lease hir life, whether the people would impute hir death to the thought or sicknesse, or thereof would laie the blame to him.

[*H*. iii. 734-735] King Richard, after his coronation,

taking his waie to Glocester to visit (in his new honour) the towne of which he bare the name of his old, deuised (as he rode) to fulfill the thing which he before had intended. And forsomuch as his mind gaue him, that, his nephues liuing, men would not reckon that he could haue right to the realme, he thought therefore without delaie to rid them; as though the killing of his kinsmen could amend his cause, and make him a kindlie king. Whervpon he sent one Iohn Greene (whom he speciallie trusted) vnto sir Robert Brakenberie, constable of the Tower; with a letter and credence also, that the same sir Robert should in anie wise put the two children to death.

This Iohn Greene did his errand vnto Brakenberie, kneeling before our ladie in the Tower. Who plainelie answered, that he would neuer put them to death to die therefore. With which answer Iohn Greene returning, re-counted the same to king Richard at Warwike, yet in his waie. Wherewith he tooke such displeasure & thought, that the same night he said vnto a secret page of his: "Ah! whom shall a man trust? Those that I haue brought vp myselfe, those that I had weent would most suerlie serue me, euen those faile me, and at my commande-ment will doo nothing for me." "Sir" (quoth his page) "there lieth one on your pallet without, that I dare well saie, to doo your grace pleasure, the thing were right hard that he would refuse." Meaning this by sir Iames Tirrell, which was a man of right goodlie personage, and for natures gifts worthie to haue serued a much better prince; if he had well serued God, and by grace obteined as much truth and good will as he had strength and wit.

The man had an high heart, & sore longed vpward, not rising yet so fast as he had hoped, being hindered & kept vnder by the meanes of sir Richard Ratcliffe, and sir William Catesbie, which, (longing for no mo parteners of the princes fauour; and, namelie, not for him, whose pride they wist would beare no peere,) kept him by secret drifts out of all secret trust: which thing this page well had marked and knowne. Wherefore, this occasion offered, of verie speciall friendship he tooke his time to put him forward, and by such wise doo him good, that all the enimies he had (except the deuill) could neuer haue doone him so much hurt. For vpon this pages words king Richard arose, (for this communication had he sitting at the draught, a conuenient carpet for such a councell,) and came out into the pallet chamber, on which he found in bed sir Iames and sir Thomas Tirrels, of person like, and brethren of bloud, but nothing of kin in conditions.

Then said the king merilie to them : " What, sirs, be ye in bed so soone ? " And calling vp sir Iames, brake to him secretlie his mind in this mischeeuous matter. In which he found him nothing strange. Wherefore on the morow he sent him to Brakenberie with a letter, by which he was commanded to deliuer sir Iames all the keies of the Tower for one night ; to the end he might there accomplish the kings pleasure, in such things as he had giuen him commandement. After which letter deliuered, & the keies receiued, sir Iames appointed the night next insuing to destroie them ; deuising before and preparing the meanes.

[*H*. iii. 746] Nothing was more maruelled at, than that the lord Stanleie had not beene taken and reputed as an enimie to the king ; considering the working of the ladie Margaret his wife, moother to the earle of Richmond. But, forsomuch as the enterprise of a woman was of him reputed of no regard or estimation, and that the lord Thomas hir husband had purged himselfe sufficientlie to be innocent of all dooings and attempts by hir perpetrated and committed ; it was giuen him in charge to keepe hir in some secret place at home, without hauing anie seruant or companie : so that from thense foorth she should neuer send letter or messenger vnto hir sonne, nor anie of his freends or confederats, by the which the king might be molested or troubled, or anie hurt or preiudice might be attempted against his realme and communaltie.

BUCKINGHAM AND RICHARD

[*H*. iii. 736] Some haue I heard say, that the duke, a little before his coronation, among other things, required of the protector the erle of Herefords lands, to the which he pretended himselfe iust inheritor. And, forsomuch as the title, which he claimed by inheritance, was somwhat interlaced with the title to the crowne by the line of king Henrie before depriued, the protector conceiued such indignation, that he reiected the dukes request with manie spitefull and minatorie words. Which so wounded his heart with hatred and mistrust, that he neuer after could indure to looke aright on king Richard, but euer feared his owne life.

BUCKINGHAM'S STATEMENT

[H. iii. 739]   When I my selfe sued vnto him for my part of the earle of Herefords lands, which his brother king Edward wrongfullie deteined and withheld from me ; and also required to haue the office of the high constableship of England, as diuerse of my noble ancestors before this time haue had, and in long descent continued : in this my first sute shewing his good mind toward me, he did not onelie first delaie me, and afterward denaie me, but gaue me such vnkind words, with such tawnts & retawnts, ye, in manner checke and checkemate, to the vttermost proofe of my patience : as though I had neuer furthered him, but hindered him ; as though I had put him downe, and not set him vp. . . .

But when I was crediblie informed of the death of the two yoong innocents, his owne naturall nephues, contrarie to his faith and promise ; to the which (God be my iudge !) I neuer agreed, nor condescended ; O Lord, how my veines panted, how my bodie trembled, and how my heart inwardlie grudged ! insomuch that I so abhorred the sight, and much more the companie, of him, that I could no longer abide in his court, except I should be openlie reuenged : the end whereof was doubtfull.

[H. iii. 735]   Sir Iames Tirrell deuised, that   [IV. iii.] [the Princes] should be murthered in their beds. To the execution whereof, he appointed Miles Forrest, one of the foure that kept them, a fellow fleshed in murther before time. To him he ioined one Iohn Dighton, his owne horssekeeper, a big, broad, square, and strong knaue.

Then, all the other being remooued from them, this Miles Forrest, and Iohn Dighton, about midnight, (the seelie children lieng in their beds,) came into the chamber, &, suddenlie lapping them vp among the clothes, so to bewrapped them and intangled them, keeping downe by

force the fether-bed and pillowes hard vnto their mouths,
that, within a while, smoothered and stifled, their breath
failing, they gaue vp to God their innocent soules into
the ioies of heauen ; leauing to the tormentors their
bodies dead in the bed. Which after that the wretches
perceiued, first by the strugling with the paines of death,
and after long lieng still, to be thoroughlie dead, they laid
their bodies naked out vpon the bed, and fetched sir Iames
to see them ; which, vpon the sight of them, caused those
murtherers to burie them at the staire foot, meetlie deepe
in the ground, vnder a great heape of stones.

Then rode sir Iames in great hast to king Richard, and
shewed him all the maner of the murther ; who gaue him
great thanks, and (as some saie) there made him knight.
But he allowed not (as I haue heard) the burieng in so vile
a corner ; saieing, that he would haue them buried in a
better place, bicause they were a kings sonnes. . . ,
Whervpon, they saie that a priest of sir Robert Braken-
beries tooke vp the bodies againe, and secretlie interred
them in such place, as, by the occasion of his death, which
onelie knew it, could neuer since come to light.

REBELLION AGAINST RICHARD

[*H*. iii. 743] Accompanied with a great power of wild
Welshmen, whom he (being a man of great courage and
sharpe speech) in maner against their willes had rather
thereto inforced and compelled by lordlie and streict
commandement, than by liberall wages and gentle
demenour ; which thing was the verie occasion why they
left him desolate [the Duke of Buckingham] with all his
power, marched through the forrest of Deane, intending
to haue passed the riuer Seuerne at Glocester, & there to
haue ioined his armie with the Courtneis, and other
westerne men of his confederacie and affinitie.

[*H*. iii. 743] King Richard, (who in the meane time
had gotten togither a great strength and puissance,)
thinking it not most for his part beneficiall, to disperse
and diuide his great armie into small branches, and
particularlie to persecute anie one of the coniuration by
himselfe, determined (all other things being set aside) with

his whole puissance to set on the chiefe head, which was
the duke of Buckingham.

[*H*. iii. 750]   King Richard was crediblie aduertised,
what promises and oths the earle and his confederates
had made and sworn togither at Rennes, and how by the
earles means all the Englishmen were passed out of
Britaine into France. Wherefore, being sore dismaid,
and in a maner desperate, bicause his craftie chieuance
tooke none effect in Britaine, he imagined & deuised how
to infringe and disturbe the earles purpose by an other
meane ; so that, by the marriage of ladie Elizabeth his
neece, he should pretend no claime nor title to the
crowne. . . .

[He] determined to reconcile to his fauour his brothers
wife queene Elizabeth, either by faire words, or liberall
promises ; firmelie beleeuing, hir fauour once obteined,
that she would not sticke to commit (and louinglie credit)
to him the rule and gouernance both of hir and hir
daughters ; and so by that meanes the earle of Richmond
of the affinitie of his neece should be vtterlie defrauded
and beguiled. . . .

[He] would rather take to wife his cousine and neece the
ladie Elizabeth, than for lacke of that affinitie the whole
realme should run to ruine ; as who said, that, if he once
fell from his estate and dignitie, the ruine of the relme
must needs shortlie insue and follow. Wherefore he sent
to the queene (being in sanctuarie) diuerse and often
messengers, which first should excuse and purge him of all
things before against hir attempted or procured, and after
should so largelie promise promotions innumerable, and
benefits, not onelie to hir, but also to hir sonne lord
Thomas, Marquesse Dorset, that they should bring hir (if
it were possible) into some wanhope, or (as men saie) into
a fooles paradise.

The messengers, being men both of wit and grauitie, so
persuaded the queene with great and pregnant reasons, &
with faire and large promises, that she began somewhat
to relent, and to giue to them no deafe eare ; insomuch
that she faithfullie promised to submit and yeeld hir selfe
fullie and frankelie to the kings will and pleasure. . . .

After she sent letters to the marquesse hir sonne, (being

then at Paris with the earle of Richmond,) willing him in anie wise to leaue the earle, and without delaie to repaire into England, where for him were prouided great honours, and honourable promotions; ascerteining him further, that all offenses on both parts were forgotten and forgiuen, and both he and she highlie incorporated in the kings heart.

[*H*. iii. 743] [The king] tooke his iournie toward Salisburie, to the intent that in his iournie he might set on the dukes armie, if he might know him in anie place incamped, or in order of battell arraied.

[*H*. iii. 754] [He] sent to Iohn duke of Norffolke, Henrie earle of Northumberland, Thomas earle of Surrie, and to other of his especiall & trustie friends of the nobilitie, which he iudged more to preferre and esteeme his wealth and honour, than their owne riches and priuate commoditie; willing them to muster and view all their seruants and tenants, and to elect and choose the most couragious and actiue persons of the whole number, and with them to repaire to his presence with all speed and diligence.

[*H*. iii. 744] [Richmond] prepared an armie of fiue thousand manlie Britons, and fortie well furnished ships. When all things were prepared in a readinesse, and the daie of departing and setting forward was appointed, which was the twelfe daie of the moneth of October, the whole armie went on shipbord, and halsed vp their sailes, and with a prosperous wind tooke the sea.

[*H*. iii. 751] [The king] most mistrusted Thomas lord Stanleie, sir William Stanleie his brother, Gilbert Talbot, and six hundred other: of whose purposes although king Richard were ignorant, yet he gaue neither confidence nor credence to anie of them; and least of all to the lord Stanleie bicause he was ioined in matrimonie with the ladie Margaret, mother to the earle of Richmond, as afterward apparantlie yee may perceiue. For when the said lord Stanleie would haue departed into his countrie to visit his familie, and to recreate and refresh his spirits, (as he openlie said, but the truth was, to the intent to be in a perfect readinesse to receiue the earle of Richmond at his first arriuall in England,) the king in no wise would suffer him to depart, before he had left as an hostage in the court George Stanleie, lord Strange, his first begotten sonne and heire.

[*H*. iii. 743] [The duke] persuaded all his complices and partakers, that euerie man in his quarter, with all diligence, should raise vp people & make a commotion. And by this means, almost in one moment, Thomas marques Dorset came out of sanctuarie, (where since the begining of K. Richards daies he had continued, whose life by the onelie helpe of sir Thomas Louell was preserued from all danger & perill in this troublous world,) gathered together a great band of men in Yorkeshire.

Sir Edward Courtneie, and Peter his brother, bishop of Excester, raised an other amie in Deuonshire and Corne-wall. In Kent, Richard Gilford and other gentlemen collected a great companie of souldiers, and openlie began warre.

[*H*. iii. 743] [Before the duke] could atteine to Seuerne side, by force of continuall raine and moisture, the riuer rose so high that it ouerflowed all the countrie adioining ; insomuch that men were drowned in their beds, and houses with the extreame violence were ouer-turned, children were caried about the fields swimming in cradels, beasts were drowned on hilles. Which rage of water lasted continuallie ten daies, insomuch that in the countrie adioining they call it to this daie, " The great water " ; or, " the duke of Buckinghams great water." By this floud the passages were so closed, that neither the duke could come ouer Seuern to his adherents, nor they to him. During the which time, the Welshmen, lingring idelie, and without monie, vittels, or wages, suddenlie scattered and departed : and, for all the dukes faire promises, threatnings, and inforcements, would in no wise either go further nor abide.

The duke (being thus left almost post alone) was of necessitie compelled to flie. . . .

Now when it was knowne to his adherents, (which were redie to giue battell,) that his host was scatred and had left him almost alone, and was fled, & could not be found, they were suddenlie amazed & striken with a sudden feare that euery man like persons desperate shifted for himselfe & fled.

[*H*. iii. 744] [The king] made proclamation, that what person could shew and reueale where the duke of Buckingham was, should be highlie rewarded : if he were a bondman, he should be infranchised and set at libertie ; if he were of free bloud, he should haue a generall pardon, and be rewarded with a thousand pounds.

[*H*. iii. 744-745] Toward night the wind changed, and the weather turned, and so huge and terrible a tempest so suddenlie arose, that, with the verie power and strength of the storme, the ships were disparkled, seuered & separated asunder : some by force were driuen into Normandie, some were compelled to returne againe into Britaine. The ship wherein the earle of Richmond was, associat onelie with one other barke, was all night tossed and turmoiled.

In the morning after, (when the rage of the furious tempest was asswaged, and the ire of blustering wind was some deale appeased,) about the houre of noone the same daie, the earle approched to the south part of the realme of England, euen at the mouth of the hauen of Pole, in the countie of Dorset ; where he might plainelie perceiue all the sea bankes & shores garnished and furnished with men of warre and souldiers, appointed and deputed there to defend his arriuall and landing. . . . Wherefore he gaue streict charge, and sore commandement, that no person should once presume to take land, and go to shore, vntill such time as the whole nauie were assembled and come togither. And, while he taried and lingered, he sent out a shipboate toward the land side, to know whether they, which stood there in such a number, and so well furnished in apparell defensiue, were his foes and enimies, or else his freends and comfortors.

They, that were sent to inquire, were instantlie desired of the men of warre keeping the coast, (which thereof were before instructed & admonished,) to descend and take land ; affirming that they were appointed by the duke of Buckingham there to await and tarie for the arriuall and landing of the earle of Richmond, and to conduct him safelie into the campe, where the duke, not far of, laie incamped with a mightie armie, and an host of great strength and power, to the intent that the duke and the earle, ioining in puissances and forces togither, might prosecute and chase king Richard being destitute of men, and in maner desperate ; and so, by that meanes, and their owne labours, to obteine the end of their enterprise which they had before begun.

The earle of Richmond, suspecting their flattering request to be but a fraud (as it was in deed), after he perceiued none of his ships to appeare in sight, he weied vp his anchors, halsed vp his sailes, &, hauing a prosperous and streinable wind, and a fresh gale sent euen by God to deliuer him from that perill and ieopardie, arriued safe and in all securitie in the duchie of Normandie ; where he (to refresh and solace his soldiers and people) tooke his recreation by the space of three daies, and cleerelie determined with part of his companie to passe all by land againe into Britaine.

[*H.* iii. 753] The lord Stanleie, hauing in his [IV. v.] band almost fiue thousand men, lodged in the same towne. But, hearing that the erle of Richmond was marching thitherward, gaue to him place, dislodging him and his, and repaired to a town ecalled Aderstone ; the re abiding the comming of the earle. And this wilie fox did this act, to auoid all suspicion on king Richards part.

For the lord Stanleie was afraid, least, if he should seeme openlie to be a fautor or aider to the earle his sonne in law, before the day of the battell, that king Richard, (which yet vtterlie did not put in him diffidence and mistrust,) would put to some cruell death his sonne and heire apparant, George lord Strange, whome king Richard (as you haue heard before) kept with him as a pledge or hostage, to the intent that the lord Stanleie his father should attempt nothing preiudiciall to him.

[*H.* iii. 754] [Richmond] could in no wise be assured of his father in law Thomas lord Stanleie, which, for feare of the destruction of the lord Strange his sonne (as you haue heard), as yet inclined to neither partie. For, if he had gone to the earle, and that notified to king Richard, his sonne had beene shortlie executed.

[*H.* iii. 753] [Richmond] was by his espials asserteined, that sir Walter Herbert, and Rice ap Thomas were in harnesse before him ; readie to incounter with his armie, and to stop their passage. Wherefore, like a valiant capteine, he first determined to set on them, and either to destroie or to take them into his fauour; and after, with all his power and puissance, to giue battell to his mortall enimie king Richard. But, to the intent his freends should know in what readinesse he was, and how he proceeded forward, he sent of his most secret and faithfull seruants with letters and instructions to the ladie Margaret his mother, to the lord Stanleie and his brother, to sir Gilbert Talbot, and to other his trustie freends; declaring to them that he, being succoured and holpen with the aid and reliefe of his freends, intended to passe ouer the riuer of Seuerne at Shrewesburie, and so to passe directlie to the citie of London.

Wherefore he required them, (as his speciall trust and confidence was fixed in the hope of their fidelitie,) that they would meet him by the waie with all diligent preparation; to the intent that he and they, at time and place conuenient, might communicate togither the deepnesse of all his doubtfull and weightie businesse. When the messengers were dispatched with these commandements and admonitions, he marched forward towards Shrewesburie: and, in his passing, there met and saluted him Rice ap Thomas, with a goodlie band of Welshmen; which, making an oth and promise to the earle, submitted himselfe wholie to his order and commandement.

[*H*. iii. 753] [There] came to [Richmond] sir Gilbert Talbot, with the whole power of the yoong earle of Shrewesburie, then being in ward; which were accounted to the number of two thousand men. And thus, his power increasing, he arriued at the towne of Stafford, and there paused.

There also came sir William Stanleie accompanied with a few persons.

[*H*. iii. 749] Iohn Vere, earle of Oxford, which (as you haue heard before) was by king Edward kept in prison within the castell of Hammes, so persuaded Iames Blunt, capteine of the same fortresse, and sir Iohn Fortescue, porter of the towne of Calis, that he himselfe was not onelie dismissed and set at libertie, but they also abandoning and leauing their fruitfull offices, did condescend to go with him into France to the earle of Richmond, and to take his part.

[*H*. iii. 742] The countesse of Richmond tooke into hir seruice Christopher Urswike, an honest and wise priest, and (after an oth of him for to be secret taken and sworne) she vttered to him all hir mind and counsell ; adhibiting to him the more confidence and truth, that he all his life had fauoured and taken part with king Henrie the sixt, and as a speciall iewell put to hir seruice by sir Lewes hir physician. So the mother, studious for the prosperitie of hir son, appointed this Christopher Urswike to saile into Britaine to the earle of Richmond, and to declare and reueale to him all pacts and agreements betweene hir & the queene agreed and concluded.

[*H*. iii. 744] [The duke] was at Salisburie, in [V. i.] the open market place, on a new scaffold, beheaded and put to death.

[*H*. iii. 754] Diuerse other noble personages, [V. ii.] which inwardlie hated king Richard woorse than a tode or a serpent, did likewise resort to him with all their power and strength, wishing and working his destruction ; who otherwise would haue beene the instrument of their casting away.

[*H*. iii. 757] Such as were present (more for dread than loue) kissed them openlie, whome they inwardlie hated. Other sware outwardlie to take part with such whose death they secretlie compassed, and inwardlie imagined. Other promised to inuade the kings enimies, which fled and fought with fierce courage against the king. Other stood still and looked on, intending to take part with the victors and ouercommers.

[*H*. iii. 755] King Richard, which was ap- [V. iii.] pointed now to finish his last labor by the very diuine iustice & prouidence of God, (which called him to condigne punishment for his mischiefous deserts,) marched to a place meet for two battels to incounter, by a village called Bosworth, not farre from Leicester : and there he pitched his field on a hill called Anne Beame, refreshed his souldiers, and tooke his rest.

[*H*. iii. 755] [Richmond's army] exceeded not fiue thousand men, beside the power of the Stanleies, wherof

three thousand were in the field, vnder the standard of sir
William Stanleie. The kings number was double so much
and more.

[*H*. iii. 755] [Richmond moved] to the towne of Ader-
ston, where the lord Stanleie and sir William his brother
with their bands were abiding. There the erle came first
to his father in law, in a litle close, where he saluted him,
and sir William his brother : and after diuerse and freendlie
imbracings, each reioised of the state of other, and suddenlie were surprised with great ioy, comfort, and hope
of fortunate successe in all their affaires and dooings.
Afterward they consulted togither how to giue battell to
king Richard if he would abide, whome they knew not to
be farre off with an huge host.

[*H*. iii. 755] After that the earle of Richmond was
departed from the communication of his freends (as you
haue heard before) he began to be of a better stomach,
and of a more valiant courage, and with all diligence
pitched his field iust by the campe of his enimies, and
there he lodged that night.

[*H*. iii. 755] The fame went, that [the king] had the
same night a dreadfull and terrible dreame : for it seemed
to him being asleepe, that he did see diuerse images like
terrible diuels, which pulled and haled him, not suffering
him to take anie quiet or rest. The which strange vision
not so suddenlie strake his heart with a sudden feare, but
it stuffed his head and troubled his mind with manie busie
and dreadfull imaginations. For incontinent after, his
heart being almost damped, he prognosticated before the
doubtfull chance of the battell to come ; *not* vsing the
alacritie and mirth *of mind* and countenance as he *was*
accustomed to doo before he came toward the battell.
And least that it might be suspected that he was abashed
for feare of his enimies, and for that cause looked so
pitiouslie ; he recited and declared to his familiar freends
in the morning his wonderfull vision and fearfull dreame.

[*H*. iii. 755] In the morning betimes, he caused his men
to put on their armour, and apparell themselues readie
to fight and giue battell.

RICHMOND'S ORATION TO HIS ARMY

[*H*. iii. 757–758] I doubt not, but *God* will rather aid vs (yea and *fight* for vs) than see vs vanquished and ouerthrowne by such as neither feare him nor his laws, nor yet regard iustice or honestie.

Our cause is so iust, that no enterprise can be of more **vertue**, both by the lawes diuine & ciuill. *For what* can be a more honest, goodlie, or godlie quarrell, than to fight against a capteine, being *an homicide* and murtherer of his owne bloud or progenie, an extreame destroier of his nobilitie, and to his and our countrie and the poore subiects of the same a deadlie mallet, a firie brand, and a burthen intollerable ? . . .

Beside this, I assure you, that there be yonder in the great battell, men brought thither for feare, and not for loue ; souldiers by force compelled, and not with good will assembled ; persons which desire rather the destruction than saluation of their maister and capteine : . . .

What mercie is in him that sleieth his trustie freends as well as his extreame enimies. . . .

Therefore labour for your gaine, & *sweat* for your right. While we were in Britaine, we had small liuings and little plentie of wealth or welfare, now is the time come to get aboundance of riches, and copie of profit ; which is the reward of your seruice, and merit of *your paines*. . . .

And this one thing I assure you, that in so iust and good a cause, and so notable a quarrell, you shall find me this daie rather a dead carrion up*on the cold* ground, than a free prisoner on a carpet in a ladies chamber. . . .

And therefore, *in the name of God and S. George*, let euerie man couragiouslie *aduance* foorth his *standard !*

RICHARD'S ARRANGEMENTS

[*H*. iii. 755] King Richard, being furnished with men & all ablements of warre, bringing all his men out of their campe into the plaine, ordered his fore-ward in a maruellous length, in which he appointed both horsmen and footmen, to the intent to imprint, in the hearts of them that looked a farre off, a sudden terror and deadlie feare, for the great multitude of the armed souldiers : and in the fore-front he placed the archers like a strong fortified trench or bulworke. Ouer this battell was capteine, Iohn duke of Norffolke, with whome was Thomas earle of Surrie, his sonne. After this long vant-gard, followed king Richard himselfe with a strong companie of chosen and approued men of warre, hauing horssemen for wings on both sides of his battell.

[*H*. iii. 759] [Norfolk] was warned by diuerse to refrain from the field, in so much that the night before he should set forward toward the king, one wrote this rime vpon his gate :

> Iacke *of Norfolke be not too bold,*
> *For Dikon thy maister is bought and sold.*

Yet all this notwithstanding, he regarded more his oth, his honor, and promise made to king Richard, like a gentleman ; and, as a faithfull subiect to his prince, absented not himselfe from his maister ; but as he faith-fullie liued vnder him, so he manfullie died with him, to his great fame and laud.

RICHARD'S ORATION

[*H*. iii. 756] Ye see . . . . how a companie of traitors, theeues, outlawes, *and runnagates* of our owne nation, be aiders and partakers of his feat and enterprise, readie at hand to ouercome and oppresse vs.

You see also, what a number of beggerlie *Britans* and fainthearted Frenchmen be with him arriued to destroie vs, our *wiues* and children. . . .

And to begin with the erle of Richmond, capteine of this rebellion, he is *a* Welsh *milkesop*, a man of small courage, and of lesse experience in martiall acts and feats of warre ; brought vp by my *moothers* meanes, and mine, like a captiue in a close cage, *in* the court of Francis duke of *Britaine*. . . .

And as for the Frenchmen and *Britans*, their valiant-nesse is such, that our noble progenitors, and your valiant parents haue them oftener vanquished and ouercome in one moneth, than they in the beginning imagined possible to compasse and finish in a whole yeare.

The Battle

[*H*. iii. 760]   When king Richard was come to Bosworth, he sent a purseuant to the lord Stanleie, commanding him to aduance forward with his companie, and to come to his presence ; which thing if he refused to doo, he sware, by Christes passion, that he would strike off his sonnes head before he dined.   The lord Stanleie answered the pur- seuant that, if the king did so, he had more sonnes aliue ; and, as to come to him, he was not then so determined. When king Richard heard this answer, he commanded the lord Strange incontinent to be beheaded : which was at that verie same season, when both the armies had sight ech of other.   But the councellors of king Richard pondered the time and cause, (knowing also the lord Strange to be innocent of his fathers offense,) & persuaded the king that it was now time to fight, & no time to execute.

Besides that, they aduised him to keepe the lord Strange as prisoner till the battell were ended, and then at leisure his pleasure might be accomplished.   So (as God would) king Richard brake his holie oth, and the lord was deliuered to the keepers of the kings tents, to be kept as prisoner.

[*H*. iii. 758]   Betweene both armies there was a great marish then (but at this present, by reason of diches cast, it is growne to be firme ground) which the earle of Rich- mond left on his right hand; for this intent, that it should be on that side a defense for his part, and in so dooing he had the sunne at his backe, and in the faces of his enimies. When king Richard saw the earles companie was passed the marish, he did command with all hast to set vpon them.

[*H*. iii. 759–760]   When the losse of the battell   [V. iv.] was imminent and apparant, they brought to [Richard] a swift and a light horsse, to conueie him awaie.   He which was not ignorant of the grudge and ill will that the common people bare toward him, casting awaie all hope of fortunate successe and happie chance to come, answered (as men saie) that on that daie he would make an end of all battels, or else there finish his life.

[*H*. iii. 759]   King Richard was admonished by his explorators and espials, that the earle of Richmond (accompanied with a small number of men of armes) was not far off. And, as he approched and marched toward him, he perfectlie knew his personage by certeine demonstrations and tokens, which he had learned and knowen of others that were able to giue him full information. Now, being inflamed with ire, and vexed with outragious malice, he put his spurres to his horsse, and rode out of the side of the range of his battell, leauing the vant-gard fighting; and like a hungrie lion ran with speare in rest toward him. The earle of Richmond perceiued well the king furiouslie comming toward him, and, bicause the whole hope of his wealth and purpose was to be determined by battell, he gladlie proffered to incounter with him bodie to bodie, and man to man.

King Richard set on so sharplie at the first brunt, that he ouerthrew the earles standard, and slue sir William Brandon his standard-bearer, (which was father to sir Charles Brandon, by king Henrie the eight created duke of Suffolke,) and matched hand to hand with sir Iohn Cheinie, a man of great force and strength, which would haue resisted him : but the said Iohn was by him manfullie ouerthrowen. And so, he making open passage by dint of sword as he went forward, the earle of Richmond withstood his violence, and kept him at the swords point, without aduantage, longer than his companions either thought or iudged : which, being almost in despaire of victorie, were suddenlie recomforted by sir William Stanleie, which came to his succors with three thousand tall men. At which verie instant, king Richards men were driuen backe and fled, & he himselfe, manfullie fighting in the middle of his enimies, was slaine ; and (as he worthilie had deserued) came to a bloudie death, as he had lead a bloudie life.

[*H.* iii. 760] The people reioised, and clapped their hands, crieng vp to heauen, " King Henrie, king Henrie ! "

When the lord Stanleie saw the good will and gladnesse of the people, he tooke the crowne of king Richard, (which was found amongst the spoile in the field,) and set it on the earles head ; as though he had beene elected king by the voice of the people, as in ancient times past in diuerse realmes it hath beene accustomed. . . .

Which, when the field was doone, and their maister

slaine, and proclamation made to know where the child was, they submitted themselues as prisoners to the lord Strange, and he gentlie receiued them, and brought them to the new proclamed king ; where, of him and of his father, he was receiued with great ioy. After this the whole campe remooued with bag and baggage.

The same night in the euening, king Henrie with great pompe came to the towne of Leicester.

[*H*. iii. 759] Of the nobilitie were *slaine Iohn duke of Norffolke.* . . .

There were slaine beside him, Walter lord Ferrers of Chartleie, *sir* Richard Radcliffe, and *Robert Brakenberie*, lieutenant of the Tower, and not manie gentleman more.

[*H*. iii. 760] [Richmond] ascended vp to the top of a little mounteine, where he not onelie praised and lauded his valiant souldiers, but also gaue vnto them his hartie thanks, with promise of condigne recompense for their fidelitie and valiant facts ; willing and commanding all the hurt and wounded persons to be cured, and the dead carcasses to be deliuered to the sepulture.

[*H*. iii. 759] Of captiues and prisoners there were a great number. For, after the death of king Richard was knowne and published, euerie man, in manner vnarming himselfe, & casting awaie his abiliments of warre, meekelie submitted themselues to the obeisance and rule of the earle of Richmond : of the which the more part had gladlie so doone in the beginning, if they might haue conuenientlie escaped from king Richards espials, which, hauing as cleere eies as Lynx, and open ears as Midas, ranged & searched in euerie quarter.

Character of Edward IV

[*H*. iii. 711] A goodlie personage, and princelie to behold, of heart couragious, politike in counsell, in aduer-sitie nothing abashed, in prosperite rather ioifull than proud, in peace iust and mercifull, in warre sharpe and fierce, in the field bold and hardie, and natheles no further (than wisdome would) aduenturous ; whose warres who so well considered, he shall no lesse commend his wise-dome where he voided, than his manhood where he vanquished. He was of visage louelie, of bodie mightie, strong, and cleane made : howbeit, in his latter daies, with ouer liberall diet, somewhat corpulent and boorelie, and nathelesse not vncomelie. He was of youth greatlie giuen to fleshlie wantonnesse.

CHARACTER OF DUKE OF CLARENCE

[H. iii. 712] George duke of Clarence was a goodlie noble prince, and at all times fortunate, if either his owne ambition had not set him against his brother, or the enuie of his enimies his brother against him.

CHARACTER OF RICHARD

[H. iii. 712] Richard, the third sonne, of whome we now intreat, was in wit and courage equall with either of them, in bodie and prowesse farre vnder them both ; litle of stature, ill featured of limmes, crooke backed, his left shoulder much higher than his right, *hard fauoured* of visage, and such as is in states called warlie, in other men otherwise ; he was malicious, wrathfull, enuious, and from afore his birth euer froward. It is for truth reported, that the duchesse his mother had so much adoo in hir trauell, that she could not be deliuered of him vncut ; and that he came into the world with the feet forward, as men be borne outward, and (as the fame runneth also) not vntoothed. . . .

None euill capteine was he in the warre, as to which his disposition was more meetly than for peace. Sundrie victories had he, & sometimes ouerthrowes ; but neuer on default as for his owne person, either of hardinesse or politike order. Free was he called of dispense, and somewhat aboue his power liberall : with large gifts he gat him vnstedfast freendship, for which he was faine to pill and spoile in other places, and got him stedfast hatred. He was close and secret, a deepe dissembler, lowlie of countenance, arrogant of heart, outwardlie companiable where he inwardlie hated, not letting to kisse whome he thought to kill : despitious and cruell, not for euill will alway, but ofter for ambition, and either for the suertie or increase of his estate.

Friend and fo was much what indifferent, where his aduantage grew; he spared no mans death whose life withstoode his purpose.

CHARACTER OF RICHMOND

[*H*. iii. 757]   A man of no great stature, but so formed and decorated with all gifts and lineaments of nature, that he seemed more an angelicall creature, than a terrestriall personage.   His countenance and aspect was cheerefull and couragious, his haire yellow like the burnished gold, his eies graie, shining, and quicke : prompt and readie in answering, but of such sobrietie, that it could neuer be iudged whether he were more dull than quicke in speaking (such was his temperance.)

HENRY VIII

[For the material dramatised in *Henry VIII* Shakespeare turned mainly to Holinshed, although he may also have made reference to such chroniclers as Hall and Foxe. It will be found that more of Holinshed's actual wording has been retained in this play than in any of the other dramas. Characterisation, episode and dialogue owe directly to the chronicler.]

THE MEETING OF THE KINGS

[*H*. iii. 858]   The daie of meeting was appointed   [I. i.] to be on the thursdaie the seauenth of June, vpon which daie the *two kings met in the vale of Andren*, accompanied with such a number of the nobilitie of both realmes, so richlie appointed in apparell, and costlie iewels, as chaines, collars of S S, & other the like ornaments to set foorth their degrees and estates, that a woonder it was to behold and view them in their order and roomes, which euerie man kept according to his appointment.

The two kings meeting in the field, either saluted other in most louing wise, first on horssebacke, and after alighting on foot eftsoones imbraced with courteous words, to the great reioising of the beholders : and, after they had thus saluted ech other, they went both togither into a rich tent of cloath of gold, there set vp for the purpose, in the which they passed the time in pleasant talke, banketting, and louing deuises, till it drew toward the euening, and then departed for that night, the one to *Guisnes*, the other to *Ard*.

[*H*. iii. 860]   The lord cardinall in statelie attire, accompanied with the duke of Buckingham and other great lords, conducted forward the French king, and in their way they incountered and met the king of England and his companie right in the vallie of Anderne, apparalled in their masking apparell, which gladded the French king.

[*H*. iii. 855]   The peeres of the realme (receiuing letters to prepare themselues to attend the king in this iournie, and no apparant necessarie cause expressed, why nor wherefore) seemed to grudge, that such a costlie iournie should be taken in hand to their importunate charges and expenses, without consent of the whole boord of the councell. But namelie the duke of Buckingham (being a man of a loftie courage, but not most liberall) sore repined that he should be at so great charges for his furniture foorth at this time, saieng : that he knew not for what cause so much monie should be spent about the sight of a vaine talke to be had, and communication to be ministred of things of no importance. Wherefore he sticked not to saie, that it was an intollerable matter to obeie such a vile and importunate person.

The duke indeed could not abide the cardinall, and speciallie he had of late conceiued an inward malice against him for sir William Bulmer's cause, whose trouble was onelie procured by the cardinall ; who first caused him to be cast into prison. Now such greeuous words, as the duke thus vttered against him, came to the cardinalls eare ; wherevpon he cast before hand all waies possible to haue him in a trip, that he might cause him to leape headlesse.

[*H*. iii. 853] The French king, desirous to continue the friendship latelie begun betwixt him and the king of England, made meanes vnto the cardinall, that they might in some conuenient place come to an interuiew togither, that he might haue further knowledge of king Henrie, and likewise king Henrie of him. But the fame went that the cardinall desired greatlie, of himselfe, that the two kings might meet ; who, mesuring by his will what was conuenient, thought it should make much with his glorie, if *in France* also, at some high assemblie of noble men, he should be seene in his vaine *pompe* and shew of dignitie : hee therefore breaketh with the king of that matter, declaring how honourable, necessarie, and conuenient it should be for him to gratifie his friend therein ; and thus with his persuasions the K. began to conceiue an earnest desire to see the French king, and therevpon appointed to go ouer to Calis, and so in the marches of Guisnes to meet with him. . . .

Moreover, now that it was concluded, that the kings of England and France should meet (as yee haue heard), then both the kings committed the order and manner of their meeting, and how manie daies the same should continue, & what preheminence each should giue to other, vnto the cardinall of Yorke, which, to set all things in a certeintie, made an instrument, conteining an order and direction concerning the premisses by him deuised and appointed.

[*H*. iii. 856–857]   On Whitsundaie, earlie in the morning, they tooke their horsses, and rode to the citie of Canturburie, the more to keepe solemne the feast of Pentecost, but speciallie *to see the queene* of England *his aunt* was the emperour his intent ; of whome ye may be sure he was most ioifullie receiued and welcomed. . . .

The chiefe cause, that mooued the emperour to come thus on land at this time, was to persuade that by word of mouth which he had before done most earnestlie by letters ; which was, that the king should not meet with the French king at anie interuiew : for he doubted least, if the king of England & the French king should grow into some great friendship and faithfull bond of amitie, it might turn him to displeasure.

But, now that he perceiued how the king was forward on his iournie, he did what he could to procure that no trust should be committed to the faire words of the Frenchmen : and that, if it were possible, the great friendship, that was now in breeding betwixt the two kings, might be dissolued. And, forsomuch as he knew the lord cardinall to be woone with rewards, as a fish with a bait, he bestowed on him great gifts, and promised him much more ; so that hee would be his friend, and helpe to bring his purpose to passe. The cardinall (not able to susteine the least assault by force of such rewards as he presentlie receiued, and of such large promises as on the emperours behalfe were made to him) promised to the emperour, that he would so vse the matter, as his purpose should be sped : onelie he required him not to disalow the kings intent for interuiew to be had ; which he desired in anie wise to go forward, that he might shew his high magnificence in France, according to his first intention.

ARREST OF BUCKINGHAM

[*H*. iii. 863]   The duke herevpon was sent for vp to
London, &, at his comming thither, was streightwaies
attached, and brought to the Tower by sir Henrie Marneie,
capteine of the gard, the sixteenth of Aprill.   There was
also attached the foresaid Chartreux monke, maister Iohn
de la Car alias de la Court, *the dukes confessor*, and sir
Gilbert Perke, priest, the dukes *chancellor*.

After the apprehension of the duke, inquisitions were
taken in diuerse shires of England of him ; so that, by the
knights and gentlemen, he was indicted of high treason,
for certeine words spoken (as before ye haue heard) by
the same duke at Blechinglie, to the lord of Aburgauennie
and therewith was the same lord attached for concelement,
and so likewise was the lord Montacute, and both led
to the Tower.

THE PROTEST OF THE COMMONS

[*H*. iii. 891-892]   The king being determined   [I. ii.]
thus to make wars in France, & to passe the sea himselfe in
person, his councell considered that aboue all things great
treasure and plentie of monie must needes be prouided.
Wherfore, by the cardinall there was deuised strange
commissions, and sent in the end of March into euerie shire,
and commissioners appointed, and priuie instructions sent
to them how they should proceed in their sittings, and
order the people to bring them to their purpose : which
was, that the *sixt part* of euerie mans *substance* should
be paid in monie or plate to the king *without delaie*, for
the furniture of his war.   Hereof followed such cursing,
weeping, and exclamation against both king & cardinall,
that pitie it was to heare. . . .

The cardinall trauelled earnestlie with the maior and
aldermen of London, about the aid of monie to be granted,
and likewise the commissioners, appointed in the shires of
the realme, sat vpon the same : but the burthen was so
greeuous, that it was generallie denied, and the commons
in euerie place so mooued, that it was like to grow to
rebellion. . . .

The duke of Suffolke, sitting in commission about this subsidie in Suffolke, persuaded by courteous meanes the rich *clothiers* to assent therto: but, when they came home, and went about to discharge and *put* from them their *spinners, carders, fullers, weauers,* and other artificers, (which they kept in worke afore time,) the people began to assemble in companies. . . . And herewith there assembled togither, after the maner of rebels, foure thousand men of Lanam, Sudberie, Hadleie, and other townes thereabouts ; which put themselues in harnesse, and rang the bels alarme, and began still to assemble in great number. . . .

The duke of Norffolke, being therof aduertised, gathered a great power in Norffolke, and came towards the commons, &, sending to them to know their intent, receiued answer, that they would liue and die in the kings causes, and be to him obedient. Herevpon he came himselfe to talke with them, and, willing to know who was their capteine, that he might answer for them all, it was told him by one Iohn Greene, a man of fiftie yeares of age, that Pouertie was their capteine, the which, with his cousin Necessitie, had brought them to that dooing. . . .

The king then came to Westminster to the cardinals palace, and assembled there a great councell, in the which he openlie protested, that his mind was neuer to aske anie thing of his commons which might sound to the breach of his lawes ; wherefore he willed to know by whose meanes the commissions were so streictlie giuen foorth, to demand the sixt part of euerie mans goods.

The cardinall excused himselfe, and said, that when it was mooued in councell how to leuie monie to the kings vse, the kings councell, and namelie the judges, said, that he might lawfullie demand anie summe by commission, and that by the consent of the whole councell it was doone ; and tooke God to witnes that he neuer desired the hinderance of the commons, but like a true councellor deuised how to inrich the king. The king indeed was much offended that his commons were thus intreated, & thought it touched his honor, that his councell should attempt such a doubtfull matter in his name, and to be denied both of the spiritualtie and temporaltie. There-

fore he would no more of that trouble, but caused letters to
be sent into all shires, that the matter should no further be
talked of : & he pardoned all them that had denied the
demand openlie or secretlie. The cardinall, to deliuer
himselfe of the euill will of the commons, purchased by
procuring & aduancing of this demand, affirmed, and
caused it to be bruted abrode, that *through* his intercession
the king had *pardoned* and released all things.

The Plot against Buckingham

⌊*H*. iii. 862-863] The cardinall, boiling in hatred
against the duke of Buckingham, & thirsting for his
bloud, deuised to make Charles Kneuet, that had beene
the dukes *surueior*, and put from him (as ye haue heard)
an instrument to bring the duke to destruction. This
Kneuet, being had in examination before the cardinall,
disclosed all the dukes life. And first he vttered, that the
duke was accustomed, by waie of talke, to saie how he
meant so to vse the matter, that he would atteine to the
crowne, *if king* Henrie chanced to *die without issue :* &
that he had talke and conference of that matter on a time
with George Neuill, lord of Aburgauennie, vnto whome
he had giuen his daughter in marriage ; and also that
he threatned to punish the cardinall for his manifold
misdooings, being without cause his mortall enimie.

The cardinall, hauing gotten that which he sought for,
incouraged, comforted, and procured Kneuet, with manie
comfortable words and great promises, that he should
with a bold spirit and countenance obiect and laie these
things to the dukes charge, with more if he knew it when
time required. Then Kneuet, partlie prouoked with
desire to be reuenged, and partlie moooued with hope of
reward, openlie confessed, that the duke had once fullie
determined to deuise meanes how to make the king away,
being *brought* into a full hope that he should be king, *by a
vaine prophesie* which one *Nicholas* Hopkins, a monke of
an house of the *Chartreux* order beside Bristow, called
Henton, sometime *his confessor*, had opened vnto him.

The cardinall, hauing thus taken the examination of
Kneuet, went vnto the king, and declared vnto him, that

his person was in danger by such traitorous purpose, as the duke of Buckingham had conceiued in his heart, and shewed how that now there is manifest tokens of his wicked pretense : wherefore, he exhorted the king to prouide for his owne suertie with speed. The king, hearing the accusation, inforced to the vttermost by the cardinall, made this answer : " If the duke haue deserued to be punished, let him haue according to his deserts."

THE INDICTMENT OF BUCKINGHAM

[*H.* iii. 864] *The* same *duke,* the tenth of Maie, in the twelfe yeare of the kings reigne at London in a place called *the Rose, within the parish* of *saint Laurence Poultnie* in Canwike street ward, *demand*ed *of* the said Charles Kneuet esquier, *what was the* talke among*est the Londoners concerning the* kings *iourneie* beyond the seas ? And the said Charles told him, that manie stood in doubt of that iourneie, least *the French*men meant some deceit towards the king. Whereto the duke answered, that it was to be feared least it would come to passe according to the *words* of *a* certeine *holie moonke :* " For there is " (saith he) " a Chartreux moonke, *that* diuerse times *hath sent to me,* willing *me* to send vnto him my chancellor : and I did send vnto him *Iohn de la Court my chapleine,* vnto *whome he* would not declare anie thing, till de la Court *had sworne* vnto him to keepe all things secret, and to tell *no creature liuing what* hee should heare of him, except it were *to me.*

" And then the said moonke told de la Court, that *neither the king nor his heires* should *prosper,* and that I should indeuour my selfe to purchase *the* good wils *of the communaltie* of England ; for I *the* same *duke* and my bloud should prosper, and haue the rule of the realme of *England.*" . . .

Then said Charles Kneuet : " *The moonke* maie *be deceiued* through *the diuels illusion :*" and that it was euill to meddle with such matters. " Well " (said the duke) " it cannot hurt me ; " and so (saith the indictment) the duke seemed to reioise in the moonks woords. And further, at the same time, the duke told the said Charles, *that,* if *the king had* miscaried now *in his last sicknesse,* he would *haue* chopped *off* the *heads* of *the cardinall,* of *sir Thomas Louell* knight, and of others ; and also said, that he had rather die for it, than to be vsed as he had beene.

On the fourth of Nouember, in the eleuenth yere of the kings reigne, *at* east *Greenwich* in the countie of Kent, [Buckingham] said vnto one Charles Kneuet esquier, (*after* that the king *had reprooued the duke* for *reteining William Bulmer,* knight, into his seruice,) that, *if* he had perceiued that he should haue *beene committed to the Tower* (as he doubted hee should haue beene), hee would haue so wrought, that the principall dooers therein should not haue had cause of great reioising : for he *would haue plaied the part* which his *father* intended to haue put in practise against king *Richard* the third *at Salisburie ; who made* earnest *sute to* haue *come* vnto the *presence* of the same king Richard : *which* sute *if* he might haue obteined, he hauing a *knife* secretlie about him, *would haue* thrust it *into* the bodie of king Richard, *as he* had *made semblance* to kneele downe before him. And, in speaking these words, *he* maliciouslie laid his *hand vpon his dagger,* and said, that, if *he were* so *euill vsed, he would* doo his best to accomplish his pretensed *purpose ;* swearing to confirme his word by the bloud of our Lord.

HENRY'S YOUNG COURTIERS

[*H.* iii. 850] And when these yoong gentle- [I. iii.] men came againe into England, they were all French, in eating, drinking, and apparell, yea, and in French vices and brags, so that all the estates of England were by them laughed at, the ladies and gentlewomen were dispraised ; so that nothing by them was praised, but if it were after the French turne ; which after turned them to displesure, as you shall heare.

[*H.* iii. 852] To whome the king answered, that he had chosen them of his councell, both for the maintenance of his honour, and for the defense of all things that might blemish the same : wherefore, if they saw anie about him misuse themselues, he committed it vnto their *reformation.* Then the kings councell caused the lord chamberleine to

call before them diuerse of the priuie chamber, (which
had beene in the French court,) and banished them the
court for diuerse considerations ; laieng nothing particularlie to their charges, & they that had offices were commanded to go to their offices. Which discharge out of
court greeued sore the hearts of these yoong men, which
were called the kings minions.

Wolsey's Banquet

[*H.* iii. 922] First, yee shall vnderstand that the
tables were set in the chamber of presence banquetwise
couered, & the lord cardinall sitting vnder the cloth of
estate, there hauing all his seruice alone : and then was
there set a ladie with a noble man, or a gentleman and a
gentlewoman, throughout all the tables in the chamber
on the one side, which were made and ioined as it were
but one table : all which order and deuise was doone by
the lord Sandes, then lord chamberleine to the king, and
by *sir Henrie Gilford, comptroller* of the kings maiesties
house.

[*H.* iii. 921–922] [Wolsey's] house was resorted to with
*noble*men and *gentlemen*, feasting and banketting ambassadors diuerse times, and all other right noblie. And when
it pleased the king for his recreation to repaire to the
cardinals house, (as he did diuerse times in the yeare,)
there wanted no preparations or furniture : bankets were
set foorth with maskes and mummeries, in so gorgeous a
sort and costlie maner, that it was an heauen to behold.
There wanted no dames or damosels meet or apt to danse
with the maskers, or to garnish the place for the time. . . .

On a time the *king* came suddenlie thither in a maske,
with a dozen *maskers* all in garments *like sheepheards,*
made of fine cloth of gold, and crimosin sattin paned, &
caps of the same, with visards of good physnomie, their
haires & beards either of fine goldwire silke, or blacke
silke ; hauing sixteene torch-bearers, besides their drums
and other persons with visards, all clothed in sattin of the
same color. And, before his entring into the hall, he
came by water to the water gate without anie noise ;
where were laid diuerse chambers and guns charged with

shot, and at his landing they were shot off, which made such a rumble in the aire, that it was like thunder: it made all the noblemen, gentlemen, ladies, and gentle-women, to muse what it should meane, comming so suddenlie, they sitting quiet at a solemne banket. . . .

Then immediatlie after, the great chamberleine and the said comptrollor sent to looke what it should meane (as though they knew nothing of the matter); who, looking out of the windowes into the Thames, returned againe and shewed him, that it *seemed they* were noblemen and *strangers* that arriued at his bridge, comming *as ambassadours from* some *forren prince*.

With that, quoth the cardinall, "I desire you, bicause *you can speake French,* to take the paines to go into the hall, there to *receiue* them according to their estates, *and* to *conduct* them *into* this chamber, *where* they *shall* see vs, and all these noble personages being merie at our *banket*; desiring them to sit downe with vs, and to take part of our fare." Then went he incontinent downe into the hall, whereas they receiued them with twentie new torches, and conueied them vp into the chamber, with such a noise of drums and flutes, as seldome had beene heard the like. At their entring into the chamber, two and two togither, *they* went *directlie before the cardinall,* where he sate, *and saluted him* reuerentlie.

To whom the lord chamberleine for them said: "Sir, for as much as *they* be strangers, and can not *speake English,* they haue desired me *to* declare vnto you, *that* they, *hauing* vnderstanding *of this* your triumphant banket, where was *assembled* such a number of excellent dames, *they could doo no lesse, vnder* support of *your* grace, *but* to repaire hither, *to view* as well their incomparable *beautie,* as for to accompanie them at mum-chance, and then to danse *with them :* and, sir, they require of your grace licence to accomplish the said cause of their comming." To whom the cardinall said he was verie well content they should so doo.

[*H.* iii. 922] Then quoth the cardinall to the lord chamberleine, "I praie you" (quoth he) "that you would shew them, that me seemeth *there should be* a nobleman *amongst them,* who is *more* meet to occupie *this*

seat and *place than* I am ; *to whome I would* most gladlie
surrender the same according to *my dutie, if I knew him.*"

Then spake the lord chamberleine to them in French,
and they rounding him in the eare, the lord chamberlein
said to my lord cardinall : " Sir " (quoth he) " *they confesse,* that among them *there is* such a noble personage,
whome, if *your grace* can appoint him *out* from the rest,
he is content to disclose himselfe, and to accept your place."
With that the cardinall taking good aduisement among
them, at the last (quoth he) " me seemeth, the gentleman
with the blacke beard should be euen hee " : and with
that he arose out of his chaire, and offered the same to
the gentleman in the blacke beard, with his cap in his hand.
The person to whom he offered the chaire was sir Edward
Neuill, a comelie knight, that much more resembled the
kings person in that maske than anie other.

The king, perceiuing the cardinall so deceiued, could
not forbeare laughing, but pulled downe his visar and
master Neuels also, and dashed out such a *pleasant*
countenance and cheere, that all the noble estates there
assembled, perceiuing the king to be there among them,
reioised verie much. . . .

[Wolsey] eftsoons desired his highnesse to take the place
of estate.   To whom the king answered, that he would
go first and shift his apparell, and so departed into my
lord cardinals chamber, and there new apparelled him :
in which time the dishes of the banket were cleane taken
vp, and the tables spred againe with new cleane perfumed
cloths ; euerie man and woman sitting still, vntill the
king with all his maskers came among them againe all
new apparelled.

THE TRIAL OF BUCKINGHAM

[*H*. iii. 865]   When the lords had taken their   [II. i.]
place, *the duke* was brought *to the barre,* and, vpon *his*
arreignement, *pleaded not guiltie,* and put himselfe vpon
his peeres.   Then was his indictment read, which the duke
denied to be true, *and* (as he was an eloquent man)
alledged reasons to falsifie the indictment ; pleading the
matter for his owne iustification verie pithilie and

earnestlie. *The kings attourneie*, against the dukes reasons, alledged *the examinations, confessions*, and *proofes of witnesses*.

The duke desired that the witnesses might bee *brought* foorth. And then came before *him* Charles Kneuet, Perke, De la Court, & *Hopkins* the *monke* of the priorie of the Charterhouse beside Bath, which like a false hypocrite had induced the duke to the treason *with his* false forged *prophesies*. Diuerse presumptions and accusations were laid vnto *him* by Charles Kneuet; *which he would faine haue* couered. The depositions were read, & the deponents deliuered as prisoners to the officers of the Tower. Then spake the duke of Norffolke, and said: "My lord, the king our souereigne lord hath commanded that you shall haue his lawes ministred with fauour and right to you. Wherefore, if you haue anie other thing to say for your selfe, you shall be heard." Then he was commanded to withdraw him, and so was led into Paradise, a house so named. The lords went to councell a great while, and after tooke their places.

Then said the duke of Norffolke to the duke of Suffolke: "What say you of sir Edward duke of Buckingham, touching the high treasons?" The duke of Suffolke answered: "He is giltie": & so said the marques and all the other earles and lords. Thus was this prince, duke of Buckingham, *found giltie of high treason*, by a duke, a marques, seuen earles, & twelue barons. The duke *was brought to the barre* sore chafing, and *swet* maruellouslie; &, after he had made his reuerence, he paused a while. The duke of Norffolke, as iudge, said: "Sir Edward, you haue heard how you be indicted by high treason; you pleaded thereto not giltie, putting your selfe to the peeres of the realme, which haue found you giltie."

Comment on the Trial

[*H*. iii. 864–865] Sauing that (I trust) I maie without offense saie, that (as the rumour then went) *the cardinall* chieflie procured the death of this noble man, no lesse fauoured and beloued of the people of this realme in that season, than the cardinall himselfe was hated and enuied. Which thing caused the dukes fall the more to be *pitied*

and lamented, sith he was the man of all other that
chieflie went about to crosse the cardinall in his lordlie
demeanor, & headie proceedings.

[*H*. iii. 855] Bicause he doubted his freends, kinnesmen,
and alies, and cheeflie the earle of Surrie, lord admerall,
(which had married the dukes daughter,) [Wolsey] thought
good first to send him some whither out of the waie, least
he might cast a trumpe in his waie. There was great
enimitie betwixt the cardinall and the earle, for that, on
a time, when the cardinall tooke vpon him to checke
the earle, he had like to haue thrust his dagger into the
cardinal.

At length there was occasion offered him to compasse
his purpose, by occasion of the earle of Kildare his comming out of Ireland. For the cardinall, knowing he was
well prouided of monie, sought occasion to fleece him of
part thereof. The earle of Kildare, being vnmarried,
was desirous to haue an English woman to wife ; and, for
that he was a suter to a widow, contrarie to the cardinals
mind, he accused him to the king of that he had not borne
himselfe vprightlie in his office in Ireland, where he was
the kings lieutenant. Such accusations were framed
against him, when no bribes would come, that he was
committed to prison, and then by the cardinals good preferment the earle of Surrie was sent into Ireland as the
kings deputie, in lieu of the said earle of Kildare ; there
to remaine rather as an exile than as lieutenant to the
king, euen at the cardinals pleasure, as he himselfe well
perceiued.

BUCKINGHAM'S SPEECH

[*H*. iii. 865] The duke of Buckingham said, " My lord
of Norffolke, you haue said as a *traitor* should be said vnto,
but I was neuer anie : but, my lords, I nothing maligne
for that you haue doone to me, but the eternall God
forgiue you my death, and I doo. I shall neuer sue to the
king for life, howbeit he is a gratious prince, and more
grace may come from him than I desire. I desire you,
my lords, and all my fellowes, to pray for me." Then
was the edge of the axe turned towards him, and he led
into a *barge*.

[*H*. iii. 865] Sir Thomas Louell desired him to sit on the cushins and carpet ordeined for him. He said, " *nay ;* for *when I* went to Westminster *I was duke of Buckingham ; now* I am but *Edward Bohune,* the most caitife of the world." Thus they landed at the Temple, where receiued him sir Nicholas Vawse & sir William Sands, baronets, and led him through the citie ; who desired euer the people to pray for him.

RUMOURS ABOUT KATHARINE

[*H*. iii. 897] [There] rose a secret brute in London that the kings confessor, doctor Longland, and diuerse other great clerks, had told the king that the marriage betweene him and the ladie Katharine, late wife to his brother prince Arthur, was not lawfull : wherevpon the king should sue a diuorse, and marrie the duchesse of Alanson, sister to the French king, at the towne of Calis, this summer : and that the vicount Rochford had brought with him the picture of the said ladie. The king was offended with those tales, and *sent* for sir Thomas Seimor, *maior* of the citie of London, secretlie charging him to see that the people ceassed from such talke.

[*H*. iii. 906] Ye haue heard how the people talked a little before the cardinals going ouer into France, the last yeare, that the king was told by doctor Longland, bishop of Lincolne, and others, that his marriage with queene Katharine could not be good nor lawfull. The truth is, that, whether this doubt was first mooued by the cardinall, or by the said Longland, being the kings confessor, the king was not onelie brought in doubt, whether it was a lawfull marriage or no ; but also determined to haue the case examined, cleered, and adiudged by learning, law, and sufficient authoritie. The cardinall verelie was put in most blame for this scruple now cast into the kings conscience, for the hate he bare to *the emperor*, bicause he would *not* grant to *him the archbishoprike of Toledo*, for the which he was a suter. And therefore he did not onelie procure the king of England to ioine in freendship with the French king, but also sought a diuorse betwixt the king and the queene, that the king might haue in marriage the duchesse of Alanson, sister vnto the French king: and (as some haue thought) he trauelled in that matter with the French king at Amiens, but the duchesse would not giue eare therevnto.

But howsoeuer it came about that the king was thus troubled in *conscience* concerning his *mariage*, this followed, that, like a wise & sage prince, to haue the doubt cleerlie remooued, he called togither the best learned of the realme; which were of seuerall opinions. Wherefore he thought to know the truth by indifferent iudges, least peraduenture *the Spaniards*, and other also in fauour of the queene, would saie, that his owne subiects were not indifferent iudges in this behalfe. And therefore he wrote his cause to Rome, and also sent to *all the* vniuersities in Italie and France, and to the great *clearkes* of all *christendome*, to know their opinions, and desired the court of Rome to send into his realme a legat, which should be indifferent, and of a great and profound iudgement, to heare the cause debated. At whose request *the whole consistorie* of the college of *Rome* sent thither Laurence Campeius, a *preest* cardinall, a man of great wit and experience. . . . and *with* him was *ioined* in *commission* the *cardinall of Yorke* and legat of England.

This cardinall came to London in October, and did intimate both to the king & queene the cause of his comming: which being knowne, great talke was had thereof.

[*H.* iii. 907] And bicause the king meant [II. ii] nothing but vprightlie therein, and knew well that the queene was somewhat wedded to hir owne opinion, and wished that she should do nothing without counsell, he bad hir choose the best clearks of his realme to be of hir counsell, and licenced them to doo the best on hir part that they could, according to the truth.

[*H.* iii. 907] The king receiued into fauour doctor Stephan Gardiner, whose seruice he vsed in matters of great secrecie and weight, admitting him in the roome of *doctor Pace*, the which, being continuallie abroad in ambassages, and the same oftentimes not much necessarie, by the cardinals appointment, at length he tooke such *greefe* therewith, that he fell out of his right wits.

HONOURS GIVEN TO ANNE BOLEYN

[*H*. iii. 928] On the first of September being [II. iii.]
sundaie, the K., being come to Windsor, created the ladie
Anne Bullongne *marchionesse of Penbroke*, and gaue to
hir *one thousand pounds* land by the *yeare*.

THE TRIAL OF KATHARINE

[*H*. iii. 907] The place where the cardinals [II. iv.]
should sit, to heare the cause of matrimonie betwixt the
king and the queene, was ordeined to be at the *Blacke
friers* in London; where in the great hall was preparation
made of seats, tables, and other furniture, according to
such a solemne session and roiall apparance. *The court*
was platted in tables and benches *in manner of a consistorie*, one seat raised higher for the iudges to sit in.   Then
as it were in the midst of the said iudges, aloft, aboue them
three degrees high, was a *cloth of estate* hanged, with a
chaire roiall vnder the same, wherein sat the king; and,
besides him, *some distance from* him sat *the queene*, and
vnder the iudges feet sat *the scribes* and other officers:
the cheefe scribe was doctor Steeuens, and the caller of
the court was one Cooke of Winchester.
  Then before the king and the iudges, within the court,
sat the archbishop of Canturburie, Warham, and all the
other bishops.   Then stood at both ends within, the counsellors learned in the spirituall laws, as well the kings as
the queenes.   The doctors of law for the king . . . had
their *conuenient* roomes.   Thus was the court furnished.
  [*H*. iii. 907] [Katharine] elected William Warham
archbishop of Canturburie, and Nicholas Weast bishop of
Elie, doctors of the laws; and Iohn Fisher, bishop of
Rochester, and Henrie Standish, bishop of St. Assaph,
doctors of diuinitie; and manie other doctors and well
learned men, which for suertie, like men of great learning,
defended hir cause, as farre as learning might mainteine
and hold it vp.
  [*H*. iii. 907] The iudges *commanded silence whilest* their
commission was *read*, both to the court and to the people
assembled.   That doone the scribes commanded the crier

to call the king by the name of " *king Henrie of England, come into the court,*" &c. With that the king answered and said, " *Heere !* " Then called he the queene by the name of " *Katharine, queene of England, come into the court,*" &c. Who made *no answer,* but rose *out of hir chaire.*

And, bicause shee could not come to the king directlie, for the distance seuered betweene them, shee went *about* by *the court, and* came *to the king, kneel*ing downe *at his feet,* to whome she said in effect as followeth :

KATHARINE'S DEFENCE

[*H.* iii. 907] " *Sir* " (quoth she) " *I desire you to doo me iustice and right, and* take some *pitie* vp*on me, for I am a poore woman, and a stranger, borne out of your dominion ; hauing heere no indifferent* counsell, & lesse *assurance of freendship.* *Alas, sir, what haue I offended you, or what* occasion of *displeasure* haue I shewed you ; intending *thus to put me* from you after this sort ? I take God to my iudge, *I haue beene to you a true & humble wife,* euer *conformable to your will* and pleasure ; that neuer contraried or gainesaid any thing thereof, and, being alwaies contented with all things wherein you had any delight, whether little or much, without grudge or displeasure, I loued for your sake all them whome you loued, whether they were my *freends or enimies.*

" *I haue beene your wife* these *twentie yeares* and more, & you *haue* had *by* me diuerse *children.* *If* there be anie iust cause that *you can* alleage against me, either of dishonestie, or matter lawfull to put me from you, I am content to depart to my shame and rebuke : and if there be none, then I praie you to let me haue *iustice* at your hand. *The king your father was* in his time *of excellent wit,* and the *king of Spaine, my father, Ferdinando, was reckoned one* of *the wisest prince*s *that reigned* in Spaine *manie years before.* *It is not to be* doubted, but *that they had gathered as wise* counsellors vn*to them of euerie realme, as to their wisedoms they thought meet, who deemed* the *marriage* betweene you and me good and *lawfull,* &c. *Wherefore, I humblie* desire *you to spare me,* vn*till I may*

know what *counsell my freends in Spaine* will aduertise
me to take, and, *if* you will *not*, then *your pleasure be
fulfilled.*"

[*H*. iii. 908] Heere is to be noted, that the queene in
presence of the whole court most greeuouslie accused the
cardinall of vntruth, deceit, wickednesse, & malice ; which
had sowne dissention betwixt hir and the king hir husband : and therefore openlie protested, that she did
vtterlie abhorre, refuse, and forsake such a *judge,* as was
not onelie a *most malicious enimie* to hir, but also a
manifest aduersarie to all right and iustice ; and therewith
did she *appeale vnto the pope,* committing hir *whole cause to
be judged* of him.

[*H*. iii. 907–908] With that she arose vp, making a
lowe curtesie to the king, and departed from thence.

The king, being aduertised that shee was readie to go
out of the house, commanded the crier to *call hir againe ;*
who called hir by these words : "*Katharine, queene of
England, come into the court !*" With that quoth maister
Griffith, "*Madame, you* be *called* againe." "On, on "
(quoth she) "it maketh no matter, *I will not tarrie,* go on
your waies !" And thus she departed, without anie
further answer at that time, or anie other, and neuer
would appeare after *in anie court.* . . .

THE KING'S SPEECH

The king, perceiuing she was departed, said these words
in effect : "For as much" (quoth he) "as the queene is
gone, I will in hir absence declare to you all, that shee
hath beene to me as true, as obedient, and as conformable
a wife, as I would wish or desire. She hath all the
vertuous qualities that ought to be in a woman of hir
dignitie, or in anie other of a baser estate ; *she is* also
surelie a *noble* woman *borne ;* hir conditions will well
declare the same."

With that quoth Wolseie the cardinall : "*Sir, I* most
humblie *require your highnesse, to declare* before all this
audience, *whether I* haue beene the cheefe and first moouer
of *this* matter *vnto your* maiestie or no, for I am greatlie
suspected heerein. . . . ."

"*My lord cardinall* " (quoth the king) "*I* can well

excuse you in this matter, marrie" (quoth he) "you haue beene rather against me in the tempting heereof, than a setter forward or moouer of the same. The speciall cause, that *mooued* me vnto this matter, was a certeine scrupulositie that pricked *my conscience, vpon certeine* words spoken at a time *by the bishop of Baion,* the *French ambassador, who had beene hither sent,* vpon *the debating* of *a marriage* to be concluded betweene *our daughter* the ladie *Marie,* and *the duke of Orleance,* second son to the king of France.

"Upon the *resolution* and *determination* whereof, *he* desired *respit* to *aduertise the king his* maister thereof, *whether our daughter* Marie should be *legitimate* in *respect* of *this* my *marriage with* this woman, being *sometimes* my *brothers wife.* Which words, once conceiued within *the* secret bottome *of my conscience,* ingendered such a scrupulous doubt, that my conscience was incontinentlie accombred, vexed, and disquieted; whereby I *thought* my selfe to be greatlie in danger of God's indignation. Which appeared to be (as me seemed) the rather, for that he sent vs no *issue male,* and all such issues male, as my said wife had by me, *died* incontinent *after* they came into the *world ;* so that I doubted the great displeasure of God in that behalfe.

"Thus, *my conscience* being tossed in the waues of a scrupulous mind, and partlie in despaire to haue anie other issue than I had alredie by this ladie now my wife, it behooued me further to consider the state of this *realme,* and *the danger* it *stood in* for lacke of a prince to succeed me. *I* thought it good in release of the weightie burthen of *my* weake *conscience.* . . . to attempt the law therin, whether I may lawfullie take another wife more lawfullie. . . . not for anie displeasure or misliking of *the* queenes *person* and age ; with whome I would be as well *contented to* continue, if *our mariage* may stand with the laws of God, as with anie woman aliue.

"In this point consisteth all this doubt that we go about now to trie by the learning, wisedome, and iudgement of you our prelats and pastors of all this our realme and dominions, now heere assembled for that purpose ; . . . Wherein, after that I perceiued my conscience so doubtfull, I mooued it in confession to *you*, *my Lord of Lincolne*, then ghostlie father. And, for so much as then you your selfe were in some *doubt*, you mooued me to aske the counsell of all these my lords : wherevpon *I mooued you, my lord of Canturburie*, first to haue your licence, in as much as you were metropolitane, to put this matter in question, and so I did of all you, my lords : to which you granted *vnder your seales*, heere to be shewed. . . ."

After that the king rose vp, and the *court* was *adiourned vntill* another *daie*.

KATHARINE AND THE CARDINALS

[*H.* iii. 908] The cardinals being in the [III. i.] queenes chamber of presence, the gentleman usher aduertised the queene that the cardinals were come to speake with hir. With that she rose vp, &, with a skeine of white thred about hir necke, came into hir chamber of presence, where the cardinals were attending. At whose comming quoth she, "*What* is *your plesure with me ?*" "*If it please* your grace " (quoth cardinall Wolseie) "*to* go *into your* privie *chamber, we* will shew *you the cause of our comming.*" "My lord " (quoth she) "if yee haue anie thing to saie, *speake it* openlie before all these folke ; for I feare nothing that yee can saie against me, but that I would all the world should heare and see it, and therefore speake your mind." Then began the cardinall to speake to hir in Latine. "Naie, *good my lord* " (quoth she) "*speake* to me *in English.*"

"Forsooth " (quoth the cardinall) "good madame, if it please you, *we come* both *to know* your mind *how you* are disposed to doo *in* this matter *betweene the king and you, and* also *to* declare secretlie *our opinions and counsell* vnto you : which we doo onelie for verie *zeale and obedience* we beare vnto *your grace.*" "*My lord* " (quoth she) "*I thanke you for your good will ; but to make* you *answer* in your request I cannot so *suddenlie*, for *I was* set *among my maids at worke*, thinking *full little* of anie *such* matter, wherein there needeth a longer deliberation, and a better head than mine to make answer : for I need *counsell* in this case which toucheth me so neere, & for anie counsell or freendship that I can find *in England,* they are not *for my profit.* What, *thinke you,* my *lords,* will *anie Englishman* counsell *me, or be freend* to me *against* the K. *pleasure* that is his *subiect ? Naie, forsooth.* And as for my counsell in whom I will put *my trust, they* be *not here, they* be in Spaine *in my owne countrie.*

"And, my lords, *I am* a poore *woman, lacking wit, to answer to* anie such noble *persons* of wisedome as you be, in so weightie a matter, therefore I praie you be good to me, poore woman, destitute of freends here in a forren region,"* . . . "and *your counsell* also I will be glad to heare." And therewith she tooke the cardinall by the hand, and led him into hir priuie chamber with the other cardinall, where they tarried a season talking with the queene.

[*H.* iii. 908.] [They wished] to persuade with hir by their wisdoms, and to aduise hir to surrender the whole matter *into the kings* hands by hir owne consent & will, which should *be much better* to hir *honour,* than to stand to *the triall of law,* and thereby to be condemned, which should seeme much to hir dishonour.

ANNE BOLEYN

[*H.* iii. 908–909] The cardinall of Yorke was   [III. ii.] aduised that the king had set his affection vpon a yoong gentlewoman named Anne, the daughter of Sir Thomas Bullen, vicount Rochford, which did wait vpon the queene. This was a great griefe vnto the cardinall, as he that perceiued aforehand, that the king would marie the said gentlewoman, if the diuorse tooke place. Wherfore he began with all diligence to disappoint that match, which, by reason of the misliking that he had to the woman, he iudged ought to be auoided more than present death. While the matter stood in this state, and that the cause of the queene was to be heard and iudged at Rome, by reason of the appeale which by hir was put in, the cardinall required *the pope* by *letters* and secret messengers, that in anie wise he should defer *the iudgement of the diuorse,* till he might frame the kings mind to his purpose.

Howbeit he went about nothing so secretlie, but that the same came to the kings knowledge, who tooke so high displeasure with such his cloked dissimulation, that he determined to abase his degree, sith as an vnthankefull person he forgot himselfe and his dutie towards him that had so highlie aduanced him to all honor and dignitie. When the nobles of the realme perceiued the cardinall to be in displeasure, they began to accuse him of such offenses as they knew might be proued against him, and thereof they made a booke conteining certeine articles, to which diuerse of the kings councell set their hands.

CAMPEGGIO'S DEPARTURE

[*H*. iii. 908] "I will not giue iudgement till I haue made relation to the pope of all our proceedings ; whose counsell and commandement in this case I will obserue: the case is verie doubtfull, and also the partie defendant will make no answer here, but dooth rather appeale from vs, supposing that we be not indifferent. Wherfore I will adiourne this court for this time, according to the order of the court of Rome." And with that the court was dissolued, and no more doone. This protracting of the conclusion of the matter, king Henrie tooke verie displeasantlie. Then cardinall Campeius tooke his leaue of the king and nobilitie, and returned towards Rome.

THE DISMISSAL OF WOLSEY

[*H*. iii. 909] The king sent the two dukes [III. ii.] of Norfolke and Suffolke to the cardinals place at Westminster, who went as they were commanded, and, finding the cardinall there, they declared that *the kings pleasure* was that he should sur*render vp the great seale into* their *hands*, and to depart simplie *vnto Asher*, which was an house situat nigh vnto Hampton court, belonging to the bishoprike *of Winchester*. The cardinall demanded of them their *commission* that gaue them such *authoritie ;* who answered againe, that they were sufficient commissioners, and had authoritie to doo no lesse by *the kings* *mouth*. Notwithstanding, he would in no wise agree in that behalfe, without further knowledge of their authoritie, saieng: that the great seale was deliuered him by the kings person, to *inioy* the ministration thereof, with the roome of the chancellor for the terme of his *life*, whereof for his suertie he had the kings *letters patents*. . . .

The dukes were faine to depart againe without their purpose, and rode to Windsore to the king, and made report accordinglie; but the next daie they returned againe, bringing with them the kings letters. Then the cardinall deliuered vnto them the great seale, and was content to depart simplie, taking with him nothing but onelie certeine prouision for his house: and after long talke betweene him and the dukes, they departed with the great seale of England, and brought the same to the king.

The Charges against Wolsey

[*H*.iii.912] [There] was brought downe to the commons the booke of articles, which the lords had put to the king against the cardinall; the chiefe whereof were these:

1 *First, that* he *without the kings assent* had procured *to be a legat,* by reason whereof he tooke awaie the right *of all bishops* and spirituall persons.

2 Item, *in all* writings which he wrote *to Rome, or* anie other *foreign prince,* he wrote *Ego & rex meus,* I and my king: as who would saie that *the king* were his *seruant.* . . .

4 Item, he *without the kings* assent carried *the* kings *great seale* with him *into Flanders, when* he was sent *ambassador to the emperour.*

5 *Item,* he, without the kings assent, *sent a commission to* sir *Gregorie de Cassado,* knight, *to conclude a league betweene* the king *&* the duke of *Ferrar, without the kings* knowledge. . . .

7 Item, *that* he *caused* the cardinals *hat to be* put *on the kings coine.* . . .

9 Item, *that* he had *sent innumerable substance to Rome,* for the obteining of his *dignities; to the* great impouerishment *of the* realme.

These articles, with *manie more*, read in the common house, and signed with the cardinals hand, was confessed by him.

[*H*. iii. 909] The king (being informed that *all those things*, that the cardinall had *doone by* his *power legatine within this* realme, were *in the* case *of* the *premunire* and *prouision*) caused his atturneie Christopher Hales to sue out *a writ* of premunire *against* him; in the which he licenced him to make his atturneie. . . .

In the kings bench, his matter for the premunire, being callen vpon, two atturneis, which he had authorised by his warrant signed with his owne hand, confessed the action; and so had iudgement *to forfeit all* his *lands, tenements, goods,* and *cattels, and to be out of the kings protection.*

[*H*. iii. 910]. *Sir Thomas Moore* [was] made *lord chancellor.*

THE MARRIAGE OF ANNE BOLEYN

[*H*. iii. 929] [Henry] staied at Calis for a conuenient wind till tuesdaie the twelfth of Nouember at midnight, and then taking his ship, landed at Douer the next daie about fiue of the clocke in the morning. And herewith vpon his returne, he married priuilie the ladie Anne Bullongne the same daie, being the fourteenth daie of Nouember, and the feast daie of saint Erkenwald; which marriage was kept so secret, that verie few knew it till Easter next insuing, when it was perceiued that she was with child.

[*H*. iii. 929] Queene *Katharine* should *no more be called queene, but princesse Dowager,* as the *widow* of *prince Arthur.*

[*H*. iii. 913] [Wolsey's] seruants departed from him to the kings seruice, and in especiall Thomas Crumwell, one of his chiefe counsell, and chiefe dooer for him in the suppression of abbeies.

WOLSEY'S REGRET

[*H*. iii. 917] " I see the matter how it is framed; but if *I had serued God* as diligentlie as *I* haue doone the *king,*

he would not haue giuen *me* ouer *in* my greie haires :
but it is the iust reward that I must receiue for the
diligent paines and studie that I haue had to doo him
seruice ; not regarding my seruice to God, but onelie to
satisfie his pleasure."

The Coronation of Anne Boleyn

[*H*. iii. 930] In the beginning of Maie, the   [IV. i.]
king caused open proclamations to be made, that all
men *that claimed* to doo anie seruice, or execute anie
office at the solemne feast *of the coronation* by the waie
of tenure, grant, or prescription, should put their grant
three weekes after Easter in the Starrechamber before
Charles *duke of Suffolke*, for that time *high steward* of
England, and the lord chancellor, and other commissioners.
The duke of Norffolke claimed *to be erle marshall*, and
to exercise his office at that feast.

[*H*. iii. 929–930]   This matter was opened with all the
circumstances to the ladie *Katharine Dowager* (for so
was she then called), the which persisted still in hir former
opinion, and would reuoke by no meanes hir appeale to
the court of Rome.   Wherevpon *the archbishop of Canturburie, accompanied with* the bishops of London, Winchester,
Bath, Lincolne, and diuers other *learned* men in great
number, rode to *Dunstable*, which is *six miles from Ampthill,
where the princesse* Dowager *laie ;* and there *by* one Doctor
Lee *she was cited* to appeare before the said archbishop
in cause of matrimonie in the said towne of Dunstable,
and at the daie of appearance she *appeared not*, but made
default ; and so she was called peremptorie euerie daie
fifteene daies togither, *and*, at the last, *for* lacke of
appearance, by the assent of all the *learned men* there
present, *she was diuorsed* from the king, *and the mariage*
declared to be void and *of none effect*.

[*H*. iii. 933]   First went gentlemen, then esquiers, then
knights, then the aldermen of the citie in their cloks of
scarlet, after them the *iudges* in their mantels of scarlet
and coiffes.   Then followed the knights of the bath being
no lords, euerie man hauing a white lace on his left sleeue ;
then followed barons and vicounts in their parlement

robes of scarlet. After them came earls, marquesses, and
dukes in their robes of estate of crimsin veluet furred
with ermine, poudered according to their degrees. After
them came the *lord chancellor* in a robe of scarlet open
before, bordered with lettise ; after him came the kings
chapell and the moonks solemnelie *singing* with procession,
then came abbats and bishops mitered, then sargeants and
officers of armes ; then after them went the *maior of
London* with his *mace,* and *garter in his cote of armes ;* then
went the *marquesse Dorset* in a robe of estate, which bare
the *sceptre of gold ;* and *the earle of* Arundell, which bare
the rod of iuorie *with the doue ;* both togither.

Then went alone the earle of Oxford, high chamberleine
of England, which bare the crowne ; after him went the
duke of Suffolke in his robe of estate also, for that daie
being *high steward* of England, hauing *a long white* rod in
his hand ; and *the* lord William Howard *with the rod of*
the *marshalship ;* and euerie knight of the garter had
on his collar of the order. Then proceeded foorth *the
queene in* a circot and *robe* of purple veluet furred with
ermine, *in hir here,* coiffe, and circlet as she had the
saturdaie ; and ouer hir was *borne* the *canopie by foure of
the* fiue *ports,* all crimsin with points of blue and red
hanging on their sleeues ; and *the bishops of London and
Winchester* bare vp the laps of the queenes robe. *The
queenes traine,* which was verie long, was borne by *the old
duches of Norffolke ;* after hir folowed *ladies* being lords
wiues. . . .

When she was thus *brought to* the high *place* made *in the*
middest of the church, betweene the *queere* and the high
altar, she was set *in a rich chaire.* And after that she
had *rest*ed *a while,* she descended downe *to the* high *altar,*
and there prostrate hir selfe while *the archbishop of Canturburie* said certeine collects : *then* she *rose,* and the bishop
annointed hir on the head and on the brest, and then she
was led vp againe ; where, after diuerse orisons, said, the
archbishop set the *crowne* of saint *Edward* on hir head,
and then deliuered hir the scepter of gold in hir right
hand, and *the rod* of iuorie with the doue in the left hand ;
and then all *the queere soong Te Deum,* &c. . . .

When the queene had a little reposed hir, the companie

returned in *the same* order that they set foorth ; and the
queene went crowned, and so did the ladies aforesaid.
. . . Now when she was out of the sanctuarie and appeered
within the palace, the trumpets plaied maruellouslie
freshlie ; then she was brought to Westminster hall, & so
to hir withdrawing chamber.

HENRY'S PALACE

[*H*. iii. 923] [Henry] came to his manour of Westminster, which before was called Yorke place : for after
that the cardinall was attainted in the premunire, & was
gone northward, he made a feoffement of the same place
to the king, and the chapiter of the cathedrall church of
Yorke by their writing confirmed the same feoffement ;
& then the king changed the name and called it the kings
manor of Westminster, and *no more Yorke place.*

THE DEATH OF KATHARINE

[*H*. iii. 939] The . . . princesse Dowager lieng at [IV. ii.]
Kimbalton, fell into hir last *sick*nesse, whereof the king
being aduertised, appointed *the* emperors *ambassador*
that was legier here with him, *named* Eustachius *Caputius,*
to go to *visit* hir, and to doo *his commendations* to hir,
and will hir to be of *good comfort.* The ambassador with
all diligence did his duetie therein, comforting hir the
best he might; but she, within six daies after, perceiuing
hir selfe to wax verie weake and feeble, and to feele death
approching at hand, caused one of hir gentlewomen to
write a *letter* to the king, *commending* to *him* hir *daughter*
and his, *beseeching him to* stand good father vnto hir:
and further desired him to *haue some* consideration of
hir gentle*women that* had serued hir, and to see them
bestowed in marriage. Further, that it would please him
to appoint that hir seruants might haue their due wages,
and a yeeres wages beside. This in effect was all that
she requested, and so immediatlie herevpon she departed
this life the seuenth of Ianuarie at Kimbalton aforesaid,
and was buried at Peterborow.

THE DEATH OF WOLSEY

[*H*. iii. 917]   [Wolsey went] to Leicester abbeie, and by
the waie waxed so *sicke* that *he* was almost fallen from *his
mule ;* so that it was night before *he came to* the abbeie of
Leicester, where at his comming in at the gates, *the abbat
with all his conuent* met him with diuerse torches light ;
whom they *honorablie receiued* and welcomed.

To whom the cardinall said : " *Father abbat*, I am *come*
hither *to lay* my *bones among* you " ; riding so still vntil
he came to the staires of the chamber, where he allighted
from his mule, and master Kingston led him vp the
staires, and as soone as he was in his chamber he *went to
bed*.   This was on the saturday at night ; and then
increased he sicker and sicker, vntill mondaie, that all
men thought he would haue died : so on tuesdaie, saint
Andrewes euen, master Kingston came to him and bad
him good morrow, (for it was about six of the clocke,)
and asked him how he did ? . . .

& incontinent the clocke stroke *eight*, and then he gaue
vp the ghost, and departed this present life : which
caused some to call to remembrance how he said the daie
before, that at eight of the clocke they should loose their
master.

THE CHARACTER OF WOLSEY

[*H*. iii. 922]   This cardinall . . . *was of a* great *stomach*,
for he compted *himselfe* equall *with princes*, & *by* craftie
suggestion gat into his hands innumerable treasure : he
forced little on *simonie*, and *was* not *pittifull*, and stood
affectionate in *his owne opinion : in* open *presence he
would* lie and *saie vntruth, and* was *double both in* speach
and meaning : he would promise much & performe little :
he was vicious *of his bodie, & gaue the clergie euill
example*.

[*H*. iii. 917]   *This cardinall* (as Edmund Campian in
his historie of Ireland describeth him) *was* a man *vndoubtedly* borne *to honor :* I thinke (saith he) some princes
bastard, no butchers sonne ; *exceeding wise ; faire spoken ;*
high minded ; full of reuenge ; vitious of his bodie ;
loftie to his enimies, were they neuer so big ; *to those*

that accepted and *sought* his freendship woonderfull courteous ; *a ripe* schooleman ; thrall to affections ; brought a bed with flatterie ; insatiable to *get,* and more *princelie in bestowing,* as appeareth by his two colleges at *Ipswich and Oxenford,* the one ouerthrowne with his fall, *the other vnfinished,* and *yet,* as it lieth for an house of students, considering all the appurtenances, incomparable thorough *Christendome ;* whereof Henrie the eight is now called founder, bicause he let it stand. He held and inioied at once the bishopriks of Yorke, Duresme, & Winchester, the dignities of lord cardinall, legat, & chancellor, the abbeie of saint Albons, diuerse priories, sundrie fat benefices " In commendam : " a great preferrer of his seruants, an aduancer of learning, stout in euerie quarell, neuer happie till this *his ouerthrow.* Wherein he shewed such moderation, and ended so perfectlie, that the houre of his death did him more honor than all the pompe of his life passed.

ANNE BOLEYN'S DAUGHTER

[*H.* iii. 934]   The seuenth of September, being sundaie, betweene three & foure of the clocke in the afternoone, *the queene* was *deliuered of a* faire yoong ladie.

[*H.* iii. 934–935]   [The christening] was appointed on the wednesdaie next following ; and was accordinglie accomplished on the same daie, with all such solemne ceremonies as were thought conuenient. The godfather at the font was the lord archbishop of Canturburie, the godmothers, the old dutches of Norffolke, & the old marchionesse Dorset, widowes ; and at the confirmation the ladie marchionesse of Excester was godmother : the child was named Elizabeth.

Upon the daie of the christening, the maior, sir Stephan Peacocke, in a gowne of crimsin veluet, with his collar of S S, and all the aldermen in scarlet, with collars and chaines, and all the councell of the citie with them, tooke their barge after dinner, at one of the clocke, and the citizens had another barge ; and so rowed to Greenwich, where were manie lords, knights, and gentlemen assembled. . . .

The old dutches of Norffolke bare the child in a mantell of purple veluet, with a long traine furred with ermine. The duke of Norffolke with his marshall rod went on the right hand of the said dutches, and the duke of Suffolke on the left hand, and before them went the officers of armes. The countesse of Kent bare the long traine of the childs mantell ; and betweene the countesse of Kent and the child went the earle of Wilshire on the right hand, and the earle of Darbie on the left hand, supporting the said traine ; in the middest, ouer the said child, was borne a canopie by the lord Rochford, the lord Huse, the lord William Howard, and by the lord Thomas Howard the elder ; after the child followed manie ladies and gentlewomen. . . .

When the ceremonies and christening were ended, Garter, cheefe king of armes, cried alowd, " God of his infinite *goodnesse send prosperous life & long to the high and mightie princesse of England, Elizabeth :* " & then the trumpets blew. Then the archbishop of Canturburie gaue to the princesse a standing cup of gold : the dutches of Norffolke gaue to hir a standing cup of gold, fretted with pearle : the marchionesse of Dorset gaue three gilt bolles, pounced, with a couer : and the marchionesse of Excester gaue three standing bolles, grauen, all gilt, with a couer. . . . Then they set forwards, the trumpets going before in the same order towards the kings palace, as they did when they came thitherwards, sauing that the gifts that the godfather and the godmothers gaue were borne before the child by foure persons, that is to saie : First, sir Iohn Dudelie bare the gift of the ladie of Excester, the lord Thomas Howard the yoonger bare the gift of the ladie of Dorset, the lord Fitzwater bare the gift of the ladie of Norffolke, and the earle of Worcester bare the gift of the archbishop of Canturburie. . . .

In this order they brought the princesse to the Q. chamber, & tarried there a while with the maior & his brethren the aldermen, and at the last the dukes of Norffolke and Suffolke came out from the K., thanking them hartilie ; who commanded them to giue thanks in his name : which being doone, with other courtesies, they departed, & so went to their barges.

MACBETH

[The story of Macbeth in Holinshed is combined, in Shakespeare's drama, with passages relating to the reign of Duff. It is needless to point out that Shakespeare has dealt freely with the original story and that the story itself has but little basis in fact.]

[*H. ii. H. S.* 168–169] After Malcolme succeeded his nephue Duncane the sonne of his daughter Beatrice : for Malcome had two daughters, the one which was this Beatrice, being giuen in mariage vnto one Abbanath Crinen, a man of great nobilitie, and thane of the Iles and west parts of Scotland, bare of that mariage the foresaid Duncane ; the other called Doada, was maried vnto *Sinell the thane of Glammis,* by whom she had issue one Makbeth a valiant gentleman, and one that if he had not beene somewhat cruell of nature, might haue beene thought most woorthie the gouernement of a realme. On the other part, Duncane was so soft and gentle of nature, that the people wished the inclinations and maners of these two cousins to haue beene so tempered and inter-changeablie bestowed betwixt them, that where the one had too much of clemencie, and the other of crueltie, the meane vertue betwixt these two extremities might haue reigned by indifferent partition in them both, so should Duncane haue proued a woorthie king, and Makbeth an excellent capteine. The beginning of Duncans reigne was verie quiet and peaceable, without anie notable trouble ; but after it was perceiued how negligent he was in punish-ing offendors, manie misruled persons tooke occasion thereof to trouble the peace and quiet state of the common-wealth, by seditious commotions which first had their beginnings in this wise.

Banquho the thane of Lochquhaber, of whom the house of the Stewards is descended, the which by order of linage hath now for a long time inioied the crowne of Scotland,

euen till these our daies. . . . gathered the finances due
to the king. . . .

Then doubting not but for such contemptuous demeanor
against the kings regall authoritie, they should be inuaded
with all the power the king could make, Makdowald one of
great estimation among them, making first a confederacie
with his neerest friends and kinsmen, tooke vpon him to
be chiefe capteine of all such rebels as would stand
against the king, in maintenance of their grieuous offenses
latelie committed against him. . . . He vsed also such
subtill persuasions and forged allurements, that in a small
time he had gotten togither a mightie power of men :
for out of the westerne Iles there came vnto him a great
multitude of people. . . . and out of Ireland . . . no
small number of *Kernes and Galloglasses*. . . .

At length Makbeth speaking much against the kings
softnesse, and ouermuch slacknesse in punishing offendors,
. . . he promised notwithstanding, if the charge were
committed vnto him and vnto Banquho, so to order the
matter, that the rebels should be shortly vanquished &
quite put downe, and that not so much as one of them
should be found to make resistance within the countrie.

And euen so it came to passe : for being sent foorth
with a new power, at his entring into Lochquhaber, the
fame of his comming put the enimies in such feare, that a
great number of them stale secretlie awaie from their
capteine Makdowald, who neuerthelesse inforced thereto,
gaue battell vnto Makbeth, with the residue which remained
with him : but being ouercome, and fleeing for refuge into
a castell (within the which his wife & children were inclosed)
at length when he saw how he could neither defend the
hold anie longer against his enimies, nor yet vpon surrender
be suffered to depart with life saued, hee first slue his wife
and children, and lastlie himselfe, least if he had yeelded
simplie, he should haue beene executed in most cruell
wise for an example to other. Makbeth entring into the
castell by the gates, as then set open, found the carcasse
of Makdowald lieng dead there amongst the residue of
the slaine bodies, which when he beheld, remitting no
peece of his cruell nature with that pitifull sight, he caused
the head to be cut off, and set vpon a poles end, and so

sent it as present to the king, who as then laie at Bertha.
The headlesse trunke he commanded to bee hoong vp
vpon an high paire of gallows. . . . Thus was iustice and
law restored againe to the old accustomed course, by the
diligent means of Makbeth. Immediatlie wherevpon
woord came that Sueno king of Norway was arriued in
Fife with a puissant armie, to sudue the whole realme
of Scotland.

[*H*. ii. *H. S.* 170] Makbeth and Banquho were sent with
the kings authoritie, who hauing with them a conuenient
power, incountred the enimies, slue part of them, and
chased the other to their ships. They that escaped and
got once to their ships, obteined of Makbeth for a great
summe of gold, that such of their friends as were slaine
at this last bickering, might be buried in saint Colmes Inch.

THE WITCHES

[*H*. ii .*H. S.* 149] But yet could [the King] not [I. iii.]
sleepe in the night time by anie prouocations that could be
deuised, but still fell into exceeding sweats, which by no
means might be restreined. . . . But about that present
time there was a murmuring amongst the people, how the
king was vexed with no naturall sicknesse, but by sorcerie
and magicall art, practised by a sort of witches dwelling
in a towne of Murrey land, called Fores. . . .

[*H*. ii. *H. S.* 149] Wherevpon learning by hir confession in what house in the towne it was where they wrought
their mischiefous mysterie, he sent foorth souldiers about
the middest of the night, who breaking into the house,
found one of the witches rosting vpon a wooden broch an
image of wax at the fier, resembling in each feature the
kings person, made and deuised (as is to be thought) by
craft and art of the diuell : an other to them sat reciting
certeine words of inchantment, and still basted the image
with a certeine liquor verie busilie.

The souldiers finding them occupied in this wise, tooke
them togither with the image, and led them into the castell,
where being streictlie examined for what purpose they went
about such manner of inchantment, they answered, to
the end to make away the king, for as the image did

waste afore the fire, so did the bodie of the king breake
foorth in sweat. And as for the words of the inchantment, they serued to keepe him still waking from sleepe,
so that as the wax euer melted, so did the kings flesh :
by the which meanes it should haue come to passe, that
when the wax was once cleane consumed, the death of the
king should immediatlie follow.

[*H.* ii. *H.* S. 170–171]   Shortlie after happened a strange
and vncouth woonder, which afterward was the cause
of much trouble in the realme of Scotland, as ye shall
after heare. It fortuned as Makbeth and Banquho
iournied towards Fores, where the king then laie, they went
sporting by the waie togither without other companie,
saue onelie themselues, passing thorough the woods and
fields, when suddenlie in the middest of a laund, there met
them three women in strange and wild apparell, resembling
creatures of elder world, whome when they attentiuelie
beheld, woondering much at the sight, the first of them
spake and said: "*All haile, Makbeth, thane of Glammis !*"
(for he had latelie entered into that dignitie and office
by the death of his father Sinell). The second of them
said: "*Haile, Makbeth, thane of Cawder !*" But the
third said: "*All haile, Makbeth,* that *heereafter shalt
be king* of Scotland !"

Then Banquho : " What manner of women " (saith he)
" are you, that seeme so little fauourable vnto me, whereas
to my fellow heere, besides high offices, ye assigne also the
kingdome, appointing foorth nothing for me at all ? "
" Yes " (saith the first of them), " we promise greater
benefits vnto thee, than vnto him, for he shall reigne in
deed, but with an vnluckie end : neither shall he leaue
anie issue behind him to succeed in his place, where
contrarilie thou in deed shalt not reigne at all, but of thee
those shall be borne which shall gouerne the Scotish
kingdome by long order of continuall descent." Herewith
the foresaid women vanished immediatlie out of their
sight. This was reputed at the first but some vaine
fantasticall illusion by Makbeth and Banquho, insomuch
that Banquho would call Mackbeth in iest, king of
Scotland ; and Mackbeth againe would call him in sport
likewise, the father of manie kings. But afterwards the

common opinion was, that these women were either the
weird sisters, that is (as ye would say) the goddesses of
destinie, or else some nymphs or feiries, indued with
knowledge of prophesie by their necromanticall science,
bicause euerie thing came to passe as they had spoken.
For shortlie after, the thane of Cawder being condemned
at Fores of treason against the king committed ; his lands,
liuings, and offices were giuen of the kings liberalitie to
Mackbeth.

The same night after, at supper, Banquho iested with
him and said : " Now Mackbeth thou hast obteined those
things which the two former sisters prophesied, there
remaineth onelie for thee to purchase that which the
third said should come to passe." Wherevpon Mackbeth
reuoluing the thing in his mind, began euen then to deuise
how he might atteine to the kingdome : but yet he thought
with himselfe that he must tarie a time, which should
aduance him thereto (by the diuine prouidence) as it had
come to passe in his former preferment. But shortlie
after it chanced that king Duncane, hauing two sonnes
by his wife which was the daughter of Siward earle of
Northumberland, he made the elder of them, called
Malcolme, prince of Cumberland, as it were thereby to
appoint him his successor in the kingdome, immediatlie
after his deceasse. Mackbeth sore troubled herewith, for
that he saw by this means his hope sore hindered (where,
by the old lawes of the realme, the ordinance was, that if
he that should succeed were not of able age to take the
charge vpon himselfe, he that was next of blood vnto him
should be admitted) he began to take counsell how he
might vsurpe the kingdome by force, hauing a iust quarrell
so to doo (as he tooke the matter) for that Duncane did
what in him lay to defraud him of all maner of title and
claime, which he might in time to come, pretend vnto the
crowne.

The woords of the three weird sisters also (of whom before ye haue heard) greatlie incouraged him herevnto, but
speciallie his wife lay sore vpon him to attempt the thing,
as she that was verie ambitious, burning in vnquenchable
desire to beare the name of a queene. At length therefore,
communicating his purposed intent with his trustie

friends, amongst whome Banquho was the chiefest, vpon
confidence of their promised aid, he slue the king at
Enuerns, or (as some say) at Botgosuane, in the sixt yeare
of his reigne. Then hauing a companie about him of such
as he had made priuie to his enterprise, he caused himselfe
to be proclamed king, and foorthwith went vnto Scone,
where (by common consent) he receiued the inuesture of
the kingdome according to the accustomed maner. The
bodie of Duncane was first conueied vnto Elgine, & there
buried in kinglie wise ; but afterwards it was remoued and
conueied vnto Colmekill, and there laid in a sepulture
amongst his predecessors, in the yeare after the birth of
our Sauiour, 1046.

The Murder

[*H. ii. H. S.* 150–151] [Donwald] conceiued such an
inward malice towards the king (though he shewed it not
outwardlie at the first) that the same continued still
boiling in his stomach, and ceased not, till through setting
on of his wife, and in reuenge of such vnthankefulnesse,
hee found meanes to murther the king within the foresaid
castell of Fores where he vsed to soiourne. For the
king being in that countrie, was accustomed to lie most
commonlie within the same castell, hauing a speciall
trust in Donwald, as a man whom he neuer suspected.

But Donwald, not forgetting the reproch which his
linage had susteined by the execution of those his kinsmen,
whome the king for a spectacle to the people had caused
to be hanged, could not but shew manifest tokens of great
griefe at home amongst his familie : which his wife
perceiuing, ceassed not to trauell with him, till she vnderstood what the cause was of his displeasure. Which at
length when she had learned by his owne relation, she
as one that bare no lesse malice in hir heart towards the
king, for the like cause on hir behalfe, than hir husband
did for his friends, counselled him (sith the king oftentimes vsed to lodge in his house without anie gard about
him, other than the garrison of the castell, which was
wholie at his commandement) to make him awaie, and
shewed him the meanes wherby he might soonest accomplish it.

Donwald thus being the more kindled in wrath by the words of his wife, determined to follow hir aduise in the execution of so heinous an act. Whervpon deuising with himselfe for a while, which way hee might best accomplish his curssed intent, at length gat opportunitie, and sped his purpose as followeth. It chanced that the king vpon the daie before he purposed to depart foorth of the castell, was long in his oratorie at his praiers, and there continued till it was late in the night. At the last, comming foorth, he called such afore him as had faith-fullie serued him in pursute and apprehension of the rebels, and giuing them heartie thanks, he bestowed sundrie honorable gifts amongst them, of the which number Donwald was one, as he that had beene euer accounted a most faithfull seruant to the king.

At length, hauing talked with them a long time, he got him into his priuie chamber, onelie with two of his chamberlains, who hauing brought him to bed, came foorth againe, and then fell to bancketting with Donwald and his wife, who had prepared diuerse delicate dishes, and sundrie sorts of drinks for their reare supper or collation, wherat they sate vp so long, till they had charged their stomachs with such full gorges, that their heads were no sooner got to the pillow, but asleepe they were so fast, that a man might haue remooued the chamber ouer them, sooner than to haue awaked them out of their droonken sleepe.

Then Donwald, though he abhorred the act greatlie in heart, yet through instigation of his wife hee called foure of his seruants vnto him (whome he had made priuie to his wicked intent before, and framed to his purpose with large gifts) and now declaring vnto them, after what sort they should worke the feat, they gladlie obeied his instructions, & speedilie going about the murther, they enter the chamber (in which the king laie) a little before cocks crow, where they secretlie cut his throte as he lay sleeping, without anie buskling at all. . . .

Donwald, about the time that the murther was in dooing, got him amongst them that kept the watch, and so continued in companie with them all the residue of the night. But in the morning when the noise was raised

in the kings chamber how the king was slaine, his bodie
conueied awaie, and the bed all beraied with bloud ; he
with the watch ran thither, as though he had knowne
nothing of the matter, and breaking into the chamber, and
finding cakes of bloud in the bed, and on the floore about
the sides of it, he foorthwith slue the chamberleins, as
guiltie of that heinous murther, and then like a mad man
running to and fro, he ransacked euerie corner within the
castell, as though it had beene to haue seene if he might
haue found either the bodie, or anie of the murtherers
hid in anie priuie place : but at length comming to the
posterne gate, and finding it open, he burdened the
chamberleins, whome he had slaine, with all the fault,
they hauing the keies of the gates committed to their
keeping all the night, and therefore it could not be otherwise (said he) but that they were of counsell in committing
of that most detestable murther.

Finallie, such was his ouer earnest diligence in the
seuere inquisition and triall of the offendors heerein, that
some of the lords began to mislike the matter, and to smell
foorth shrewd tokens, that he should not be altogither
cleare himselfe. But for so much as they were in that
countrie, where he had the whole rule, what by reason
of his friends and authoritie togither, they doubted to
vtter what they thought, till time and place should better
serue therevnto, and heere vpon got them awaie euerie
man to his home.

[*H. ii. H. S.* 158] Thus might he seeme happie to all
man, hauing the loue both of his lords and commons ;
but yet to himselfe he seemed most vnhappie, as he that
could not but still liue in continuall feare, least his wicked
practise concerning the death of Malcolme Duffe should
come to light and knowledge of the world. For so
commeth it to passe, that such as are pricked in conscience
for anie secret offense committed, haue euer an vnquiet
mind. And (as the fame goeth) it chanced that a voice
was heard as he was in bed in the night time to take his
rest, vttering vnto him these or the like woords in effect :
" Thinke not Kenneth that the wicked slaughter of
Malcolme Duffe by thee contriued, is kept secret from the
knowledge of the eternall God : thou art he that didst

conspire the innocents death, enterprising by traitorous
meanes to doo that to thy neighbour, which thou wouldest
haue reuenged by cruell punishment in anie of thy
subiects, if it had beene offered to thy selfe. It shall
therefore come to passe, that both thou thy selfe, and thy
issue, through the iust vengeance of almightie God, shall
suffer woorthie punishment, to the infamie of thy house
and familie for euermore. For euen at this present are
there in hand secret practises to dispatch both thee and
thy issue out of the waie, that other maie inioy this
kingdome which thou doost indeuour to assure vnto
thine issue."

The king with this voice being striken into great dread
and terror, passed that night without anie sleepe comming
in his eies.

[*H*. ii. *H*. *S*. 171]   Malcolme Commore and Donald
Bane the sons of king Duncane, for feare of their liues
(which they might well know that Mackbeth would
seeke to bring to end for his more sure confirmation
in the estate) fled into Cumberland, where Malcolme
remained, till time that saint Edward the sonne of Ethelred
recouered the dominion of England from the Danish
power, the which Edward receiued Malcolme by way of
most friendlie enterteinment : but Donald passed ouer
in*to Ireland,* where he was tenderlie cherished by the king
of that land.

[*H*. ii. *H*. *S*. 151–152]   For the space of six [II. iv.]
moneths togither, after this heinous murther thus committed, there appeered no sunne by day, nor moone by
night in anie part of the realme, but still was the skie
couered with continuall clouds, and sometimes such outragious winds arose, with lightenings and tempests, that
the people were in great feare of present destruction. . . .

Monstrous sights also that were seene within the
Scotish kingdome that yeere were these : *horsses* in
Louthian, being of singular *beautie and swiftn*esse, did
eate their owne flesh, and would in no wise taste anie
other meate. . . . There was a sparhawke also strangled
by an owle. Neither was it anie lesse woonder that the
sunne, as before is said, was continuallie couered with
clouds for six moneths space. But all men vnderstood

that the abhominable murther of king Duffe was the
cause heereof.

[*H. ii. H. S.* 172] The pricke of conscience [II. iii.]
(as it chanceth euer in tyrants, and such as atteine to
anie estate by vnrighteous means) caused him euer to
feare, least he should be serued to the same cup, as he
had ministred to his predecessor. The woords also of
the three weird sisters would not out of his mind, which
as they promised him the kingdome, so likewise did they
promise it at the same time vnto the posteritie of Banquho.
He willed therefore the same Banquho, with his sonne
named Fleance, to come to a supper that he had prepared
for them; which was in deed, as he had deuised, present
death at the hands of certeine murderers, whom he hired
to execute that deed; appointing them to meete with the
same Banquho and his sonne without the palace, as they
returned to their lodgings, and there to slea them, so that
he would not haue his house slandered, but that in time
to come he might cleare himselfe, if anie thing were laid
to his charge vpon anie suspicion that might arise.

It chanced yet, by the benefit of the darke night, that,
though the father were slaine, the sonne yet, by the helpe
of almightie God reseruing him to better fortune, escaped
that danger; and afterwards hauing some inkeling (by
the admonition of some friends which he had in the
court) how his life was sought no lesse than his fathers,
who was slaine not by chancemedlie (as by the handling
of the matter Makbeth woould haue had it to appeare)
but euen vpon a prepensed deuise: wherevpon to auoid
further perill he fled into Wales.

[*H. ii. H. S.* 174] But to returne vnto Makbeth, in
continuing the historie, and to begin where I left, ye shall
vnderstand that, after the contriued slaughter of Banquho,
nothing prospered with the foresaid Makbeth: for in
maner euerie man began to doubt his owne life, and durst
vnneth appeare in the kings presence; and euen as there
were manie that stood in feare of him, so likewise stood
he in feare of manie, in such sort that he began to make
those awaie by one surmized cauillation or other, whome
he thought most able to worke him anie displeasure.

At length he found such sweetnesse by putting his

nobles thus to death, that his earnest thirst after bloud
in this behalfe might in no wise be satisfied : for ye must
consider he wan double profit (as hee thought) hereby :
for first they were rid out of the way whome he feared,
and then againe his coffers were inriched by their goods
which were forfeited to his vse, whereby he might better
mainteine a gard of armed men about him to defend his
person from iniurie of them whom he had in anie suspicion.
Further, to the end he might the more cruellie oppresse
his subiects with all tyrantlike wrongs, he builded a
strong castell on the top of an hie hill called Dunsinane,
situate in Gowrie, ten miles from Perth, on such a proud
height, that, standing there aloft, a man might behold
well neere all the countries of Angus, Fife, Stermond, and
Ernedale, as it were lieng vnderneath him. This castell,
then, being founded on the top of that high hill, put the
realme to great charges before it was finished, for all the
stuffe necessarie to the building could not be brought vp
without much toile and businesse. But Makbeth, being
once determined to haue the worke go forward, caused
the thanes of each shire within the realme, to come and
helpe towards that building, each man his course about.

At the last, when the turne fell vnto Makduffe, thane of
Fife, to build his part, he sent workemen with all needfull
prouision, and commanded them to shew such diligence
in euerie behalfe, that no occasion might bee given for the
king to find fault with him, in that he came not himselfe
as other had doone, which he refused to doo, for doubt
least the king, bearing him (as he partlie vnderstood) no
great good will, would laie violent hands vpon him, as
he had doone vpon diuerse other. Shortlie after, Makbeth
comming to behold how the worke went forward, and
bicause he found not Makduffe there, he was sore offended,
and said : " I perceiue this man will neuer obeie my
commandements, till he be ridden with a snaffle ; but I
shall prouide well inough for him."

Neither could he afterwards abide to looke [IV. i.]
vpon the said Makduffe, either for that he thought
his puissance ouer great ; either else for that he had
learned of certeine wizzards, in whose words he put great
confidence, (for that the prophesie had happened so right,

which the three faries or weird sisters had declared
vnto him,) how that he ought to take heed of Makduffe,
who in time to come should seeke to destroie him.

And suerlie herevpon had he put Makduffe to death,
but that a certeine witch, whome hee had in great trust,
had told that he should neuer be slaine with man *borne
of* anie *woman,* nor *vanquished till* the *wood* of *Bernane*
came *to* the castell of *Dunsinane.* By this prophesie
Makbeth put all feare out of his heart, supposing he might
doo what he would, without anie feare to be punished
for the same, for by the one prophesie he beleeued it was
vnpossible for anie man to vanquish him, and by the
other vnpossible to slea him. This vaine hope caused
him to doo manie outragious things, to the greeuous
oppression of his subiects. At length Makduffe, to auoid
perill of life, purposed with himselfe to passe into England,
to procure Malcolme Cammore to claime the crowne of
Scotland. But this was not so secretlie deuised by
Makduffe, but that Makbeth had knowledge giuen him
thereof : for kings (as is said) haue sharpe sight like vnto
Lynx, and long ears like vnto Midas. For Makbeth had,
in euerie noble mans house, one slie fellow or other in
fee with him, to reueale all that was said or doone within
the same, by which slight he oppressed the most part of
the nobles of his realme.

Immediatlie then, being aduertised where- [IV. ii.]
about Makduffe went, he came hastily with a great
power into Fife, and foorthwith besieged the castell
where Makduffe dwelled, trusting to haue found
him therein. They that kept the house, without anie
resistance opened the gates, and suffered him to enter,
mistrusting none euill. But neuerthelesse Makbeth most
cruellie caused the wife and children of Makduffe, with all
other whom he found in that castell, to be slaine. Also
he confiscated the goods of Makduffe, proclaimed him
traitor, and confined him out of all the parts of his realme ;
but Makduffe was alreadie escaped out of danger, and
gotten into England vnto Malcolme Cammore, to trie
what purchase hee might make by means of his support,
to reuenge the slaughter so cruellie executed on his wife,
his children, and other friends.

At his comming vnto Malcolme, he [IV. iii.] declared into what great miserie the estate of Scotland was brought, by the detestable cruelties exercised by the tyrant Makbeth, hauing committed manie horrible slaughters and murders, both as well of the nobles as commons; for the which he was hated right mortallie of all his liege people, desiring nothing more than to be deliuered of that intollerable and most heauie yoke of thraldome, which they susteined at such a caitifes hands.

Malcolme, hearing Makduffes woords, which he vttered in verie lamentable sort, for meere compassion and verie ruth that pearsed his sorowfull hart, bewailing the miserable state of his countrie, he fetched a deepe sigh; which Makduffe perceiuing, began to fall most earnestlie in hand with him, to enterprise the deliuering of the Scotish people out of the hands of so cruell and bloudie a tyrant, as Makbeth by too manie plaine experiments did shew himselfe to be: which was an easie matter for him to bring to passe, considering not onelie the good title he had, but also the earnest desire of the people to haue some occasion ministred, whereby they might be reuenged of those notable iniuries, which they dailie susteined by the outragious crueltie of Makbeths misgouernance. Though Malcolme was verie sorowfull for the oppression of his countriemen the Scots, in maner as Makduffe had declared; yet doubting whether he were come as one that ment vnfeinedlie as he spake, or else as sent from Makbeth to betraie him, he thought to haue some further triall, and therevpon, dissembling his mind at the first, he answered as followeth:

"I am trulie verie sorie for the miserie chanced to my countrie of Scotland, but though I haue neuer so great affection to relieue the same, yet, by reason of certeine incurable vices, which reigne in me, I am nothing meet thereto. First, such immoderate lust and voluptuous sensualitie (the abhominable founteine of all vices) followeth me, that, if I were made king of Scots, I should seeke to defloure your maids and matrones, in such wise that mine intemperancie should be more importable vnto you, than the bloudie tyrannie of Makbeth now is."

Heerevnto Makduffe answered : " This suerlie is a verie
euill fault, for manie noble princes and kings haue lost
both liues and kingdomes for the same ; neuerthelesse
there are women enow in Scotland, and therefore follow
my counsell. Make thy selfe king, and I shall conueie the
matter so wiselie, that thou shalt be so satisfied at thy
pleasure, in such secret wise that no man shall be aware
thereof."

Then said Malcolme, " I am also the most auaritious
creature on the earth, so that, if *I were king*, I should
seeke so manie waies to get lands and goods, that I would
slea the most part of all the nobles of Scotland by surmized
accusations, to the end I might inioy *their lands*, goods,
and possessions. . . . Therefore " saith Malcolme, " suffer
me to remaine where I am, least, if I atteine to the
regiment of your realme, mine vnquenchable *auarice* may
prooue such that ye would thinke the displeasures, which
now grieue you, should seeme easie in respect of the
vnmeasurable outrage, which might insue through my
comming amongst you."

Makduffe to this made answer, how it was a far woorse
fault than the other : " for *auarice* is the *root* of all
mischiefe, and for that crime the most part of our *kings*
haue beene *slain* and brought to their finall end. Yet
notwithstanding follow my counsell, and take vpon thee
the crowne. There is gold and riches inough in Scotland
to satisfie thy greedie desire." Then said Malcolme againe,
" I am furthermore inclined to dissimulation, telling of
leasings, and all other kinds of deceit, so that I naturallie
reioise in nothing so much, as to betraie & deceiue such
as put anie trust or confidence in my woords. Then sith
there is nothing that more becommeth a prince than
constancie, *veritie*, truth, and *iustice*, with the other
laudable fellowship of those faire and noble vertues which
are comprehended onelie in soothfastnesse, and that
lieng vtterlie ouerthroweth the same ; you see how vnable
I am to gouerne anie prouince or region : and therefore,
sith you haue remedies to cloke and hide all the rest of my
other vices, I praie you find shift to cloke this vice amongst
the residue."

Then said Makduffe : " This yet is the woorst of all, and

there I leaue thee, and therefore saie : Oh ye vnhappie and miserable Scotishmen, which are thus scourged with so manie and sundrie calamities, ech one aboue other ! Ye haue one curssed and wicked tyrant that now reigneth ouer you, without anie right or title, oppressing you with his most bloudie crueltie. This other, that hath the right to the crowne, is so replet with the inconstant behauiour and manifest vices of Englishmen, that he is nothing woorthie to inioy it ; for by his owne confession he is not onelie auaritious, and giuen to vnsatiable lust, but so false a traitor withal, that no trust is to be had vnto anie woord he speaketh. Adieu, Scotland, for now I account my selfe a banished man for euer, without comfort or consolation : " and with those woords the brackish teares trickled downe his cheekes verie abundantlie.

At the last, when he was readie to depart, Malcolme tooke him by the sleeue, and said : " Be of good comfort, Makduffe, for I haue none of these vices before remembred, but haue iested with thee in this manner, onelie to prooue thy mind ; for diuerse times heeretofore hath Makbeth sought by this manner of meanes to bring me into his hands, but the more slow I haue shewed my selfe to condescend to thy motion and request, the more diligence shall I vse in accomplishing the same." Incontinentlie heerevpon they imbraced ech other, and, promising to be faithfull the one to the other, they fell in consultation how they might prouide for all their businesse, to bring the same to good effect.

[H. ii. H. S. 175] Soone after, Makduffe, re- [V.] pairing to the borders of Scotland, addressed his letters with secret dispatch vnto the nobles of the realme, declaring how Malcolme was confederat with him, to come hastilie into Scotland to claime the crowne, and therefore he required them, sith he was right inheritor thereto, to assist him with their powers to recouer the same out of the hands of the wrongful vsurper.

In the meane time, Malcolme purchased such fauor at king Edwards hands, that old Siward earle of Northumberland was appointed with ten thousand men to go with him into Scotland, to support him in this enterprise, for recouerie of his right. After these newes were spread abroad in Scotland, the nobles drew into two seuerall factions, the one taking part with Makbeth, and the other with Malcolme. Herevpon insued oftentimes sundrie bickerings, & diuerse light skirmishes ; for those that were of Malcolmes side would not ieopard to ioine with their enimies in a pight field, till his comming out of England to their support. But after that Makbeth perceiued his enimies power to increase, by such aid as came to them foorth of England with his aduersarie Malcolme, he recoiled backe into Fife, there purposing to abide in campe fortified, at the castell of Dunsinane, and to fight with his enimies, if they ment to pursue him ; howbeit some of his friends aduised him, that it should be best for him, either to make some agreement with Malcolme, or else to flee with all speed into the Iles, and to take his treasure with him, to the end he might wage sundrie great princes of the realme to take his part, & reteine strangers, in whome he might better trust than in his owne subiects, which stale dailie from him ; but he had such confidence in his prophesies, that he beleeued he should neuer be vanquished, till Birnane wood were brought to Dunsinane ; nor yet to be slaine with anie man, that should be or was born of anie woman.

[*H. ii. H. S.* 176] Malcolme, following hastilie after Makbeth, came the night before the battell vnto Birnane wood ; and, when his armie had rested a while there to refresh them, he commanded *euerie* man to get *a bough* of some tree or other of that wood in his hand, as big as he might beare, and to march foorth therewith in such wise, that on the next morrow they might come closelie and without sight in this manner within view of his enimies. On the morrow when Makbeth beheld them comming in this sort, he first maruelled what the matter ment, but in the end remembred himselfe that the prophesie which he had heard long before that time, of the comming of Birnane wood to Dunsinane castell, was likelie to be now fulfilled. Neuerthelesse, he brought his men in order of battell, and exhorted them to doo valiantlie ; howbeit his enimies had scarselie cast from them their boughs, when Makbeth perceiuing their numbers, betooke him streict to flight ; whom Makduffe pursued with great hatred euen till he

came vnto Lunfannaine where Makbeth perceiuing that
Makduffe was hard at his backe, leapt beside his horsse,
saieng : "Thou traitor, what meaneth it that thou
shouldest thus in vaine follow me that am not appointed
to be slaine by anie creature that is borne of a woman ?
come on therefore, and receiue thy reward which thou hast
deserued for thy paines," and therwithall he lifted vp
his swoord, thinking to haue slaine him.

But Makduffe, quicklie auoiding from his horsse, yer he
came at him, answered (with his naked swoord in his hand)
saieng : "It is true, Makbeth, and now shall thine
insatiable crueltie haue an end, for I am euen he that thy
wizzards haue told thee of ; who was neuer borne of my
mother, but *ripped* out of her *wombe* : " therewithall he
stept vnto him, and slue him in the place. Then cutting
his head from his shoulders, he set it vpon a pole, and
brought it vnto Malcolme. This was the end of Makbeth,
after he had reigned 17 yeeres ouer the Scotishmen.

[*H. i. H. E.* 192] About the thirteenth yeare of king
Edward his reigne (as some write) or rather about the
nineteenth or twentieth yeare, as should appeare by the
Scotish writers, Siward the noble earle of Northumberland
with a great power of horssemen went into Scotland, and
in battell put to flight Mackbeth that had vsurped the
crowne of Scotland, and, that doone, placed Malcolme
surnamed Camoir, the sonne of Duncane, sometime king
of Scotland, in the gouernement of that realme, who
afterward slue the said Mackbeth, and then reigned in
quiet. . . . .

It is recorded also, that, in the foresaid battell, in which
earle Siward vanquished the Scots, one of Siwards sonnes
chanced to be slaine, whereof although the father had good
cause to be sorowfull, yet, when he heard that he died of
a wound which he had receiued in fighting stoutlie, in
the forepart of his bodie, and that with his face towards
the enimie, he greatlie reioised thereat, to heare that he
died so manfullie. But here is to be noted, that not
now, but a little before (as *Henrie Hunt* saith) that earle
Siward went into Scotland himselfe in person, he sent
his sonne with an armie to conquere the land, whose hap
was there to be slaine: and when his father heard the

newes, he demanded whether he receiued the wound
whereof he died, in the forepart of the bodie, or in the
hinder part : and when it was told him that he receiued it
in the forepart : " I reioise (saith he) euen with all my
heart, for *I would not wish* either to my sonne nor to my
selfe any other kind of *death*."

[*H*. ii. *H.S.* 176] Malcolme Cammore thus recouering
the relme (as ye haue heard) by support of king Edward,
in the 16 yeere of the same Edwards reigne, he was
crowned at Scone, the 25 day of Aprill, in the yeere of our
Lord 1057.   Immediatlie after his coronation he called a
parlement at Forfair, in the which he rewarded them with
lands and liuings that had assisted him against Makbeth,
aduancing them to fees and offices as he saw cause, &
commanded that speciallie those, that bare the surname
of anie offices or lands, should haue and inioy the same.
He created manie earles, lords, barons, and knights.
Manie of them, that before were thanes, were at this time
made earles, as Fife, Menteth. . . . Leuenox. . . .
Cathnes, Rosse, and Angus. These were the first earles
that haue beene heard of amongst the Scotishmen (as
their histories doo make mention.   Manie new surnames
were taken vp at this time amongst them, as Cauder
. . . Seiton. . . . with manie other that had possessions
giuen them, which gaue names to the owners for the time.

KING LEAR

[The story of King Lear and his three daughters is told in *The True Chronicle History of King Leir*, published in 1605. From it and from Holinshed Shakespeare seems to have taken most of his material, although passages in *The Mirour for Magistrates* (1587), Warner's *Albions England* (1586), and Spenser's *The Faerie Queene* (1591-1596) have been cited as possible sources of various scenes. The old *Leir* is a tragi-comedy, ending, as with Holinshed, on the King's reaccession to his throne. Shakespeare's tragic treatment of the theme necessitated the introduction of Lear's madness, for which no direct original has been found. It seems probable that the mention of Apollo is due to Holinshed's mention of a temple to that deity erected in Troynovant, the mythical name of London.]

[*H.* i. 12-13] Leir the sonne of Baldud was admitted ruler ouer the Britaines, in the yeare of the world 3105, at what time Joas reigned in Juda. This Leir was a prince of right noble demeanor, gouerning his land and subiects in great wealth. He made the towne of Caerleir now called Leicester, which standeth vpon the riuer of Sore. It is written that he had by his wife three daughters without other issue, whose names were Gonorilla, Regan, and Cordeilla, which daughters he greatly loued, but specially Cordeilla the yoongest farre aboue the two elder. When this Leir therefore was come to great yeres, & began to waxe vnweldie through age, he thought to vnderstand the affections of his daughters towards him, and preferre hir whome he best loued, to the succession ouer the kingdome. Whervpon he first asked Gonorilla the eldest, how well she loued him : who calling hir gods to record, protested that she loued him more than hir owne life, which by right and reason should be most deere vnto hir. With which answer the father being well pleased, turned to the second, and demanded of hir how well she loued him : who answered (confirming hir saiengs with great othes) that she loued him more than toong could expresse, and farre aboue all other creatures of the world.

Then called he his yoongest daughter Cordeilla before him, and asked of hir what account she made of him, vnto whome she made this answer as followeth : " Knowing the great loue and fatherlie zeale that you haue alwaies borne towards me (for the which I maie not answere you otherwise than I thinke, and as my conscience leadeth me) I protest vnto you, that I haue loued you ever, and will continuallie (while I liue) loue you as my naturall father. And if you would more vnderstand of the loue that I beare you, assertaine your selfe, that so much as you haue, so much you are worth, and so much I loue you, and no more." The father being nothing content with this answer, married his two eldest daughters, the one vnto Henninus the duke of Cornewall, and the other vnto Maglanus the duke of Albania, betwixt whome he willed and ordeined that his land should be diuided after his death, and the one halfe thereof immediatlie should be assigned to them in hand : but for the third daughter Cordeilla he reserued nothing.

Neuertheless it fortuned that one of the princes of Gallia (which now is called France) whose name was Aganippus, hearing of the beautie, womanhood, and good conditions of the said Cordeilla, desired to haue hir in mariage, and sent ouer to hir father, requiring that he might haue hir to wife ; to whome answer was made, that he might haue his daughter, but as for anie dower he could haue none, for all was promised and assured to hir other sisters alreadie. Aganippus notwithstanding this answer of deniall to receiue anie thing by way of dower with Cordeilla, tooke hir to wife, onlie moued thereto (I saie) for respect of hir person and amiable vertues. This Aganippus was one of the twelue kings that ruled Gallia in those daies, as in the British historie it is recorded. But to proceed.

After that Leir was fallen into age, the two dukes that had married his two eldest daughters, thinking it long yer the gouernment of the land did come to their hands, arose against him in armour, and reft from him the gouernance of the land, vpon conditions to be continued for terme of life : by the which he was put to his portion, that is, to liue after a rate assigned to him for the maintenance of his estate, which in processe of time was diminished as well by Maglanus as by Henninus. But the greatest griefe that Leir tooke, was to see the vnkindnesse of his daughters, which seemed to thinke that all was too much which their father had, the same being neuer so little : in so much that going from the one to the other, he was brought to that miserie, that scarslie they would allow him one seruant to wait vpon him.

In the end, such was the vnkindnesse, or (as I maie saie) the vnnaturalnesse which he found in his two daughters, notwithstanding their faire and pleasant words vttered in time past, that being constreined of necessitie, he fled the land, & sailed into Gallia, there to seeke some comfort of his yongest daughter Cordeilla, whom before time he hated. The ladie Cordeilla hearing that he was arriued in poore estate, she first sent to him priuilie a certeine summe of monie to apparell himselfe withall, and to reteine a certeine number of seruants that might attend vpon him in honorable wise, as apperteined to the estate which he had borne : and then so accompanied, she appointed him to come to the court, which he did, and was so ioifullie, honorablie, and louinglie receiued, both by his sonne in law Aganippus, and also by his daughter Cordeilla, that his hart was greatlie comforted : for he was no lesse honored, than if he had beene king of the whole countrie himselfe.

Now when he had informed his sonne in law and his daughter in what sort he had beene vsed by his other daughters, Aganippus caused a mightie armie to be put in a readinesse, and likewise a great nauie of ships to be rigged, to passe ouer into Britaine with Leir his father in law, to see him againe restored to his kingdome. It was accorded, that Cordeilla should also go with him to take possession of the land, the which he promised to leaue vnto hir, as the rightfull inheritour after his decesse, not-withstanding any former grant made to hir sisters or to their husbands in anie maner of wise.

Herevpon, when this armie and nauie of ships were readie, Leir and his daughter Cordeilla with hir husband tooke the sea, and arriuing in Britaine, fought with their enimies, and discomfited them in battell, in the which Maglanus and Henninus were slaine ; and then was Leir restored to his kingdome, which he ruled after this by the space of two yeeres, and then died, fortie yeeres after he first began to reigne.

CYMBELINE

[A tale of Boccaccio, telling of the conspiracy against a husband, forms the main theme of *Cymbeline*, but the setting, with its struggles between the Britons and the Romans, is taken from the material contained in Holinshed concerning Cymbeline (the real Cunobelinus) who lived in the first century A.D. This material is clearly legendary, and the play makes no pretence to historical accuracy. It is frankly a romance, and has to be considered as such, although it is interesting to trace Shakespeare's reading in this work which evidently appealed to him from his first days to his last.]

[*H*.i. 32–33] Kymberline or Cimbeline the sonne of Theomantius was of the Britains made king after the deceasse of his father, in the yeare of the world 3944, after the building of Rome 728, and before the birth of our Sauiour 33. This man (as some write) was brought vp at Rome, and there made knight by Augustus Cesar, under whome he serued in the warres, and was in such fauour with him, that he was at libertie to pay his tribute or not. . . . Touching the continuance of the yeares of Kymbelines reigne, some writers doo varie, but the best approoued affirme, that he reigned 35 years and then died, & was buried at London, leauing behind him two sonnes, Guiderius and Aruiragus.

But here is to be noted, that although our histories doo affirme, that as well this Kymbeline, as also his father Theomantius liued in quiet with the Romans, and continuallie to them paied the tributes which the Britains had couenanted with Julius Cesar to pay, yet we find in the Roman writers, that after Julius Cesars death, when Augustus had taken vpon him the rule of the empire, the Britains refused to paie that tribute : whereat as *Cornelius Tacitus* reporteth, Augustus (being otherwise occupied) was contented to winke ; howbeit, through earnest calling vpon to recouer his right by such as were desirous to see the vttermost of the British kingdome ; at

length, to wit, in the tenth yeare after the death of Julius
Cesar, which was about the thirteenth yeare of the said
Theomantius, Augustus made prouision to passe with an
armie ouer into Britaine, & was come forward vpon his
iournie into Gallia Celtica : or as we maie saie, into these
hither parts of France.

But here receiuing aduertisements that the Pannonians,
which inhabited the countrie now called Hungarie, and the
Dalmatians whome now we call Slauons had rebelled, he
thought it best first to subdue those rebells neere home,
rather than to seeke new countries, and leaue such in
hazard whereof he had present possession, and so turning
his power against the Pannonians and Dalmatians, he
left off for a time the warres of Britain. . . . But whether
this controuersie which appeareth to fall forth betwixt
the Britans and Augustus, was occasioned by Kymbeline,
or some other prince of the Britains, I haue not to auouch :
for that by our writers it is reported, that Kymbeline
being brought vp in Rome, & knighted in the court of
Augustus, euer shewed himselfe a friend to the Romans,
& chieflie was loth to breake with them, because the youth
of the Britaine nation should not be depriued of the
benefit to be trained and brought vp among the Romans,
whereby they might learne both to behaue themselues
like ciuill men, and to atteine to the knowledge of feats
of warre.

[*H*. ii. 45] About the same time also there came vnto
Kimbaline king of the Britains an ambassador from
Augustus the emperor, with thanks, for that entring into
the gouernement of the British state, he had kept his
allegiance toward the Romane empire : exhorting him to
keepe his subiects in peace with all their neighbors, sith
the whole world, through meanes of the same Augustus,
was now in quiet, without all warres or troublesome
tumults.

CASSIBELAN'S TRIBUTE

[*H*. i. 30–31] Cassibellane in the end was forced to
fall to a composition in couenanting to paie a yearlie
tribute of three thousand pounds.

The Revolt of Guiderius (transferred to Cymbeline)

[*H*. ii. *H. S.* 45] Kimbaline king of the Britains died,
who for that he had beene brought vp in Rome, obserued
his promised obedience towards the empire ; but Guiderius
succeeding, disdained to see the libertie of his countrie
oppressed by the Romans, and therefore procuring the
Britains to assist him, assembled a power, and inuaded
the Romans with such violence, that none escaped with
life, but such as saued themelues within castels & fortresses.

The Landing of Caesar

[*H*. i. 25] Peace being thus established after [III. i.]
the fourth day of the Romans arriuall in Britain, the 18
ships which (as ye haue heard) were appointed to conuey
the horssemen ouer, loosed from the further hauen with
a soft wind. Which when they approched so neere the
shore of Britaine, that the Romans which were in Cesars
campe might see them, suddenlie there arose so great a
tempest, that none of them was able to keepe his course,
so that they were not onelie driuen in sunder (some being
caried againe into Gallia, and some westward) but also
the other ships that lay at anchor, and had brought ouer
the armie, were so pitifullie beaten, tossed and shaken,
that a great number of them did not onelie lose their
tackle, but also were caried by force of wind into the high
sea ; the rest being likewise so filled with water, that they
were in danger by sinking to perish and to be quite lost.

[*H*. i. 28] The next day, as he had sent foorth such
as should haue pursued the Britains, word came to
him from Quintus Atrius, that his nauie by rigour of a
sore and hideous tempest was greeuouslie molested, and
throwne vpon the shore, so that the cabels and tackle
being broken and destroied with force of the vnmercifull
rage of wind, the maisters and mariners were not able to
helpe the matter.

[*H*. i. 27] Thus writeth Cesar touching his first
iournie made into Britaine. But the British historie
(which *Polydor* calleth the new historie) declareth that
Cesar in a pitcht field was vanquished at the first encounter,
and so withdrew backe into France.

[*H*. i. 30] Thus according to that which Cesar himselfe and other autentike authors haue written, was Britaine made tributarie to the Romans by the conduct of the same Cesar. But our histores farre differ from this, affirming that Cesar comming the second time, was by the Britains with valiancie and martiall prowesse beaten and repelled, as he was at the first, and speciallie by meanes that Cassibellane had pight in the Thames great piles of trees piked with yron, through which his ships being entred the riuer, were perished and lost. And after his comming a land, he was vanquished in battell, and constrained to flee into Gallia with those ships that remained.

[*H*. i. 27] The same historie also maketh mention of one Belinus that was generall of Cassibellanes armie, and likewise of Nenius brother to Cassibellane, who in fight happened to get Cesars swoord fastened in his shield by a blow which Cesar stroke at him.

TROINOVANT

[*H*. i. 23] By reason that king Lud so much esteemed that citie before all other of his realme, inlarging it so greatlie as he did, and continuallie in manner remained there, the name was changed, so that it was called Caerlud, that is to saie, Luds towne : and after by corruption of speech it was named London.

MULMUCIUS

[H. i. 15-16] He also made manie good lawes, which were long after vsed, called Mulmucius lawes, turned out of the British speech into the Latine by *Gildas Priscus*, and long time after translated out of latine into english by Alfred king of England, and mingled in his statutes. . . .

After he had established his land, and set his Britains in good and conuenient order, he ordeined him by the aduise of his lords a crowne of gold, & caused himselfe with great solemnitie to be crowned, according to the custom of the pagan lawes then in vse : & bicause he was the first that bare a crowne heere in Britaine, after the

opinion of some writers, he is named the first king of
Britaine, and all the other before rehearsed are named
rulers, dukes, or gouernors.

THE EXPLOIT OF BELARIUS (FROM A SCOTO-DANISH BATTLE)

[*H*. ii. *H. S.* 155]   The fight was cruell on both   [V. iii.]
sides : and nothing hindered the Scots so much, as going
about to cut off the heads of the Danes, euer as they might
ouercome them.   Which maner being noted of the Danes,
and perceiuing that there was no hope of life but in
victorie, they rushed foorth with such violence vpon their
aduersaries, that first the right, and then after the left wing
of the Scots, was constreined to retire and flee backe, the
middle-ward stoutly yet keeping their ground : but the
same stood in such danger, being now left naked on the
sides, that the victorie must needes haue remained with
the Danes, had not a renewer of the battell come in time,
by the appointment (as is to be thought) of almightie God.
    For as it chanced, there was in the next field at the same
time an husbandman, with two of his sons busie about his
worke, named Haie, a man strong and stiffe in making and
shape of bodie, but indued with a valiant courage.   This
Haie beholding the king with the most part of the nobles,
fighting with great valiancie in the middle ward, now
destitute of the wings, and in great danger to be oppressed
by the great violence of his enimies, caught a plow-beame
in his hand, and with the same exhorting his sonnes to doo
the like, hasted towards the battell, there to die rather
amongest other in defense of his countrie, than to remaine
aliue after the discomfiture in miserable thraldome and
bondage of the cruell and most vnmercifull enimies.   There
was neere to the place of the battell, a long lane fensed on
the sides with ditches and walles made of turfe, through
the which the Scots which fled were beaten downe by the
enimies on heapes.
    Here Haie with his sonnes, supposing they might best
staie the flight, placed themselues ouerthwart the lane,
beat them backe whome they met fleeing, and spared
neither friend nor fo : but downe they went all such as

came within their reach, wherewith diuerse hardie personages cried vnto their fellowes to returne backe vnto the battell, for there was a new power of Scotishmen come to their succours, by whose aid the victorie might be easilie obteined of their most cruell aduersaries the Danes : therefore might they choose whether they would be slaine of their owne fellowes comming to their aid, or to returne againe to fight with the enimies. The Danes being here staied in the lane by the great valiancie of the father and the sonnes, thought verely there had beene some great succors of Scots come to the aid of their king, and therevpon ceassing from further pursute, fled backe in great disorder vnto the other of their fellowes fighting with the middle ward of the Scots.

The Scots also that before was chased, being incouraged herewith, pursued the Danes vnto the place of the battell right fiercelie. Wherevpon Kenneth perceiuing his people to be thus recomforted, and his enimies partlie abashed, called vpon his men to remember their duties, and now sith their aduersaries hearts began (as they might perceiue) to faint, he willed them to follow vpon them manfully, which if they did, he assured them that the victorie vndoubtedly should be theirs. The Scots incouraged with the kings words, laid about them so earnestlie, that in the end the Danes were constreined to forsake the field, and the Scots egerlie pursuing in the chase, made great slaughter of them as they fled. This victorie turned highlie to the praise of the Scotish nobilitie, the which fighting in the middle ward, bare still the brunt of the battell, continuing manfullie therein euen to the end. But Haie, who in such wise (as is before mentioned) staied them that fled, causing them to returne againe to the field, deserued immortall fame and commendation : for by his meanes chieflie was the victorie atchiued.

EVERYMAN'S LIBRARY AND EVERYMAN PAPERBACKS: A Selection

* indicates the volumes also in paperback: for their series numbers in Everyman
Paperbacks add 1000 to the EML numbers given.

EUL stands for Everyman's University Library.

For copyright reasons some of the following titles are not available in the U.S.A.

BIOGRAPHY

ESSAYS AND CRITICISM

FICTION

RELIGION AND PHILOSOPHY

SCIENCES: POLITICAL AND GENERAL

TRAVEL AND TOPOGRAPHY